Utilizing Educational Data Mining Techniques for Improved Learning:

Emerging Research and Opportunities

Chintan Bhatt
Charotar University of Science and Technology, India

Priti Srinivas Sajja
Sardar Patel University, India

Sidath Liyanage
University of Kelaniya, Sri Lanka

A volume in the Advances in Educational Technologies and Instructional Design (AETID) Book Series

IGI Global
DISSEMINATOR OF KNOWLEDGE

Published in the United States of America by
IGI Global
Information Science Reference (an imprint of IGI Global)
701 E. Chocolate Avenue
Hershey PA, USA 17033
Tel: 717-533-8845
Fax: 717-533-8661
E-mail: cust@igi-global.com
Web site: http://www.igi-global.com

Library of Congress Cataloging-in-Publication Data

Names: Bhatt, Chintan M., 1988- editor. | IGI Global.
Title: Utilizing educational data mining techniques for improved learning: emerging research and opportunities /
Chintan Bhatt, Priti Srinivas Sajja, and Sidath Liyanage, editors.
Description: Hershey, Pennsylvania : Information Science Reference (an imprint of IGI Global), 2019.
Identifiers: LCCN 2019015786| ISBN 9781799800101 (Hardcover) | ISBN 9781799800118 (Softcover) | ISBN 9781799800125 (eBook)
Subjects: LCSH: Education--Data processing. | Computer-assisted instruction. | Data mining. | Big data.
Classification: LCC LB1028.43 .U85 2019 | DDC 371.33/4--dc23 LC record available at https://lccn.loc.gov/2019015786

This book is published in the IGI Global book series Advances in Educational Technologies and Instructional Design (AETID) (ISSN: 2326-8905; eISSN: 2326-8913)

British Cataloguing in Publication Data
A Cataloguing in Publication record for this book is available from the British Library.

Advances in Educational Technologies and Instructional Design (AETID) Book Series

ISSN:2326-8905
EISSN:2326-8913

Editor-in-Chief: Lawrence A. Tomei, Robert Morris University, USA

MISSION

Education has undergone, and continues to undergo, immense changes in the way it is enacted and distributed to both child and adult learners. In modern education, the traditional classroom learning experience has evolved to include technological resources and to provide online classroom opportunities to students of all ages regardless of their geographical locations. From distance education, Massive-Open-Online-Courses (MOOCs), and electronic tablets in the classroom, technology is now an integral part of learning and is also affecting the way educators communicate information to students.

The **Advances in Educational Technologies & Instructional Design (AETID) Book Series** explores new research and theories for facilitating learning and improving educational performance utilizing technological processes and resources. The series examines technologies that can be integrated into K-12 classrooms to improve skills and learning abilities in all subjects including STEM education and language learning. Additionally, it studies the emergence of fully online classrooms for young and adult learners alike, and the communication and accountability challenges that can arise. Trending topics that are covered include adaptive learning, game-based learning, virtual school environments, and social media effects. School administrators, educators, academicians, researchers, and students will find this series to be an excellent resource for the effective design and implementation of learning technologies in their classes.

COVERAGE

- Web 2.0 and Education
- Instructional Design Models
- Educational Telecommunications
- Online Media in Classrooms
- Adaptive Learning
- Game-Based Learning
- Digital Divide in Education
- Higher Education Technologies
- Social Media Effects on Education
- K-12 Educational Technologies

IGI Global is currently accepting manuscripts for publication within this series. To submit a proposal for a volume in this series, please contact our Acquisition Editors at Acquisitions@igi-global.com or visit: http://www.igi-global.com/publish/.

The Advances in Educational Technologies and Instructional Design (AETID) Book Series (ISSN 2326-8905) is published by IGI Global, 701 E. Chocolate Avenue, Hershey, PA 17033-1240, USA, www.igi-global.com. This series is composed of titles available for purchase individually; each title is edited to be contextually exclusive from any other title within the series. For pricing and ordering information please visit http://www.igi-global.com/book-series/advances-educational-technologies-instructional-design/73678. Postmaster: Send all address changes to above address.

Titles in this Series

For a list of additional titles in this series, please visit:
https://www.igi-global.com/book-series/advances-educational-technologies-instructional-design/73678

Blended Online Learning and Instructional Design for TPACK Emerging Research and Opportunities
Margaret L. Niess (Oregon State University, USA)
Information Science Reference • ©2019 • 213pp • H/C (ISBN: 9781522588795) • US $145.00

Handbook of Research on Assessment Practices and Pedagogical Models for Immigrant Students
Jared Keengwe (University of North Dakota, USA) and Grace Onchwari (University of North Dakota, USA)
Information Science Reference • ©2019 • 454pp • H/C (ISBN: 9781522593485) • US $255.00

Recent Advances in Applying Identity and Society Awareness to Virtual Learning
Andrew G. Stricker (The Air University, USA) Cynthia Calongne (Colorado Technical University, USA) Barbara Truman (University of Central Florida, USA) and Fil J. Arenas (The Air University, USA)
Information Science Reference • ©2019 • 370pp • H/C (ISBN: 9781522596790) • US $195.00

Handbook of Research on Faculty Development for Digital Teaching and Learning
Alev Elçi (Aksaray University, Turkey) Linda L. Beith (Roger Williams University, USA) and Atilla Elçi (Aksaray University, Turkey)
Information Science Reference • ©2019 • 624pp • H/C (ISBN: 9781522584766) • US $285.00

Evidence-Based Approaches to Becoming a Culturally Responsive Educator Emerging Research and Opportunities
Anthony Broughton (Claflin University, USA)
Information Science Reference • ©2019 • 178pp • H/C (ISBN: 9781522588672) • US $155.00

For an entire list of titles in this series, please visit:
https://www.igi-global.com/book-series/advances-educational-technologies-instructional-design/73678

IGI Global
DISSEMINATOR OF KNOWLEDGE

701 East Chocolate Avenue, Hershey, PA 17033, USA
Tel: 717-533-8845 x100 • Fax: 717-533-8661
E-Mail: cust@igi-global.com • www.igi-global.com

Table of Contents

Foreword xi

Preface xiii

Chapter 1
Role of Information and Communication Technologies in Transforming Teaching and Learning Environments 1
Deepam Goyal, National Institute of Technical Teachers Training and Research, India
Nitika Goyal, Guru Nanak College, India

Chapter 2
Improvement of the Transmission of Information for ICT Techniques Through CBEDE Methodology 13
Reinaldo Padilha França, State University of Campinas (UNICAMP), Brazil
Yuzo Iano, State University of Campinas (UNICAMP), Brazil
Ana Carolina Borges Monteiro, State University of Campinas (UNICAMP), Brazil
Rangel Arthur, State University of Campinas (UNICAMP), Brazil

Chapter 3
Towards Increasing the Efficiency of E-Learning Systems Using Recommendation System Approach 35
Zameer Gulzar, BSAR Crescent Institute of Science and Technology, India
L. Arun Raj, BSAR Crescent Institute of Science and Technology, India
A. Anny Leema, VIT University, India

Chapter 4
Predicting the Academic Performance of Students Using Utility-Based Data Mining 56
Sidath R. Liyanage, University of Kelaniya, Sri Lanka
K. T. Sanvitha Kasthuriarachchi, University of Kelaniya, Sri Lanka

Chapter 5
Data Mining in Global Higher Education: Opportunities and Challenges for Learning 86
Evan G. Mense, Southeastern Louisiana University, USA
Pamela A. Lemoine, Troy University, USA
Michael D. Richardson, Columbus State University, USA

Chapter 6
Intelligent Tutoring System 121
Abhishek Singh Rathore, Shri Vaishnav Vidyapeeth Vishwavidyalaya, India
Siddhartha Kumar Arjaria, Rajkiya Engineering College, India

Related Readings 145

About the Contributors 159

Index 164

Detailed Table of Contents

Foreword xi

Preface xiii

Chapter 1
Role of Information and Communication Technologies in Transforming Teaching and Learning Environments 1
Deepam Goyal, National Institute of Technical Teachers Training and Research, India
Nitika Goyal, Guru Nanak College, India

No aspect of human life has remained untouched by information and communication technologies (ICT) at present. Various forms of media like radio, computers, televisions, computers, etc. keep on surrounding us right from the moment we wake up in the morning till we go to bed at night. The electronic media, which have become an inseparable part of our daily lives, fall under the umbrella of a single entity known as ICT. As the society has moved one step ahead from being information society to acquiring the status of knowledge society, the knowledge and use of ICT tools has become even more important. ICT has a deep impact on every sphere of human life and education is no exception. Use of information communication technologies has promoted drastic changes in work environment, transformed the ways of handling and exchanging information, and has an everlasting impact on teaching-learning pedagogy. This chapter presents the role of ICT transforming the teaching and learning environments. The limitation of ICT and the challenges in implementation have also been discussed.

Chapter 2
Improvement of the Transmission of Information for ICT Techniques Through CBEDE Methodology 13
Reinaldo Padilha França, State University of Campinas (UNICAMP), Brazil
Yuzo Iano, State University of Campinas (UNICAMP), Brazil
Ana Carolina Borges Monteiro, State University of Campinas (UNICAMP), Brazil
Rangel Arthur, State University of Campinas (UNICAMP), Brazil

There is no single and universal definition for ICT (information and communication technology). The term is normally adopted to all devices, networking components, applications, and systems that allow combined people, companies, and organizations (i.e., businesses, nonprofit agencies, governments, and enterprises) to interact in the digital world, the modern era. In this digitally globalized world, we deal with a huge set of data all the time. Data refers to facts, events, actions, activities, and transactions which have been and can be recorded (i.e., the raw material from which information is produced), nurturing the infrastructure and components that enable modern computing. Based on this, the present study aims to implement a discrete events-based model with advanced modulation format DQPSK in a simulation environment, the Simulink of MATLAB software, aiming to improve the transmission of information in communication systems. The results show better computational performance related to memory utilization related to compression of the information, showing an improvement of up to 92.6%.

Chapter 3
Towards Increasing the Efficiency of E-Learning Systems Using Recommendation System Approach 35
Zameer Gulzar, BSAR Crescent Institute of Science and Technology, India
L. Arun Raj, BSAR Crescent Institute of Science and Technology, India
A. Anny Leema, VIT University, India

Data mining approaches have been tried in e-learning systems for information optimization and knowledge extraction to make decisions. In recent years, the recommendation system has gained popularity in every field be it e-commerce, entertainment, sports, healthcare, news, etc. However, in e-learning system, the recommender systems were not effectively utilized in comparison to other domains and thus emerged as a bottleneck for almost all e-learning systems for not offering flexible delivery of the learning resources. Current e-learning systems lack personalization features, and the information is presented in a static way despite their varying learning objectives and needs. The aim of recommender system is to personalize the information with respect to learner interest. The objective of this study is to highlight various algorithmic techniques that can be used to improve information retrieval process to provide effective recommendations to learners for improving their performance and satisfaction level.

Chapter 4
Predicting the Academic Performance of Students Using Utility-Based Data Mining....56
Sidath R. Liyanage, University of Kelaniya, Sri Lanka
K. T. Sanvitha Kasthuriarachchi, University of Kelaniya, Sri Lanka

Data mining in education has become an important topic in the sphere of influence of data mining. Mining educational data encompasses developing models, plotting data, and utilizing machine learning algorithms to derive patterns on educational data by attempting to uncover hidden patterns, create information for hidden relationships using educational statistics, and perform many more operations that are unfeasible using traditional computational tools. This research aims to identify the main factors that influence the academic performance of learners in tertiary education system in Sri Lanka. A conceptual framework and an analytical framework on factors affecting the academic performance was constructed with this aim. The analytical framework was then validated with the data collected from technology learners in a tertiary educational institute.

Chapter 5
Data Mining in Global Higher Education: Opportunities and Challenges for Learning....86
Evan G. Mense, Southeastern Louisiana University, USA
Pamela A. Lemoine, Troy University, USA
Michael D. Richardson, Columbus State University, USA

Historically, educators in higher education have searched for reliable means and methods to increase student learning. Many techniques and strategies have been used and even some have taken the form of laws to incorporate certain approaches to learning. However, there has not been one method proved effective in all situations for all students. One of the biggest challenges that global educational institutions face is the explosive growth of educational data and how to use this data to improve the quality of instructional and managerial decisions. Global higher education leaders embraced data-driven practices as an opportunity to improve efficiency, objectivity, transparency, and innovation. As a result, global higher education institutions are producing a large amount of student related data every year. Technology has given educators in higher education access to methods for assessing learning and engagement. Educational data mining is a relatively new process in global higher education that provides a tool to analyze this data and extract valuable information.

Chapter 6
Intelligent Tutoring System..121
Abhishek Singh Rathore, Shri Vaishnav Vidyapeeth Vishwavidyalaya, India
Siddhartha Kumar Arjaria, Rajkiya Engineering College, India

With digitization, a rapid growth is seen in educational technology. Different formal and informal learning contents are available on the internet. Intelligent tutoring system provides personalized e-learning to the learners. Different attributes like historical data, real-time data, behavioral, and cognitive are usually used for personalization. Based on the personalization, the intelligent tutoring system aims to provide easy and effective understanding. Recent research highlights the effect of learner's behavior and emotions on effective teaching-learning process. This chapter provides a brief description of the intelligent tutoring system, current developments, instructional techniques, proposed solution, and future recommendations. The emphasis of the study is to provide insights on self-regulated learning.

Related Readings...145

About the Contributors...159

Index...164

Foreword

Advances in Information and Communication Technology (ICT) in the last years have reshaped the teaching and learning process at all educational levels. Learning facilitators, such as school teachers and university tutors, have a new powerful collection of educational practices, methods and tools based on electronic equipment and data management.

This teaching and learning toolbox can be used to effectively communicate, create, disseminate, store, and manage information, related to the learning material and the activity of students. ICT-based approaches to teaching and learning can lead to more interactive sessions and provide more creative and personalised options for students, which, in turn can lead to a better development of the student skill set and a better preparation of the students to deal with ongoing technological changes.

The ever-increasing adoption of ICT solutions in education leads to the generation of large data quantities to be stored and managed effectively, providing a direct application field for data science research. Considering that the vast majority of academic institutions are currently using virtual learning environments and that eLearning courses are currently more common than ever further emphasises the need for efficient storage and management of the data that these activities produce or require.

This book focusses on the potential of the contribution of data science models, techniques and approaches towards improved learning, its current limitations and the challenges raised by this application. Issues related to information transferring in communication systems and the effect of data compression to memory utilisation and transmission speed are investigated. One of the chapter proposes the integration of a recommendation system into existing e-learning systems to allow personalisation of the information and the way it is represented according to the learner's interests. This book also presents a study of the factors that affect academic performance and an investigation of how data mining can be used to summarise the student-related data that are annually accumulated by academic institutions, to extract meaningful conclusions about student engagement and to assess the efficiency of learning. Finally, a tutoring system that allows for personalised, self-regulated learning according to the learner's profile is presented.

The topic of this module is interdisciplinary, as it brings together data science, machine learning, big data analytics, human computer interaction and educational research. Each of the editors of this volume is an expert on some of these research fields. Their collaboration guarantees the validity of the presentation and the value of the content for the research community.

Yannis Korkontzelos
Edge Hill University, UK

Preface

The Information and Communication Technology (ICT) has become a trivial tool for doing any business. Due to high applicability and support provided by the ICT, it has become further easy for many businesses to extremely utilize it. Such high utilization of the ICT generates ever increasing pool of information; which is difficult to manage with traditional ICT tools. Modern education has increased its reach through ICT tools and techniques. This business deals with lots of data about students, learning material, institutional details, teachers and other details related to the domain. There are many educational approaches are popular starting from traditional classroom approaches to virtual and eLearning and mobile learning. Further existence of many platforms makes the related data handling and data mining procedures very challenging and effort taking. Utilization of data mining techniques to manipulate education data, which may be big, may increase quality and effectiveness of safekeeping, delivery and use of knowledge for quality education. We may think to manage the educational data in smart or intelligent manner with help of modern artificial intelligent manner. Similarly we may apply data and web mining techniques on dedicated cloud or grid platform for an educational institute.

This edited volume includes documentation of original research work on utilization of modern data mining and handling techniques to support education business in various perspectives. The major objectives of the book are:

- To introduce data mining and data science models, techniques and approaches;
- To provide new models, platforms, tools and protocols in domain for educational data analysis and modelling;
- Application of intelligent techniques to the field;
- To introduce innovative hybrid system models and techniques dedicated to data mining and data science;

The book will be helpful for professors, tutors, individuals, researchers, scientists, academicians, students and libraries for their need to handle educational as well as big data in their domains. The models and techniques described here also may be applicable to many businesses in customised manner at various levels. This book will be helpful to the academicians, practitioners, researchers and learners to carry out similar experiment to effectively handle their respective businesses.

We thank All Mighty for giving us capabilities and strength for the making this book happen. We are very thankful to the IGI Global Publication for providing us a platform to give a shape to the idea of the edited volume on the educational data mining. Their support in editing, designing and other related activities is really thoughtful and appreciable. We are also thankful to all our contributors, without whom this book would not have been possible. A special thank from all of us is for our reviewers for their valuable comments and suggestions.

We also thank our respective institution, students and our families for their continuous support and encouragement.

We hope that the book will create awareness about the issues and problems related to the domain and its content helps in finding solutions related to it.

Chintan Bhatt
Charotar University of Science and Technology, India

Priti Srinivas Sajja
Sardar Patel University, India

Sidath Liyanage
University of Kelaniya, Sri Lanka

Chapter 1
Role of Information and Communication Technologies in Transforming Teaching and Learning Environments

Deepam Goyal
National Institute of Technical Teachers Training and Research, India

Nitika Goyal
Guru Nanak College, India

ABSTRACT

No aspect of human life has remained untouched by information and communication technologies (ICT) at present. Various forms of media like radio, computers, televisions, computers, etc. keep on surrounding us right from the moment we wake up in the morning till we go to bed at night. The electronic media, which have become an inseparable part of our daily lives, fall under the umbrella of a single entity known as ICT. As the society has moved one step ahead from being information society to acquiring the status of knowledge society, the knowledge and use of ICT tools has become even more important. ICT has a deep impact on every sphere of human life and education is no exception. Use of information communication technologies has promoted drastic changes in work environment, transformed the ways of handling and exchanging information, and has an everlasting impact on teaching-learning pedagogy. This chapter presents the role of ICT transforming the teaching and learning environments. The limitation of ICT and the challenges in implementation have also been discussed.

DOI: 10.4018/978-1-7998-0010-1.ch001

INTRODUCTION

In this era of digitalization, Information and Communication Technologies (ICT) is moving towards playing a bigger role in the field of education. It has gone far away from just playing a supportive role in education to being an indispensable part of our education system and its importance is going to increase more rapidly with the passage of time [Hawkridge et al., 2018; Brosnan, 2001].

Grading and theoretical learning are inseparable parts of the traditional education system in India. Nowadays, the era of tough competition demands practical knowledge, skills and analytical thinking for survival in the professional world. The conventional style of education has proved to be a failure at every level of education system i.e. school, college and universities [Bandura, 2014]. With the introduction of information and communication technologies in education, it is now feasible to exhibit the theoretical concepts through practical demonstrations with the help of videos, simulation and presentations etc. Thus information and communication technologies has been helping to enhance the quality of education and making the students more employable [Van Lieshout et al., 2018].

Social media, a by-product of information and communication technology, helps in enhancing the knowledge of students by helping them in exchanging ideas, opinions and information with each other. Thus, information and communication technology helps in adding to the knowledge of students by other means also along with increasing the effectiveness of formal education methods (Goyal et al., 2017). But the saddest part of this revolutionary change is that it has failed to leave the desired impact in this field due to social nature of the education process. Education is a teaching-learning process where teachers use to play a vital role in nation building. However, the introduction of ICT, though having numerous benefits, has shaped the education in a manner that it has become just student centric. A novel approach for handling the Multi-Input Multi-Output Student Academic Performance Prediction (MIMOSAPP) problem has been proposed to anticipate the future assessment of a student after being enrolled into a university (Son & Fujita, 2018). The similarities and differences among the various leaning models has been illustrated with the assumption that an instructor should be in control of the learning environment *viz.* pace and material (Leidner and Javenpaa, 1995). It has been inferred that no particular model is the best approach; indeed, different learning approaches will be appropriate depending on the circumstances – course, content, student experience, maturity, intelligence, and instructor goals, skills, and preferences, among others. The various dimensions of the learning theories have been shown in Figure 1.

Figure 1. Dimensions of the learning theories

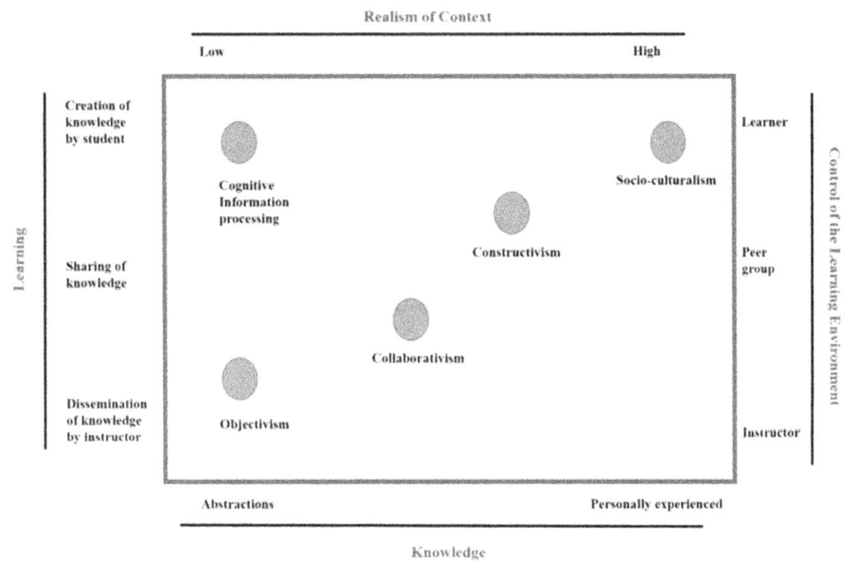

Information and communication technologies can be defined as a collection of resources and tools used to create, store, transfer and control information. The elements of ICT consist of computer systems, communication mediums such as internet, telephones and broadcasting media such as radio, television etc. (Blurton, 1999, Owen et al., 2018). Nowadays, it is a matter of great interest that how technology should be harnessed in order to increase the competence and add value at every stage of the education system both at the administrative as well as teaching-learning framework. Various functions of information and communication technologies in the field of education have been described below (Erstad & Voogt, 2018):

1. ICT: An Aid to Students

Information and communication technologies provides an effective tool to assist students for various activities such as making assignments, conducting surveys, collecting data and other research related activities etc.

2. ICT: A Bridge Between Teaching and Learning

ICT provides a feasible medium for the teachers to teach effectively and the students to learn effortlessly. Various forms of information and communication technologies based education such as educational network, drill and practice exercises, simulations etc. have proved to be useful in making teaching-learning process more effective.

3. ICT: A Tool for Effective Management

Various ICT elements are used for effective management of educational organizations. Such tools not only make many processes fast but also reduce errors which were present due to human limitations.

EMERGING METHODS OF ICT INTEGRATION

Use of computers in the field of education has been getting to new heights due to the endeavors of Government and educational institutions. Nowadays, individuals are well versed with the knowledge of various tools and applications of information and communication technology and utilize them effectively for making the learning process easy and interesting [Goyal & Goyal, 2016]. Given below are some of the effects of integration of ICT in the field of education.

E-Learning

In e-learning process, there is complete or partial use of an information network- such as the internet, an intranet (LAN) or extranet (WAN) in teaching-learning process. A subset of E-learning i.e. web based learning, makes effective use of internet browser in the teaching pedagogy [Lim et al., 2018].

Blended Learning

A learning process which merges the strengths of the traditional classroom teaching process along with the latest technological advancements in order to make the teaching- learning process more effective is known as Blended learning. An example of blended learning is Modular object-oriented dynamic learning environment. In such an environment, a teacher facilitates out of class learning using ICT tools along with the classroom teaching.

Active Learning

Active learning aims at enhancing the analytical skills of students to inquire about and analyse new things by providing them exceptional information through information and communication technologies based tools. The students are encouraged to do in-depth analysis of real life problems and learn practical applications of theoretical concepts. Thus students learn how to deal with real life situations using information and communication technologies tools and techniques. The traditional method of learning was somehow based on cramming or rote learning whereas information and communication technologies has made this approach student centric by promoting learner engagement. Active learning has made the learning process more student centric by allowing students to make a choice of what to learn and when to learn.

Collaborative Learning

Collaborative learning, facilitated by information and communication technologies tools, helps the learners, teachers and experts to have coordinated interaction irrespective of their different locations. ICT based learning system provides a platform to students belonging to various cultures and nation to share their cultural values, experiences and ideas with each other. Hence ICT promotes teamwork, communication skills and global awareness among students.

Creative Learning

ICT does not act as a simple tool used just to duplicate the received information but helps students to add their creativity into the existing information and develop real world products using this knowledge.

Imperative Learning

ICT based education overcomes one of the biggest limitations of conventional learning approach that is demarcation between various disciplines and separation between theory and practical by providing an integrative teaching-learning pedagogy.

Evaluative Learning

The student centric and analytical nature of information and communication technologies based learning has helped in developing a learning environment which exhibits the ability of logical reasoning among students. Unlike the traditional education system, which is based on print based education, information and communication technologies based education presents the students with a platform which provides them the opportunity to learn by exploring and discovering new things in place of just listening and cramming.

U-Learning

U-learning, descriptively termed as Ubiquitous learning, has been termed so due to almost omnipresence of the technology nowadays. The most important contribution of ICT in the field of education has come forward in the form of distance learning. U-learning provides a learning environment which facilitates the students to learn anytime and anywhere. Rapid development of U-learning has picked up the pace due to advancements in the field of technology. Ever increasing computing power and improving communication technology have played an important role in evolution of ubiquitous learning. Table 1 shows the implications introduced by information and communication technologies in terms of various pedagogic aspects [Lim et al., 2018; Erstad & Voogt, 2018; Voogt & Odenthal, 1999; Wijnen et al., 2000].

Table 1. Comparison of emerging methods of ICT integration

Aspect	Active learning	Collaborative	Creative	Integrative	Evaluative
Traditional Pedagogy	• Teacher centric approach • Whole class instruction • Few activities involved • Teacher determines the pace of the programme	• Everyone for him/herself • Focus on Individual • Groups of Homogeneous nature	• Already known solutions are applied to the problems • Reproductive learning	• Separate subjects • Individual teachers • Discipline based • Theory and practice remain distinct	Traditional pedagogy
Emerging Pedagogy for the information society	• Student centric approach • Learning in small groups • A wide range of activities • Learner determines the pace of program	• Supporting each other • Focus on teams • Groups of Heterogeneous nature	• Focus on deriving new alternatives for problem solving • Productive learning	• Integration between subjects • Teams of teachers • Thematic • Theory and practice are integrated	Emerging pedagogy for the information society

TYPES OF ICT/ MEDIA TECHNOLOGIES

Based on the characteristics, media technologies can be classified in the following two types:

- **Synchronous Media:** For using synchronous media the participants need to be present at the same time even though in different locations.
- **Asynchronous Media:** Such media allows the participants of the learning process to be at "different times" and "different places".

Table 2. lists various forms of synchronous and asynchronous media available these days.

LIMITATIONS OF ICT USE IN EDUCATION

A modern technology, Information and Communication Technology, has numerous advantages as it acts as an aid to various human activities, but at the same time, ICT has also given rise to many complications in human life also.

One of the limitations of the use of ICT in the field of education is that often the choice is made on basis of technological advancements rather than requirements of education. The problem generally faced while introducing information and communication technologies is that the management usually acquires an ICT tool without taking into prior consideration the needs of the students, teachers and the course requirements [Sarkar, 2012]. Thus, the targeted group does not get the benefit of these tools even after spending a huge amount of money on it.

Especially in developing economies where education system is already overburdened with various multilevel confrontations every day, the increasing

Table 2. Asynchronous and Synchronous media

Asynchronous Media	Synchronous Media
Computer file transfers	Computer conferencing such as chat and internet telephony
Virtual conferences	Broadcast radio and television
Multimedia products, offline Web based learning formats	Audio-graphics
Audio and video tapes and CDs	Audio conferencing, as in a telephone conference
E-mail	Teleconferencing

demand of implementation of ICT to fulfil educational needs has been adding fuel to the fire. The most basic requirements of implementing ICT are: electricity and communication lines. These facilities are found missing in many parts of the developing nations. Thus it is not possible to introduce IT in the institutes which fall under such areas.

The concluding remarks of the author of Programme for International Student Assessment (PISA) survey stated that the students who occasionally use computer at the institutes give better performance when compared to the students who do not use computer at all but those fellows who regularly use computer at school and home give worse performance than the students who never use it [Livingstone, 2012]. Thus the result is that information and communication technologies act as an aid to education but only if its use is restricted and extensive use of the ICT tools may also create hindrance in education. It proves that the increase in performance level is not directly proportional to the introduction of information and communication technologies tools in education.

ICT cannot be utilized in the field of education in an efficient manner unless the teachers develop required proficiency and enthusiasm for experimenting with ICT tools. The most crucial factor behind lack of teachers' interest in application of information and communication technologies in education is non-availability of efficient training programs required to make the teachers well verse in use of technology. Moreover, the student centric approach of information and communication technologies based education has been creating a huge gap between student and teachers.

Gholami et al. emphasized that ICT plays an equally significant role in providing equal opportunities to underprivileged sections of the society as is played by education and economic literacy. At the same time, it was also stressed upon that it may act as a pillar for social development but not necessarily for economic growth [Gholami et al., 2010].

ICT IMPLEMENTATION: CHALLENGES AHEAD

ICT also bring along various challenges along with numerous benefits. The most important among these is the higher cost associated with purchase, installation and maintenance of ICT tools. This scenario becomes even worse in case of developing nations as introducing ICT in a developing economy involves higher cost in comparison of developed economies [Sarkar, 2012].

Another challenge in implementation of ICT in education is piracy. Use of pirated software is not only illegal and unethical but also adds to maintenance cost thus increasing the absolute cost of implementing ICT tools. Although there is great benefit of introduction of ICT tools in education for students but some faculties do not have IT background and they feel uncomfortable while embedding these tools into teaching-learning process.

According to Williams, technology should not be taken as a distinct entity and not a part of the society, in fact, it is a social product as every footstep in the direction of innovations in the field of technology has a socially, politically or economically motivated directing force behind it [Pollock & Williams, 2016]. Thus the revolutionary inventions in the field of ICT not only promote globalization but also have great influence on the educational policies, objectives and plans. The most significant factor which needs to be considered is which type of ICT tools should be integrated in the field of education and how these tools should be implemented so as to make the most of it.

The concept that ICT is making educational facilities available 'anytime-anywhere' is not applicable universally as millions of children belonging to underprivileged families do not have access to internet or computer [DCSF, 2008]. Thus ICT in education is creating 'Digital Divide' on the lines of social and economical divide.

According to Warschauer, the greatest dilemma caused by implementation of ICT tools is that on one hand ICT is considered as an aid to social inclusion whereas on the other hand it is looked upon as a reason behind Digital divide [Warschauer, 2004]. Thus the widening gap created by ICT, known as digital divide, can be filled by effective implementation of ICT in various institution and communities by not mere installing the equipments but by developing such skills among people belonging to different sects that they could utilize the technology for various social and economical purposes.

One of the most critical thing to be taken care of while implementing ICT in education is that it should provide a balance between the global and local context as only a perfect blend of these two can only enhance the quality of education [Kumpulainen & Rajala, 2017]. Local context and the regional languages should not be ignored while making available the international study material and information publishing to the students. The cultural foundation of the education system should remain intact while providing a global platform to the learning system.

There are numerous challenges which have come into light by introduction of ICT in the field of education but if ICT is supposed to create problems in education system, it is a solution to most of the problems as well.

CONCLUSION

It is almost universally accepted fact that the development of a nation entirely depends upon the quality of the education policy and its effective implementation. Application of technology in education has completely transformed the teaching methods used by teachers and learning methods adopted by students. ICT, despite of having numerous limitations, prove to be a valuable mean to achieve this excellence.

Right to education is one of the fundamental rights of a human being. Education not only develops a human at professional but also on personal front. The rapid advancement in the field of technology has given a new platform known as distance and open learning to the distance learners thus removing the barriers between a human being and education. But implementing ICT in education should not be the ultimate target but ICT should be used as a tool to achieve the overall quality and improve accessibility to education. If implemented with this motive, ICT can play a significant role for great reforms in the education system.

Disclosure Statement

No potential conflict of interest was reported by the authors.

ACKNOWLEDGMENT

This research received no specific grant from any funding agency in the public, commercial, or not-for profit sectors.

REFERENCES

Bandura, A. (2014). Social cognitive theory of moral thought and action. In *Handbook of moral behavior and development* (pp. 69–128). Psychology Press.

Blurton, C. (1999). *New directions of ICT-use in education*. UNESCO's World Communication and Information Report.

Brosnan, T. (2001). Teaching using ICT. University of London.

DCSF. (2008). *All parents to get regular online reports on their children's progress*. Available online at: http://www.dcsf.gov.uk/pns/DisplayPN.cgi?pn_id=2008_0006

Erstad, O., & Voogt, J. (2018). The twenty-first century curriculum: issues and challenges. Second Handbook of Information Technology in Primary and Secondary Education, 19-36.

Gholami, R., Higón, D. A., Hanafizadeh, P., & Emrouznejad, A. (2010). Is ICT the key to development? *Journal of Global Information Management*, *18*(1), 66–83. doi:10.4018/jgim.2010091104

Goyal, N., & Goyal, D. (2016). Impact of E-Commerce in India: Issues & Challenges. *International Journal of Advanced Research in Computer Science*, *7*(6), 192–194.

Goyal, N., Goyal, D., & Dang, R. K. (2017). Impact of Social Networking on Youth's Dynamism. *Indian Journal of Science and Technology*, *10*(14), 1–5. doi:10.17485/ijst/2017/v10i14/110844

Hawkridge, D., Vincent, T., & Hales, G. (2018). *New information technology in the education of disabled children and adults*. Routledge. doi:10.4324/9780429486890

Kumpulainen, K., & Rajala, A. (2017). Dialogic teaching and students' discursive identity negotiation in the learning of science. *Learning and Instruction*, *48*, 23–31. doi:10.1016/j.learninstruc.2016.05.002

Leidner, D. E., & Jarvenpaa, S. L. (1995). The use of information technology to enhance management school education: A theoretical view. *Management Information Systems Quarterly*, *19*(3), 265–291. doi:10.2307/249596

Lim, C. P., Tinio, V. L., Smith, M., & Bhowmik, M. K. (2018). Achieving equity, quality, and efficiency in education. Routledge International Handbook of Schools and Schooling in Asia, 369.

Livingstone, S. (2012). Critical reflections on the benefits of ICT in education. *Oxford Review of Education*, *38*(1), 9–24. doi:10.1080/03054985.2011.577938

Owen, S., Palekahelu, D., Sumakul, T., Sekiyono, E., & White, G. (2018). Systematic educational change and teacher skill-building in developed and developing countries: The importance of teacher peer learning groups. *Teacher Development*, *22*(4), 447–463. doi:10.1080/13664530.2017.1403370

Pollock, N., & Williams, R. (2016). *How industry analysts shape the digital future*. Oxford University Press. doi:10.1093/acprof:oso/9780198704928.001.0001

Sarkar, S. (2012). The role of information and communication technology (ICT) in higher education for the 21st century. *Science*, *1*(1), 30–41.

Son, L. H., & Fujita, H. (2019). Neural-fuzzy with representative sets for prediction of student performance. *Applied Intelligence*, *49*(1), 172–187. doi:10.100710489-018-1262-7

Van Lieshout, M., Egyedi, T. M., & Bijker, W. E. (2018). *Social Learning Technologies: The introduction of multimedia in education*. Routledge. doi:10.4324/9781315204659

Voogt, J., & Odenthal, L. (1999). *With a view to the future: A study of innovative use of ICT in education*. Enschede, The Netherlands: University of Twente, Faculty of Educational Science and Technology.

Warschauer, M. (2004). *Technology and social inclusion: Rethinking the digital divide*. MIT press. doi:10.7551/mitpress/6699.001.0001

Wijnen, W. H. F. W., Zuylen, J. G. G., Mulders, D. J. W. M., & Delhoofen, P. J. W. M. (2000). Naar een nieuw evenwicht: uitwerkingen van de zes hoofdkenmerken van ontwerpgericht onderwijs [Towards a new balance: Elaborations of the six core characteristics of design-oriented education]. *OGO-Brochure*, 2.

Chapter 2
Improvement of the Transmission of Information for ICT Techniques Through CBEDE Methodology

Reinaldo Padilha França
State University of Campinas (UNICAMP), Brazil

Ana Carolina Borges Monteiro
State University of Campinas (UNICAMP), Brazil

Yuzo Iano
State University of Campinas (UNICAMP), Brazil

Rangel Arthur
State University of Campinas (UNICAMP), Brazil

ABSTRACT

There is no single and universal definition for ICT (information and communication technology). The term is normally adopted to all devices, networking components, applications, and systems that allow combined people, companies, and organizations (i.e., businesses, nonprofit agencies, governments, and enterprises) to interact in the digital world, the modern era. In this digitally globalized world, we deal with a huge set of data all the time. Data refers to facts, events, actions, activities, and transactions which have been and can be recorded (i.e., the raw material from which information is produced), nurturing the infrastructure and components that enable modern computing. Based on this, the present study aims to implement a discrete events-based model with advanced modulation format DQPSK in a simulation environment, the Simulink of MATLAB software, aiming to improve the transmission of information in communication systems. The results show better computational performance related to memory utilization related to compression of the information, showing an improvement of up to 92.6%.

DOI: 10.4018/978-1-7998-0010-1.ch002

INTRODUCTION

Information and Communication Technologies (ICT) correspond to all technologies that interfere and mediate the informational and communicative processes. Furthermore, they can be understood as a set of integrated technological resources that provide, through the functions of hardware, software and telecommunications, the automation and communication of business processes, scientific research and teaching and learning. The disruptive potential of the current waves of technological innovation related to Information and Communication Technologies, brought changes in several sectors and scopes. An example is the recent educational processes, due to the development and technological independence, are not enough to the learning conditions of the current society, which has the need of independence in the search for information and knowledge construction. This requirement of change is due to the fast technological changes that modern man is subjected to in relation to the digital era and the information in which he finds himself (Chen & Schulz, 2016; Salinas et al., 2017).

Communication is a necessity and something that has been present in human life since the earliest times. Exchanging information, recording facts, expressing ideas and emotions are factors that have contributed to the evolution of ways of communicating. Thus, over time, man has perfected his ability to relate. It is also responsible for great advances, due to the exchange of messages and consequent exchange of experience, was the engine of great discoveries. In the modern world communicating has become a true science where it is necessary to learn all the time to communicate efficiently and effectively, wherein the digital era of social networks transmit the information quickly and concisely. Where digital transformation is not only a concept for the future, but a reality today (Chen & Schulz, 2016).

Digital communication is, first of all, the digitization of the information media, being simultaneously considered and integrated into the communication as a complete ecosystem, an environment that encompasses and acts in the three dimensions. From a pragmatic point of view, digital communication composes the communication actions to be performed on the web, social networks, and mobile devices. Within this framework, emerging ICTs have changed lifestyles and relationships among individuals in modern spaces. From this, the exchange of information across the network and its innumerable communication platforms diffuses new practices of collaborative and creative interaction and provokes more participation society with the modern world, seeking to overcome the limits of the opinion and consulting sphere (Van Laar et al.2017).

Following an increasing tendency in the adoption of information and communication technologies not only by schools, companies, organizations or intuitions of diverse areas, mainly with the dissemination of data and information through the digital devices in the contemporary every day. There is a variety of information that digital processing provides: image, sound, movement, manipulable representations of data and systems, all integrated and immediately available, that offer a new framework of content sources that can be object accessible to all users (Birt et al., 2017).

Based on this, the present chapter aims to present a model of information transmission based on discrete event concepts that provide the improvement of data transmission positively impacting in increasing efficiency in sending and receiving data by reducing the consumption of system memory during this process.

ICT (Information and Communication Technology)

There is no single and universal definition for ICT (Information and Communication Technology), can be defined as a set of technological resources, used in an integrated way, with a common goal. These terms are generally accepted as all-inclusive, network components, applications, and systems that allow combined people, companies and organizations (businesses, nonprofit agencies, governments, and enterprises) to interact in the digital world. They are used in a variety of ways, in industry (in the automation process for example), in commerce (management in various forms of advertising), in the investment sector (simultaneous information, immediate communication, directly impacting feedback information) and in education (in the teaching process, as in distance education for example). One of the most favored areas with the ICTs is the educational one, in the modality of face-to-face education, they are seen as potentiating the learning processes (Birt et al., 2017; Hilty & Aebischer, 2015).

ICT also represents an advance in distance education, with the creation of virtual learning environments, students have the possibility to relate, exchange information and experiences. Teachers have the possibility to work in groups, debates, forums, among other ways to make learning more meaningful, creating an environment where the management of own knowledge depends on the infrastructure and the will of each individual, stimulating self-learning (Cuthell, 2017).

We are living in the Information Age, its democratization allied to digital inclusion, can become a milestone. However, it is necessary to differentiate information and knowledge. But before we have to allude about data, known as the raw material of information (the data that constitutes it). Data can be defined as raw information, that is, untreated. Information is treated data, this data meeting has meaning and understanding about a given situation. It is through the information that we can make decisions. The gathering of information gives way to knowledge, which is about a level above, because it is the understanding of the reality of certain information. Knowledge can constitute ideas and experiences in which only information would not be able to, so it can be understood that knowledge is information worked. Most of the decisions taken in and around the world are based on data and information. In short, Information is the key guiding force of the world today (Chen & Schulz, 2016; Janich, 2018).

ICT is responsible for the study, development, implementation, storage, and distribution of information. It can be done by hardware and software as a means of computer system, are a part of the emerging technologies which refer to the use of computerized means to store, process and disseminate all types of information or educational training processes. Refers to the combination of manufacturing and services that capture, transmit and display data and information electronically, deals with the use of computers and computer applications to transform, store, manage, protect, disseminate and locate the necessary data for any human activity. Through the internet, new communication and information systems were created, forming a real network. Creations such as e-mail, chat, forums, online group agenda, virtual communities, webcam, among others, have revolutionized human relationships (Kaware & Sain 2015).

ICT encompasses both the internet-enabled sphere as well as the mobile one powered by wireless networks, being able to reach technologies of the type telephones, cellphone, radio and television broadcast, all of which are still widely used today, composing alongside the most diverse pieces of technology cutting edge ICT. This diverse hardware, software and telecommunication capabilities provide automation and better communication in companies, scientific research and also teaching and learning processes. Therefore, in addition to bringing benefits to the internal processes of a company, organizations, and institutions, ICT also improves communication (Nath, Liu 2017; Meade & Islam 2015).

In this ample scope, data are a description of the world, being the Information making meaning from the data, and based on the data, one can conclude diverse aspects and relative issues in the world. This conclusion is the information itself is the processed data. One of the most significant advantages of information and communication technology is undoubtedly the greater integration it brings to the corporate environment. Tools such as video conferencing and instant messaging have provided more corporate mobility, transformed business communication, and enabled many employees to exchange ideas and information even when they were in different locations (El Kadiri et al., 2016).

As for education, the inclusion of computers and several applications aim at this segment improves the learning process and makes it easier for education to reach all individuals, bringing information to any place that has access to the internet, including increasing digital inclusion. For a wider use of information, it is must be communicated to people, and to serve as communication to them, which without such basic purpose there is no sense. It is only when the information is used, that is, the intention of the creation of information as well as its communication would be served. ICT delivers the people and users of the environments in which are employed a series of resources that allow better communication, reducing geographic barriers and bringing more information and interaction to various corners of the planet (Hussain, 2017; Cidrim & Madeiro, 2017).

DATA SCIENCE

Since the 1970's every two years our processing capacity has almost doubled. With this huge increase in the amount of data and processing power, a new concept emerged, Big Data. This concept refers to information technology, that means a large set of stored data. Being validated in relation to the 5V's: Velocity, Volume, Variety, Veracity, and Value. Being a term widely used these days to name very large or complex data sets, which traditional data processing applications cannot handle due to volume. Because they are generated at high speed and variety, they need innovative and economical ways to process, organize and store them, in order to allow better understanding for decision making and process automation (Hilbert, 2016).

Together came the need to analyze and try to extract from this large volume of data useful information, comes Data Science. Data science is a field that has existed for 30 years, but has gained more prominence in recent years due to some factors such as the emergence and popularization of Big Data and the development of areas such as machine learning. Following the same simplified allusion of concepts, Data Science basically analyzes the problems encountered, the hypothesis of solving and analyzing results, is a field that covers anything related to data cleaning, preparation, and analysis. It is a comprehensive term for the techniques used in order to extract data and gain insight through information (data set) (Van der Aalst, 2016; Lande, et al., 2018).

Data Science is the disciplined study of data (analysis) and information inherent to the business, whether or not this data is structured, aimed at extracting knowledge or insights for possible decision-making, and all the views that may surround a particular subject. Similar to computing, data science can be applied to different domains of knowledge and not restricted to a single industry, as traditional analysis tends to be. It combines with big data and machine learning, as well as techniques from other interdisciplinary areas such as statistics, economics, engineering, computing and its subfields as a database and cluster analysis. It is a science that studies information, its process of capture, transformation, generation and, subsequently, data analysis. It differs from statistical analyzes and computer science in its method that is applied to data collected using scientific principles (Van der Aalst, 2016; Lande, et al., 2018).

Data Science can also be understood as the way to generate knowledge, to make science from the data. In this way, everything begins with data, which are nothing but inputs, the raw material that will be transformed into knowledge, and through this process of transformation, these data need to be organized, processed and analyzed. While Big Data performs analytics of the data generated in relation to the business or company evaluated, simplifying it further is a keyword used to describe immense unstructured and structured data volumes flooding organizations of all sizes on a day-to-day (Hilbert, 2016; De Mauro, Grimaldi, 2015).

Data Analytics makes analyzes of the available data in search of a solution to the problems faced. It is the science of examining raw data in order to find patterns and draw conclusions about this information, applying an algorithmic or mechanical process to obtain information. In this way, the possibilities of using Data Science can range from an Internet search, digital advertising, recommendation systems, image recognition, logistics, healthcare, e-commerce, financial services, until price comparison (De Mauro & Grimaldi, 2015; Gandomi & Haider, 2015).

Discrete Events and Entities: Definitions and Applications

In order to solve a wide range of problems from the communications-related areas, Discrete Events (DES) can be seen as a powerful tool. Its wide applicability occurs in models of representation of systems connected to sequences of transactions of data packets, bits among others. The modeling of discrete events focused on communication usually takes place through input-output models, interactive models that provide input data and specific responses to these, the character of these responses usually reveal the behavior of the system and depending on the proposal developed generating an optimal solution for the same (Cassandras & Lafortune, 2009).

A model is a physical or mathematical representation of a system that aims to evaluate the behavioral changes of a system in the function of several variables and parameters involved, or even the evaluation of modifications (proposals) introduced in the system under study. The discrete events are derived from the results of actions taken in a system, and can be classified as an occurrence responsible for the change in the state of the system in which they act. They are used to model systems that change their state in discrete moments in time, from the occurrence of events, and may be of all kinds, where they are generally capable of producing state changes at random intervals of time, generating data and consequently the information. Discrete event simulation, as its name implies, is event-driven (Cassandras & Lafortune, 2009; Artuso & Christiansen, 2014).

The simulation of discrete events, in practice, is the most used, however, there may be mixed or combined systems that have discrete and continuous events. In this chapter, we propose to develop a model of discrete-event computational simulation where the model is rotated, without changing the input data creating a solid and concise proposal for data validation (information). It covers the study of simulation models whose variables change state instantaneously at specific points of time, the temporal evolution of the real state of any real system can be considered as the sum of partial behaviors of certain system elements, which are usually denominated by entities. Discrete entities will be, for example, customers and patients in a clinic, emails on a web server, data packets being transmitted in a system, and in general all elements that are likely to change state. Discrete events encompass systems with medium to a high level of detail, and are generally applied for modeling systems with a low level of abstraction (Artuso & Christiansen, 2014).

These entities are discrete in an event simulation. For a better understanding, the entities within a system are the customers seeking service and the events are the arrival of a new customer, the beginning of the service and the end of the service (equivalent to the customer's exit from the system). This technique has been used to model concepts with a high-level of abstraction, ranging from the exchange of emails on a server to the transmission of data packets between devices connected in a network, can be used to manage people data and the entire extent of a communication system. In this way, the diversity of applications that the technique of the discrete event provides, showing its importance in several areas of knowledge, as well as in engineering (area of the proposal of this research), was remarkable, being able to apply it in a telecommunication system, more specifically in the transmission of data in a channel (Dammasch & Horton, 2008).

Thus, entities are defined as discrete items of interest in a discrete event simulation. However, the meaning of an entity depends on what is being modeled and the type of system used, is an object of the simulation with its own characteristics. The system is viewed as a set of entities or transactions that flow through the system. These entities are described, characterized and identified by their attributes. This occurs because the presence of certain attributes may be able to affect the way events are treated or cause changes as the entity flows through the process. In this context is important to emphasize that the concepts entities and events are different. Events are instantaneous discrete incidents that can change a state variable, an output, and/or an occurrence from another event. In turn, an entity is somewhat dependent on what is being modeled and the type of system. One of the objectives of a model with discrete events is to reproduce the activities of the entities that compose the system and, from there, to know the behavior and performance of the system. Thus, entities are the transactions or tasks that move along the system, generating a flow, which are the paths that the entity will go through the system (Artuso & Christiansen, 2014; Dammasch & Horton, 2008).

AWGN Channel

The function of a communications channel is to provide the physical connection between a transmitter and a receiver, whether that connection is made through a wire or through a connection in a multiplexed medium. This data transport, many times uses two types of media: physical and electromagnetic. An example of use is the satellite communication channel, with an AWGN (Additive White Gaussian Noise) channel where strong attenuations and often large signal propagation delays predominate. The term AWGN is used in mathematical modulations to characterize those channels where the type of noise responsible for degrading the communication is a white noise added to the signal (Bossert, 1999).

The AWGN (Additive White Gaussian Noise) channel model is considered the most used model, since it has greater applicability in several physical channels. Its main characteristic is to introduce a statistically modeled noise into the transmitted signals. White noise is a random signal and has a mathematical modeling that considers infinite bandwidth, zero mean and zero correlation between its amplitudes taken at different time instants. This way, the value of the amplitude of the noise in a certain instant is independent of that observed at any other instant of any time. The Gaussian term is due to the fact that this type of noise has a Gaussian probability density function with zero mean, with standard deviation equal to its RMS voltage and equal variance, or similar to the dissipated power of a resistor of 1W, using conventional schemes of modulation and coding for this type of channel (Lakshmanan & Nikookar, 2006; Barnela & Kumar, 2014).

Modulation Types

The concepts of DPSK and PSK are different from each other. DPSK is abbreviation by Differential Phase Shift Keying, and is responsible for facilitating modulation of the non-coherent type. While, PSK comes from the term Differential Phase Shift Keying and acts on coherent demodulations. The coherent demodulation is directly connected to the carrier, which is modulated for the purpose of obtaining signal in the passband. This signal is reproduced on the receiver and is subsequently used for demodulation in the visible bandwidth to get a message. At this point, when the frequency of the carrier and the transmitted signal are equal, a noise generation occurs. As a result, there is a laborious process in the generation of the breeder received by the receiver. One of the characteristics of the DPSK modulation is that the change of the transmissions for each transmitted signal is dependent on the previous one and can be used as a local carrier. Equality leads to cancellation of signals, such characteristic allows demodulation. In this way, the phase of the modulated signal is shifted compared to the previous phase element (Ling, et al., 2017).

One variation of QPSK (Quadrature Phase Shift Keying) is DQPSK (Differential Quadrature Phase Shift Keying). The difference of this type of modulation is in the fact that instead of sending a symbol corresponding to a pure phase parameter, where this symbol represents a phase variation. In QPSK modulation, the transmission of the information is given by the absolute phase of each symbol. In DQPSK modulation, the symbols represent sets of bits. These symbols are responsible for a certain phase variation in the carrier signal. In the carrier, the respective bits are determined based on the phase change of the previous symbol (Ling et al., 2017).

The analysis of the data transmitted by each of the models can be done through the constellation. In the case of the DQPSK constellation, there are 4 possible states 0, π, + π/2, -π/2, where each symbol represents two bits of information. The division of the binary pattern is equal to QPSK, except when a bit string is shifted to about π/4 or π/2. Compared to the states for QPSK, there are a total of 8 status positions. These types of modulation are widely used in airborne systems in association with other modulation techniques. Figure 1. shows the DQPSK constellation diagram for the displaced version π/4, as well as its constellation rotated by 45 ° from the previous point, as explained above (Koike-Akino, et al., 2008).

Figure 1. Theoretical DQPSK constellation

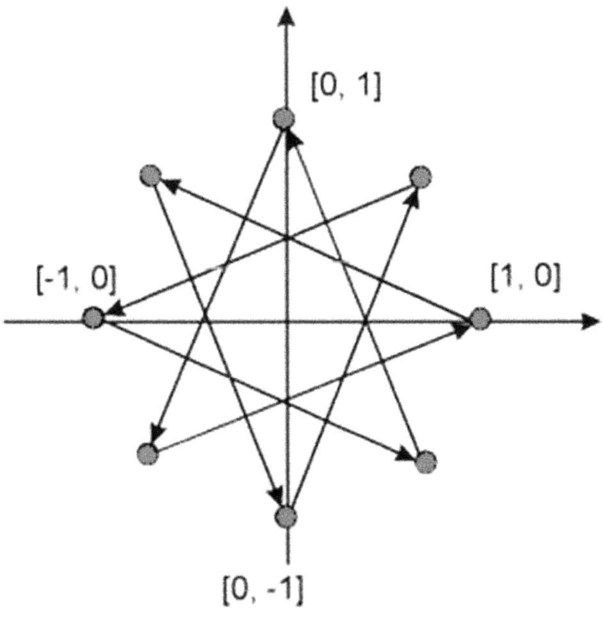

METHODOLOGY OF CBEDE MODEL

The discrete event mainly relates to the modeling representing the system as a sequence of operations performed on entities (transactions) of certain types of data packets, bits, or data structure. Discrete events allow the development of an idea through effectively modeling, supported by data and facts, i.e. discrete entities. In the specific case of this chapter, the bits in the transmission stream of a channel allow to perceive the context of the problem in a study, to simulate and evaluate the results of the developed proposal. This technique is usually used to model concepts having a high level of abstraction, i.e., clients in a queue, emails on a server, flow of vehicles on a highway, a transmission of data packets, and so forth. This session proposes a system model simulation built upon an AWGN channel with the advanced modulation format called differential quadrature phase shift keying (DQPSK) in order to improve the transmission capacity of information content through the channel.

A bit treatment with discrete events methodology inserted in the bit generation step applied in a low abstraction level is the differential and main contribution of this research. The results show better computational performance regarding the memory utilization of the information transmission channel. The modulation formats DQPSK is widely used in satellite broadcasting, in various cellular wireless standards such as GSM, CDMA, LTE, 802.16 fixed and mobile WiMAX, Satellite as also CABLE TV applications, the DQPSK modulation is a particular form of QPSK modulation, in which instead of being sent a symbol corresponding to a pure phase parameter, this symbol represents a phase change.

Based on these concepts the CBDE (Coding of Bits for Entities by means of Discrete Events) methodology is developed. The development of the methodology was performed on Intel Core i3 hardware, which contains two processing cores, Intel Hyper-Threading Technology and 4GB of RAM. In order to improve ICT environments, the CBEDE methodology is applied in a communications system in a DPSK demodulation format. The entire process occurs in the Matlab Simulink Simulation environment.

The DQPSK modulation is employed in this study because it is considered a robust modulation scheme in terms of noise modulation, allowing the demodulation with the success of a high level of distortion.

Four libraries were used:

1. **Communications System™:** Designed to design, simulate and analyze systems. It is able to model dynamic communication systems;
2. **DSP System™:** It is capable of designing and simulating systems with signal processing;

3. **Simulink®:** A block diagram environment for multi-domain simulation. Its function is supporting system-level projects for the modeling and simulation of telecommunication systems,
4. **Library SimEvents®:** Is classified as a discrete event simulation mechanism and components to develop systems models oriented to specific events

The CBEDE methodology is based on the development of an AWGN hybrid channel. This channel has the characteristic of introducing the technique of discrete events during the generation phase of the bits. The focus of this study is on bits 0 and 1.

The signals corresponding to bits 0 and 1 are generated and modulated in DPSK format. This will use the phase shift of the modulation format itself (Figure 2). Subsequently, it will follow in the AWGN channel, following the parameters present in Table 1. The demodulated signal will be demodulated in order to execute the calculation for BER. In this way, the signals corresponding to bits 0 and 1 are generated and modulated in DPSK format. This process is shown in Figure 2. This signal then follows the AWGN channel.

It is important that bit processing is present in the step of generation bits by means of discrete event techniques, in order to make it appropriate for certain purposes. In this way, the signal based on discrete events is susceptible to treatment through

Figure 2. Traditional Model of a Telecommunication System

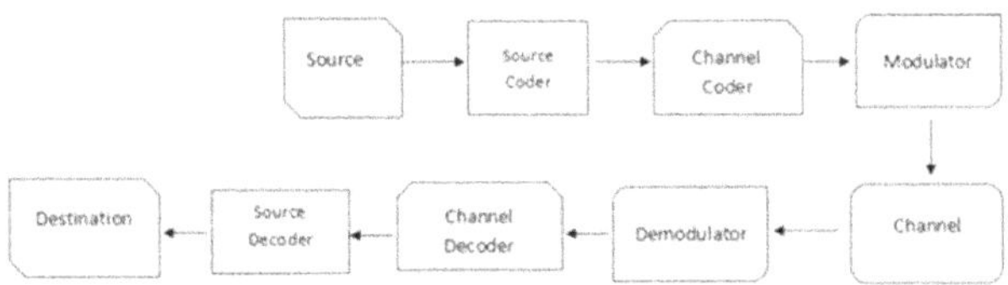

Table 1. Parameters channel models DQPSK

AWGN DQPSK	
Sample Time	1 second
Simulation time	10000 seconds
Eb/N0	0 a 20 dB
Symbol period	1 second
Input signal power	1 watt
Initial seed in the generator	37
Initial seed on the channel	67

the Simevents library. The next step consists of converting the signal to the specific format for the process, i.e. the event-based signals (bit 0 and 1) must be converted to the time-based signal format (Table 1). Entity Sink has the function of finalizing the modeling of discrete events by SimEvents. Entity Sink acts by locating the specific point where the conversion will take place. This conversion must follow the output data parameters, i.e. the bit. In this context, the Real-Word Value function preserves the input signal. Then, a rounding process takes place for the smallest closest integer, due to the performance of the floor function.

Sampling is defined by Zero-Order Hold (ZOH), which uses discrete samples at regular intervals. The ZOH is responsible for describing the conversion efficiency of the signal to the time domain. As a consequence, there is the reconstruction and the maintenance of the signal, respecting each value in its determined interval of time. All this logic is presented in Figure 3.

Subsequently, the signal is modulated with the advanced modulation format DQPSK and passing through an AWGN channel, according to the same parameters specified in Table 1. The signal will be demodulated to evaluate the bit error rate (BER) of the channel. The relative values of the BER are sent to the MATLAB workspace to verify equality and generate the BER graph of the signal, as shown in Figure 4.

Figure 3. Proposed bit precoding

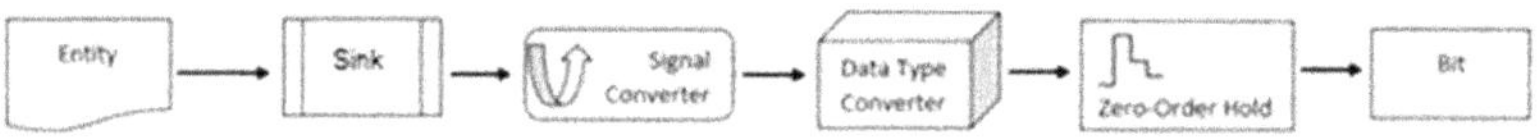

Figure 4. Model of a telecommunication system with the proposal

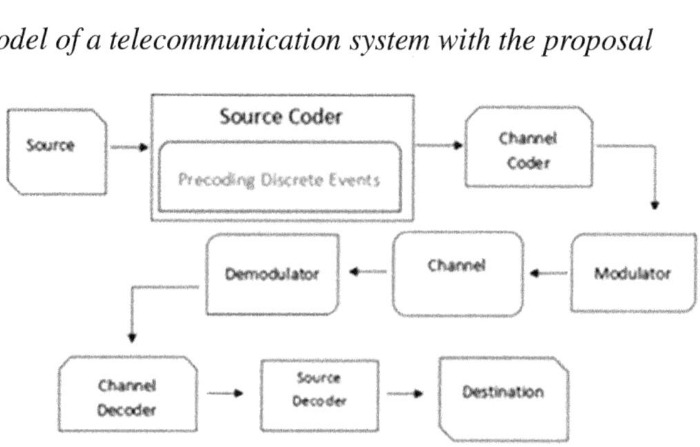

Figure 5. Generation M-ary numbers for bits 0 and 1

[0,M-1] -> [0,2-1] -> 0,1

Figure 6. Traditional model of a telecommunication system

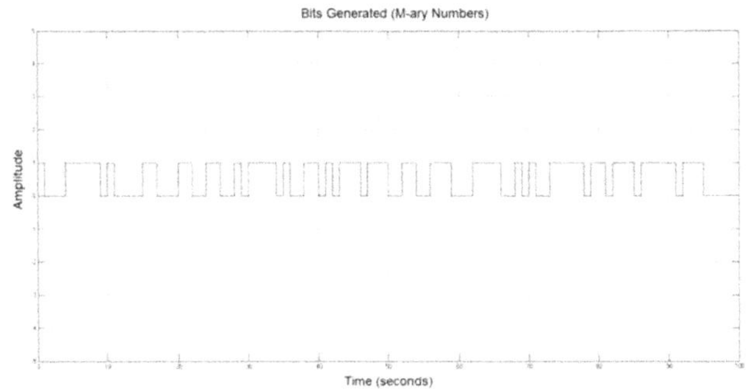

In the proposed model, Figure 2. and 4., the signals corresponding to bits 0 and 1 will be generated, respecting the rule and mathematical logic shown in Figure 5. below.

This rule and mathematical logic with respect to PSK M-ary numbers generate randomly distributed integers in the interval [0, M-1], where M is the definition for bit representation, following the nomenclature of the MATLAB software. Figure 6. shows the respective generation of the bits by means of this logic.

The “size” and “isequal” functions are responsible for verifying the signal equality, as well as the BER. These functions act by means of mathematical comparisons that compose that the signals are of the same size, that is, together with the BER, show that the same amount of bits is being transmitted in both the CBEDE and the traditionally used methodology. The equality of signals is obtained when the (true) logical value corresponds to 1. Otherwise, the value will be false (zero). In this way, it is possible to prove that the CBEDE proposition does not add and does not remove information to the initially transmitted signal.

Results and Discussion

The results presented in this section show an AWGN transmission channel with DQPSK modulation, being used the Simulink simulation environment of the MATLAB. The model from Figure 7. simulated with 20 dB, incorporates the

Figure 7. Transmission Flow for DQPSK

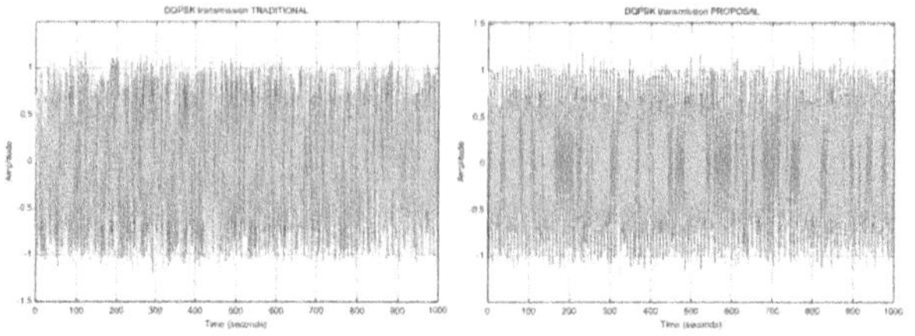

traditional method (left) and the proposed innovation of this chapter (right), showing the signal transmission flow (corresponding to bits 0 and 1), being generated and then modulated in DQPSK, passing through the AWGN channel. Figure 8. shows the constellations for 20 dB for the proposed (left) and the traditional methods (right).

It is known that it is in the first simulation where the allocation of the variables of a system occurs. Based on this, the analyzes of the first simulation of both models were performed: the traditional one and the CBEDE. The models developed were investigated from the perspective of memory consumption evaluation. These parameters were chosen because they are considered paramount in the viewpoint of users.

In this context, for memory calculation, the "sldiagnostics" function was used, where the "TotalMemory" variable received the sum of all the memory consumption processes used in the model, by the "ProcessMemUsage" parameter. This parameter counting the amount of memory used in each process, throughout the simulation, returning the total in MB (megabyte). Thus, the experiments were carried out

Figure 8. Simulated DQPSK Constellations

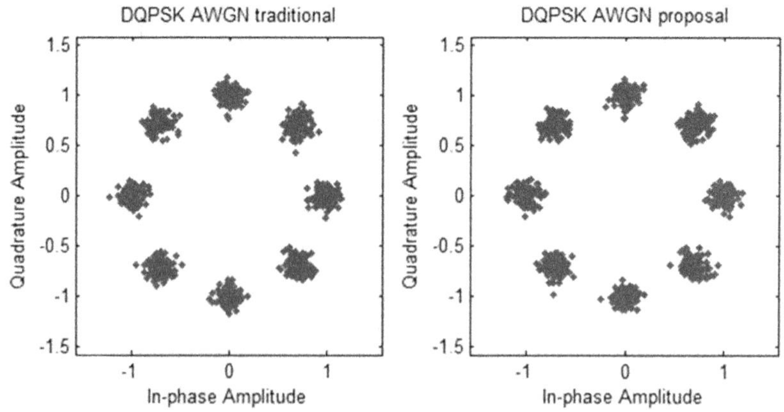

Figure 9. First simulations (memory) model DQPSK

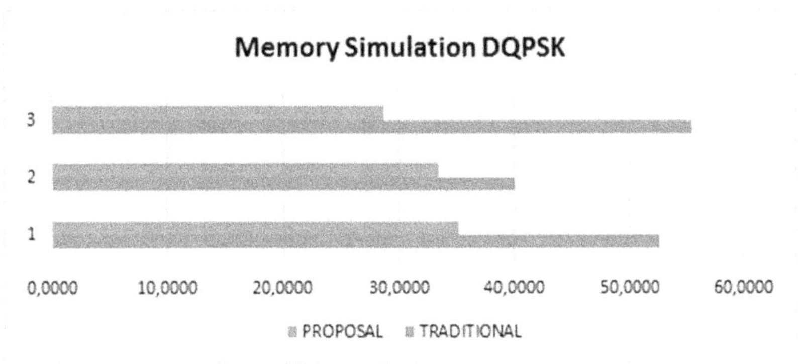

through 3 simulations of each model developed in order to develop the analysis of this chapter, as shown in Figure 9.

The results obtained by the "size" and "isequal" functions, the DQPSK modulation were analyzed through its constellation, by means of the "compass" function. The major feature of graph format has a compass shape, where *n* is the number of elements in Z. In turn, the location of the tip of each arrow will be determined by the real and imaginary components of Z, relative to the constellation of the signal. In the same way and with the same intention will be used the diagram of the constellation. In the same way, Figure 10. shows the comparative between the traditional methodology and the CBEDE methodology, being simulated 20 dB. In this context, the traditional methodology corresponds to a channel without discrete events.

Figure 10. Vectors DQPSK

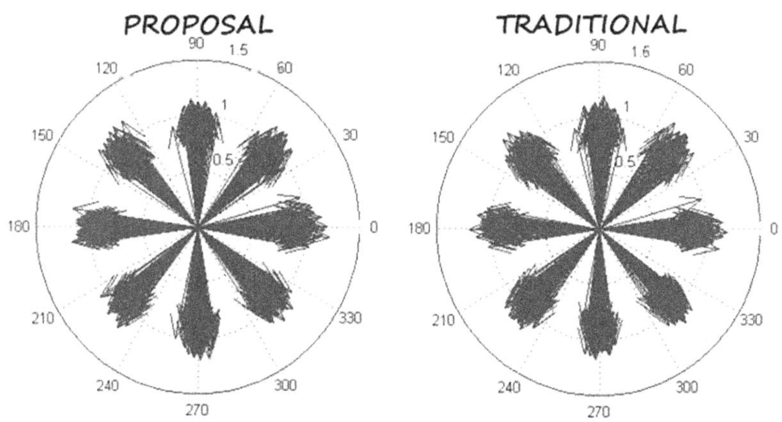

Table 2. Amounts of memory consumption

	TRADITIONAL	PROPOSAL
Simulation		
1	52,5781	35,2500
2	40,0547	33,5391
3	55,5000	28,8164

As important as developing the methodology is an improvement of the transmission of a signal that shows better performance, is to make the know-how available to the academic community, as well as to contribute to the area of study of the proposal as well as the theme that this chapter deals with. The respective amounts of memory consumption shown in Figure 9 are found previously are in Table 2:

To analyze the relationship between the simulation methodology (proposed x traditional method), and the impact on the physical layer of the channel, scripts were made in the MATLAB for processing of the graph BER. Figure 11. displays the performance of the models during transmission with noise ranging from 0 to 14 dB.

This proposal brings a new approach to signal transmission. In this case, the transmission is performed in the discrete domain with the implementation of discrete entities in the bit generation process. Thus, information compression is a

Figure11. BER between the models DQPSK

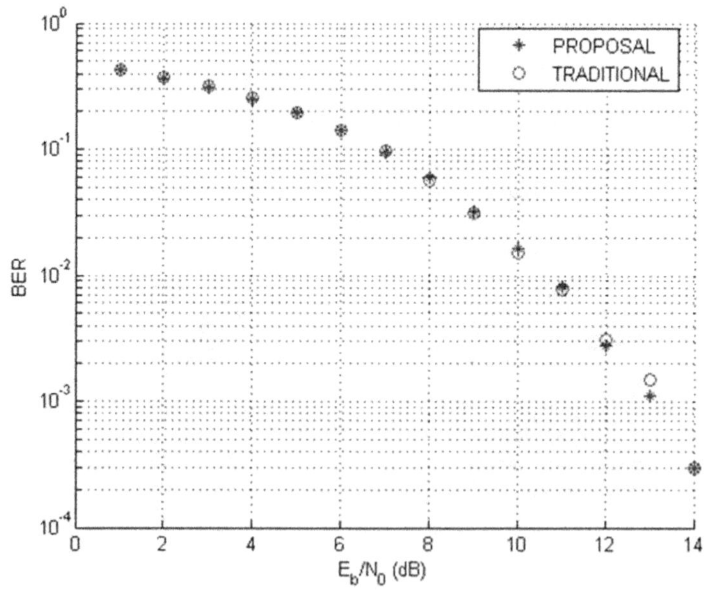

byproduct, since the proposal acts on the bits, having a substantial impact on the compression methods performed in higher layers (for example, format types such as HEVC, MPEG-4 AVC / H.264, JPG, PNG, among others) in a communication system, for example, affecting all the media information (data of examinations of the most varied types) that can be transmitted, resulting in a higher quality of both sending and receiving.

In this way is possible to increase the capacity of information transmission for communication systems. Given the above, the technique of discrete events can be applied in the treatment of bits in its generation stage, being responsible for their conversion into discrete entities. This process is the result of a methodology used in a lower level of application, which acts on the physical layer, than the already used, usually in the transport layer. Able to reduce the consumption of computational resources, such as memory, which is an important parameter to meet the needs of an increasingly technological world.

Considering that speed is a key issue when choosing a methodology, whether it is used by a user, companies or universities, the CBEDE methodology can be seen as a great allied to computing systems within educational environments allied to ICT. For this, it is important to invest in methodologies that improve the systems with ICT and that intermediate the learning of the users. With the result reaching up to 92.6% in the improvement of memory consumption of the CBEDE methodology can be employed in this process, since the interest is in the best and highest quality of teaching and learning systems, and from the point of view of data and of the user, the greater concern is in the speed of the transmission.

Currently, the computing system with ICT is linked to computers and mobile phones, it is necessary that users access this type of information on their device quickly and efficiently, the use of cell phones today is much larger than that of a computer due to its mobility. Therefore, such transmission and exchange of information should be as effective as possible.

The slowness related to the speed and lightness of communication in the system structure used by these users, can often generate device crashes, inconvenience to the user and sometimes even loss of data, or delays and inefficiency in the educational process of these users.

When this happens, often the reliability of the ICT platform in use can be put to the test by the user who from that moment prefer to migrate to other teaching modalities, or even other platforms. This bad impression can be intensified when this situation occurs with companies and universities.

Thus, in order to break this bad impression and generate greater reliability, the CBEDE methodology can also be seen as a great ally. This is because the experiments demonstrate a lower reaching up to 92.6% memory consumption in data transmission, being better than the traditional methodologies, which do not require the use of discrete events.

FUTURE RESEARCH DIRECTIONS

Future research on the CBEDE methodology includes simulations on a wider variety of hardware, including other processors, as well as other platforms, such as eLearning platforms, which distribute learning materials to students, make track student achievement, set assessment tasks, receive completed assessment tasks from students, as well as host moderated discussions and answer questions, have the ability to build a personal resource library, in the same way that access this learning environment from a variety of devices, since the CBEDE methodology has this property of providing better quality of content transmission aligned with information and teaching in communication systems. In the same way that other physical platforms and hardware will be targeted for research as they are the most common on the market today and future trends.

In the same way that the proposal will be modeled and implemented in these communication systems in order to analyze its performance. In addition, testing of data transmission in systems optimized via mobile devices is expected due to its greater popularization even more in recent years, since it is well known that in recent years the production, exchange, and consultation of data gigantically increase, and bearing in mind the CBEDE methodology is very useful in strengthening and enriching the quality of ICT tools that provide a better transmission of this information.

CONCLUSION

Our society constantly goes through moments of transformation, we are in the era of digital information, related to the new information and communication technologies, which are gradually interconnected with the educational activity. Thus, information and communication technologies (ICT) bring new forms and methods of knowledge production in the school environment. Technological innovations allow to improve the relation school/teacher; teacher/student and student/student. To do so, it is necessary to understand the use of computerized tools, disseminate them and develop proposals for improvements to this trend that is already a reality, where with this bias the methodology CBEDE brings an option of better transmission of this information throughout the system.

The revolution of computing, as well as the digital media, have brought with it countless impacts that, in turn, have reached several social areas, one of them is education, where technology is increasingly present in schools, universities, technology, the Internet and its applications, or through projects involving education and technology, which has brought a new scenario of content sharing due to this technological avalanche, however for this scenario to be fruitful, environments must be deployed to transmit and receive this information effectively, where CBEDE has a strong efficient impact in this regard, providing a more fluid transmission of data.

With this focus, this chapter shows a proposal for improvement with the differential of this research, the use of discrete events applied in the physical layer of a medium transmission, the bit itself, being this a low-level of abstraction, the results show better computational performance related to memory utilization related to the compression of the information, showing an improvement of up to 92.6%. This demonstrates that the CBEDE has great potential in the improvement of the communication for educational environments oriented to ICT, being able to improve already existing processes to increase the performance of communication response and transmission of the information between all the devices in the system, reaching positively the system where it is employed as a whole, because the flow of data will consume fewer resources and, therefore, can improve the interactions between the users, providing the most effective use of the diversity information, media, and software, that aid in this learning.

The objective reached in this chapter was to use discrete events being applied to the lowest level of abstraction possible within a communication system, as is done in bit generation. Since the use of technological resources in the teaching process is increasingly necessary, it makes the classroom more attractive, it provides students with a differentiated form of teaching, stimulating learning, however, it is necessary to develop environments and platforms every time efficient and effective. And as a result, make the educational technological environment through ICT more productive, faster and with better performance.

REFERENCES

Artuso, M., & Christiansen, H. L. (2014). Discrete-event simulation of coordinated multi-point joint transmission in LTE-Advanced with constrained backhaul. In *Proceedings of IEEE Eleventh International Symposium on Wireless Communication Systems* (pp. 106-110). IEEE. 10.1109/ISWCS.2014.6933329

Barnela, M., & Kumar, D. S. (2014). Digital modulation schemes employed in wireless communication: A literature review. *International Journal of Wired and Wireless Communications*, *2*(2), 15–21.

Birt, J., Wells, P., Kavanagh, M., Robb, A., & Bir, P. (2017). *ICT literature review*. Academic Press.

Bossert, M. (1999). *Channel coding for telecommunications*. John Wiley & Sons, Inc.

Cassandras, C. G., & Lafortune, S. (2009). *Introduction to discrete event systems*. Springer Science & Business Media.

Chen, Y. R. R., & Schulz, P. J. (2016). The effect of information communication technology interventions on reducing social isolation in the elderly: A systematic review. *Journal of Medical Internet Research*, *18*(1), e18. doi:10.2196/jmir.4596 PMID:26822073

Cidrim, L., & Madeiro, F. (2017). Information and Communication Technology (ICT) applied to dyslexia: Literature review. *Revista CEFAC*, *19*(1), 99–108. doi:10.1590/1982-021620171917916

Cuthell, J. P. (2017). *Virtual learning*. Routledge. doi:10.4324/9781315202907

Dammasch, K., & Horton, G. (2008). *Entities with combined discrete-continuous attributes in discrete-event-driven systems*. Academic Press.

De Mauro, A., Greco, M., & Grimaldi, M. (2015, February). What is big data? A consensual definition and a review of key research topics. In AIP conference proceedings (Vol. 1644, No. 1, pp. 97-104). AIP.

El Kadiri, S., Grabot, B., Thoben, K. D., Hribernik, K., Emmanouilidis, C., Von Cieminski, G., & Kiritsis, D. (2016). Current trends on ICT technologies for enterprise information systems. *Computers in Industry*, *79*, 14–33. doi:10.1016/j.compind.2015.06.008

Gandomi, A., & Haider, M. (2015). Beyond the hype: Big data concepts, methods, and analytics. *International Journal of Information Management*, *35*(2), 137–144. doi:10.1016/j.ijinfomgt.2014.10.007

George, G., Osinga, E. C., Lavie, D., & Scott, B. A. (2016). *Big data and data science methods for management research*. Academic Press.

Hilbert, M. (2016). Big data for development: A review of promises and challenges. *Development Policy Review*, *34*(1), 135–174. doi:10.1111/dpr.12142

Hilty, L. M., & Aebischer, B. (Eds.). (2015). *ICT innovations for sustainability* (Vol. 310). Springer. doi:10.1007/978-3-319-09228-7_1

Hussain, D. (2017, September). The Development of ICT Tools for E-inclusion Qualities. In *International Conference on Interactive Collaborative Learning* (pp. 734-740). Springer.

Janich, P. (2018). *What Is Information?* (Vol. 55). U of Minnesota Press. doi:10.5749/j.ctt212176r

Kaware, S. S., & Sain, S. K. (2015). ICT application in education: An overview. *International Journal of Multidisciplinary Approach & Studies*, *2*(1), 25–32.

Koike-Akino, T., Popovski, P., & Tarokh, V. (2008, November). Denoising maps and constellations for wireless network coding in two-way relaying systems. In *IEEE GLOBECOM 2008-2008 IEEE Global Telecommunications Conference* (pp. 1-5). IEEE. 10.1109/GLOCOM.2008.ECP.727

Lakshmanan, M. K., & Nikookar, H. (2006). A review of wavelets for digital wireless communication. *Wireless Personal Communications*, *37*(3-4), 387–420. doi:10.100711277-006-9077-y

Lande, D., Andrushchenko, V., & Balagura, I. (2018, August). Data Science in Open-Access Research on-Line Resources. In *2018 IEEE Second International Conference on Data Stream Mining & Processing (DSMP)* (pp. 17-20). IEEE. 10.1109/DSMP.2018.8478565

Ling, S. O. A., Zen, H., Othman, A. K. B. H., Adnan, M., & Bello, O. (2017). *A Review on Cooperative Diversity Techniques Bypassing Channel Estimation*. arXiv preprint arXiv:1711.10643

Meade, N., & Islam, T. (2015). Forecasting in telecommunications and ICT—A review. *International Journal of Forecasting*, *31*(4), 1105–1126. doi:10.1016/j.ijforecast.2014.09.003

Nath, H. K., & Liu, L. (2017). Information and communications technology (ICT) and services trade. *Information Economics and Policy*, *41*, 81–87. doi:10.1016/j.infoecopol.2017.06.003

Salinas, Á., Nussbaum, M., Herrera, O., Solarte, M., & Aldunate, R. (2017). Factors affecting the adoption of information and communication technologies in teaching. *Education and Information Technologies*, *22*(5), 2175–2196. doi:10.100710639-016-9540-7

Van der Aalst, W. (2016). Data science in action. In *Process Mining* (pp. 3–23). Berlin: Springer. doi:10.1007/978-3-662-49851-4_1

Van Laar, E., van Deursen, A. J., van Dijk, J. A., & de Haan, J. (2017). The relation between 21st-century skills and digital skills: A systematic literature review. *Computers in Human Behavior*, *72*, 577–588. doi:10.1016/j.chb.2017.03.010

Chapter 3
Towards Increasing the Efficiency of E-Learning Systems Using Recommendation System Approach

Zameer Gulzar
https://orcid.org/0000-0002-7767-2855
BSAR Crescent Institute of Science and Technology, India

L. Arun Raj
BSAR Crescent Institute of Science and Technology, India

A. Anny Leema
https://orcid.org/0000-0002-0704-2794
VIT University, India

ABSTRACT

Data mining approaches have been tried in e-learning systems for information optimization and knowledge extraction to make decisions. In recent years, the recommendation system has gained popularity in every field be it e-commerce, entertainment, sports, healthcare, news, etc. However, in e-learning system, the recommender systems were not effectively utilized in comparison to other domains and thus emerged as a bottleneck for almost all e-learning systems for not offering flexible delivery of the learning resources. Current e-learning systems lack personalization features, and the information is presented in a static way despite their varying learning objectives and needs. The aim of recommender system is to personalize the information with respect to learner interest. The objective of this

DOI: 10.4018/978-1-7998-0010-1.ch003

study is to highlight various algorithmic techniques that can be used to improve information retrieval process to provide effective recommendations to learners for improving their performance and satisfaction level.

INTRODUCTION

The 21st century in developing countries witnessed a growth of learner's and educational setups that are continuously moving towards modern technology which is becoming persistent within a diverse form of the learning environment. The range of these scientific platforms is from the tools that support auxiliary learning to the classroom activity. These advancements are full of learning techniques which refers to a collection of technologies supporting a new form of teaching and learning known as e-learning. All across the world, the educational sector from the past two decades has shown ever-increasing assimilation of communication and learning technologies (Laurillard, 2013). The education sector nowadays is altogether a different story due to technology transformation. The internet plays a critical role in a way the information access is provided to the users across the countries without any hitch which was impractical before. Thus, the facet of education is being renovated each day by which a variety of innovations are provided due to technological evolution. Currently, many varieties of the finest technologies are available for education, but the basic task is to get more concerned about the optimum use of these technical resources to make learning at higher education very effective

A general certainty among modern society is that learning technology can transform the old age concept of teaching and learning by making it attractive, exited and more relevant with respect to the learner. So, the inclusion of communication technology will drastically make changes to the quality of education and learner experience (Karasavvidis, 2014) . E-learning systems are certainly an expansion for uplifting higher education to entirely different heights. E-learning is being used inefficiently in institutions of developing countries, while it is extensively being incorporated in business sectors with the help of the Learning Management System (LMS). The primary objective of e-learning is to provide a system where the faculty finds it easy and convenient to handle the learning material or resource as per the progress and requirement of a learner is concerned. The Educational Data Mining (EDM), which is a mechanism in the modern learning system that compiles the learner data consistently to keep a check on learners' development and performance. Unfortunately, a vast number of e-learning approaches were unsuccessful to come out with a normal evaluation of the learner's development based on the data retrieved.

E-learning is a future tool that will counter the challenges of an educational system in developing countries. E-learning allows having a glance at conventional approaches to learning and also opening the latest educational opportunities. It is being viewed as the need of the hour that Information-based and knowledge-based society absolutely must have a modern means of the education system. Understanding challenges and issues by introducing e-learning is of vital importance to the researchers involved in e-learning and will have a significant role in forming future practices of learning (Robin, 2011). In the modern age of unique information and communication growth, the extant procedure of traditional education is fast disappearing into oblivion. The e-learning has become the backbone of the current educational system and learners' in pursuit of knowledge perpetually resort to the employment of technology to obtain high-quality information, notes, and appraisals to communicate when needed. The overall e-learning system is versatile or multifaceted nature which covers a wide variety of methods and techniques to open the access to ever-increasing educational population (Alfadly, 2013). In e-learning systems, the pliability of time, pace, place and personal learning environment is the main reason behind its popularity and success in developed countries. E-learning has become an important policy for most of the top institutes in developing countries as well which finds it suitable for better and fast information delivery (Arunachalam, 2014).

E-learning has added a new scale to the process of teaching and learning from inside as well as beyond the classroom and still looking at opportunities of becoming more helpful by using modern learning management systems and other technology tools. E-learning plays a vital role in developing countries to improve higher education, thereby performing an essential role in contributing to the sustainable development and knowledge economy of the country. But it is disheartening to see that most of the institutions commit a grave mistake of adopting and setting up e-learning mechanism without proper concern from their faculty and delve deep to check various features which impact on the acceptance of the system within a given framework. Mostly, Institutes turn a blind eye to strategic modules required in their strategic implementation and the fundamental backbones of e-learning (Pedagogical, Technological, and Managerial). Consequently, these institutes landed up in outsourcing it or do not reach anywhere and invariably the system will be ineffective and ultimately detached from the mechanism. The rudiments of acceptance and utilization of the e-learning have to be revealed to promote the advancement of the system. It is highly essential to concurrently take into consideration several constraints such as adoption, workload, and motivational parameters, for the proper execution of the e-learning. For e-learning to be genuinely useful, it has to provide learner-centric facilities. The success and the failure of any e-learning system depend on their performance and how well they are in retrieving relevant information according to the requirement of a particular learner.

The widespread development of web-based technologies is becoming popular and, they aim is to provide various Information types based on the requirement of users. In e-learning services, to give a better user experience, more and more methods and techniques are evolved to reduce the efforts of users. This is the opportunity which Recommender System (RS) have grabbed and seen the most significant use cases on the web. Recommender System aims to help a user in retrieving exciting information from historical data and matching it with user preferences. During the last two decades, the Recommender System has gained immense support and attention from the users and more or Less becoming ubiquitous as the information overload is intensified with the advancement of new technologies (Lei, 2014). Nowadays, Recommender System is the most important and widely used tools which have marked its presence in almost every software application to filter an ample of information to help in personalization and provide the basic relevant information that is likely to the interest of the user of the system. Recommender system is basically a subset or a division of the information filtering concept, which shows an immense potential to assist its users to create a personal environment for learning and to recognize the most relevant objects from a large pool of objects by suggesting them to a user based on the preferences, interest, and ratings of other learners'. The basic recommendation process is shown in figure 1.

To enhance the learning quality is the prerequisite of the century and the new pattern which can attract faculty and learners' is the function of personalization in e-learning systems. Personalization is very useful to improve the quality of research and learning experience and provides an answer that one size fit for all doesn't provide. Personalization in the form of recommendations has gained recognition and significant interest in day-to-day life as people trust and seek others recommendations for decision making. Personalization means to cater to the needs of an individual learner based on their interests (Imran et al, 2016). While reflecting the social

Figure 1. Recommendations process in general

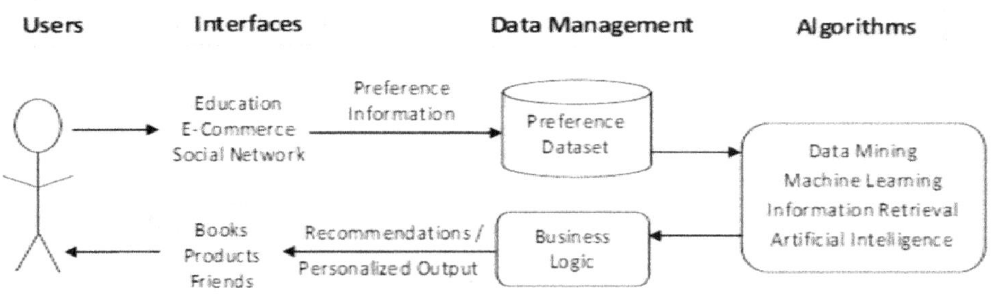

behaviour of supporting users in taking decisions for making a wise choice with least efforts, Recommender System have been adopted in a variety of fields like social networks, YouTube, e-health, and e-commerce sites (Fakoya et al, 2015).

Recommendation Systems

Believing the fact that modern means of learning systems can act as a catalyst to elevate the quality of education. Hence, the e-learning system guarantee not only the delivery of learning objects but also maintains a high standard with the desired learning output. Since e-learning system is focusing on an approach which is learner-centric still the major problem with the current e-learning system is the approach of one-size-fits-all that does not allow catering the individual learner interests and requirements. As a result, personalization of content, courses and other educational objects has become an essential issue in e-learning system as the basic users of the system are the learners' with an almost different style of learning, background, capabilities, interests and the personality. Personalization through recommender approach represents a change and a big leap from one-size-fits-all default approach of e-learning systems to a customized provision of choosing learning objects. The recommendation process is based on the relevancy assessment and learners' interest. Personalizing learners' need based on the learner's knowledge, the area of interest, preferences and other requirements would increase their learning experience.

The resources of learning in the educational scenario are heterogeneous in nature and are available in different formats. The possibility of a learner to access the most relevant items is intensively researched as it is of great concern. So, in the context of e-learning, the recommendation system is an application software agent who recommends interesting and useful resources to a learner using expertise, preferences, and ratings of other learners'. Recommendation Systems work on the specific types of information filtering and data mining techniques to recommend information items like courses, images, web pages, books, videos, news which is expected to be in the preference list of the user. Recommender Systems' basically are techniques and tools that offer suggestions to its user and thus helps in a variety of decision-making process (Lei, 2014). The most basic element which constitutes a recommendation system is the event, the session and the recommendation process. An event is an external action performed by the user and is a call to the system to perform some operations. Similarly, the process of recommendation is the actions which are executed in a particular sequence by the recommender system to produce a specific set of recommendations. An event in a recommendation can have more than one session, and the basic unit in a recommendation event is the items available need to be recommended. The item represents an object that a Recommender System suggests to its users like course, material, image, video, books etc. For each event, a recommendation window is created with a filter to create and filling the window to finally wrap and display the recommended items. The recommendations systems are traditionally divided into different categories (Burke, 2007; Bobadilla, 2013) as shown in Figure 2.

Recommender System in E-Learning

The basic use-case for Recommender System to personalize items has been mentioned, in the filtering of the e-commerce items, and entertainment options. As far as this study was able to find their usage in the e-learning system or Learning Management System for learning object selection has been minimum. The personalization of content, courses and other educational objects became an important feature of e-learning systems. A large number of learners'' with an almost different background, style of learning, personality, interests and capabilities are the primary users of the system. Personalization occurs when e-learning system is designed as per the requirements of the learner.

E-learning repository contains a huge number of objects and the object chosen by any learner may not be fit for them according to the pedagogy. For example, the resources recommended to a learner who is searching for "Data Mining" for writing an assignment is different than those learners' writing a research article on the same topic, because the requirements and the mode of education differs. The graduate student is doing formal learning while as research is an informal mode of learning which may combine different domains also. Hence, the learners' are treated contextually and, thus contextual information will be measured as a key source of suitable recommendations. However, in other domains, the recommendations are solely done on the basis of the user's interest.

Figure 2. Categorization of recommendation systems

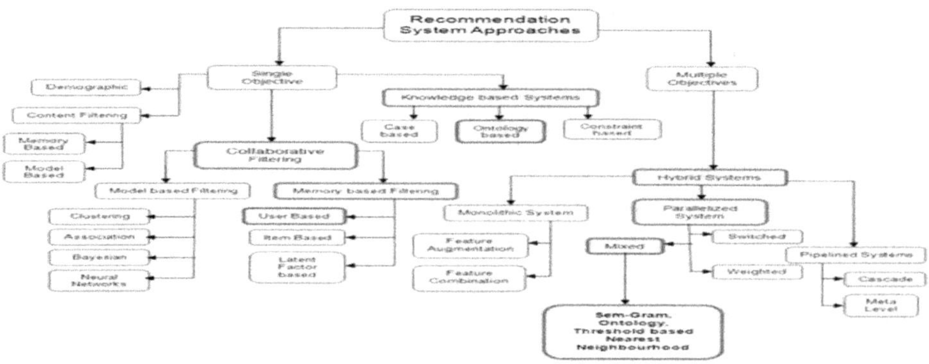

Figure 3. Recommender system classification

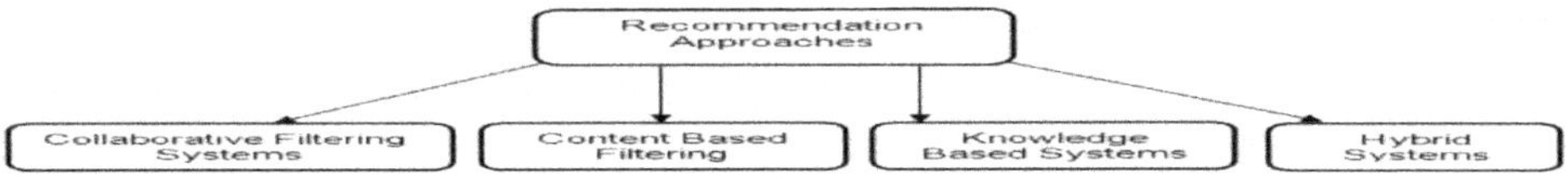

In the e-learning context, the recommender system should be able to recommend the items to the learner based on the requirement or the previous action of the learner. The most critical issue in e-learning systems for a learner is that they need tailored access to information based on the preferences and requirement, and this issue can be mitigated using the Recommendation System approach. Recommender System will analyze the information automatically according to the user preferences, and the most interesting one is presented to him in a large space of possible choices (Ricci, Rokach, Shapira and Kantor, 2011). The recommendations could be related to objects like courses, tasks, books, pictures, similar learners' or any other educational resource. Earlier due to the availability of substantial commercial databases Recommender System have been tried by e-commerce for purchasing goods but little attention has been paid off using recommendation system in e-learning systems, and certain essential things make recommendation system diverse in e-learning systems from the rest of the domains.

Recommender System Approaches

Recommendation Systems (RSs) are extremely handy in the non-formal learning environment because learners' need diverse courses to learn according to the domain of interest in order to improve learning effects, reducing learning difficulties, and especially to the trial-error method. Recommender system supports a user by providing some potential choices from a set of alternatives which are of user's interest. Recommendation system can be built with a variety of approaches, but according to Literature the categorization of a recommender system is usually done (Adomavicius and Tuzhilin, 2005) on the basis of the following criteria.

- The Information retrieval technique applied in a recommender system
- The methodology (like collaborative, Content, and Hybrid techniques) used to recommend items in a recommender system
- The application area or domain of recommended items

On the above-mentioned criterion, Figure 2. shows the in-depth recommendation system classification used for personalization depending on the information they use to suggest an item. The Collaborative Filtering (CF), Content-Based Filtering (CBF), Knowledge-Based Systems (KBS) and Hybrid Systems (HS) are the main categories and are described below.

Collaborative Filtering Systems

Collaborative Filtering is an extensively used technique for personalizing the items using Recommender System. Collaborative Filtering works by evaluating the relationship between the users and interdependencies among items, to build a database of connections between them. So CF can be either based on items or user based and the algorithms which are mainly used for this filtering are Cosine based Correlation and Pearson Correlation. For user-based CF, the system uses ratings provided by the users or a group for generating recommendations and for Item-based CF recommendations are generated by accessing collaborative behaviour of similar users in the past as of the targeted users (Kyung-Yong et al, 2004).

In order to recommend learning courses that are suitable to the students as per the learning level, collaborative systems were developed. Keeping in view complications that students are facing CF helps to improve the learning performance by recommending the courses that are more suitable to a respective students level of learning. To make the correlation between student skills and their profiles, the curriculum development, student skill model, Delphi analysis were utilized. The resulting analysis made it clear that the students obtained a better result and with more contentment with CF methods rather than facing a difficult time with a time trial and error methodology (Ji-won, Jae-choon, Hye-sung, Heui-seok, 2016).

A two-stage recommender system was proposed by (Pei-Chann, 2016) based on collaborative filtering to predict student grading in combination with faculty ratings to recommend courses for graduate students. Karl Pearson correlation and cosine similarity were used to calculate the affinity whereas collaborative filtering in the form of cluster approach based on the Artificial Immune Network (AIN) theory is used to recognize the similar learner. The study involves a dataset of both faculties, as well as student but the ratings from faculty do not intervene with predictions. To mitigate the problem of sparsity issue in Collaborative filters (Wang, Wang and Yeung, 2015) came up with a novel method of Collaborative Deep Learning (CDL) which uses a hierarchical Bayesian model, where deep representation learning is jointly performed for user content information, and CF is done for the feedback or rating matrix. The Collaborative Topic Regression (CTR) is an attractive methodology that firmly couples the two components which learn from two unique sources of information. The experimental results have shown the significant improvements in the results, but the hidden representation which CTR has learnt might be ineffective at the times when secondary information is sparse. Similarly (Almahairi et al, 2015) was determined to improve Latent Dirichlet Allocation (LDA) based CF by introducing a Collaborative Filtering based Recommender System. The system works by integrating reviews in the form of side information as a way of representing the resultant product regularization. They were moved by the success of the LDA based CF approach and proposed two review models based on Neural Network (NN) and Recurrent Neural Network (RNN) to study their effect on CF. NN has the capacity to perform resultant product regularization but interestingly the RNN seems to weaken the model's ability to act regularize the resultant product.

Content Based Filtering

Content-Based Recommender System (CBRS) attempt to solve recommendation problem by searching the items for a new user that are similar to the liking of the past users considering the item content. This means that the item preferences of one user should correlate with the same item of another user. The recommendation framework for e-learning systems was proposed by (Ghauth and Aniza, 2010) which based on excellent learners' ratings that indicate the quality of learning materials while recommending the learning materials of similar content. The authors tried to address the problem of growing e-learning material and recommend the material for a specific topic. The system was based on the concepts of Social Learning (SL) and Peer Learning (PL) theories which encourage persuade learners' to learn among themselves. This content-based recommendation system has shown noteworthy progress in test results in e-learning as compared to the e-learning systems without recommendation feature. But again learner rating deviations will affect the result which results in a lower accuracy rate.

A novel Content Based recommendation approach was suggested by (Jieun and Seoung, 2017) which use a network of multiple attribute system for reflecting several other attributes much effectively during the calculation of correlations among the items while recommending them. To ensure that various items should be recommended to the users, they employ clustering with the mechanism of centrality, to check interdependence between items and determine their interaction pattern structure. The method mitigates the problems of overspecialization and sparsity and even claims to overcome the cold start problem by using the past data of the users. Unlike Collaborative Recommender System which captures the user behaviour easily and effectively, even where user historical consumption overlies and is relatively high, but the range of the content remains static. On the other hand, the Content-Based

Recommender System may undergo frequent changes in much web application and there are users whose historical records are either not available or not enough for generating recommendations and thus ended up in cold start problem leaving this collaborative recommendation technique unproductive.

The overall scenario related to content-based RS's is that they are simple to implement but, in some situations, it is not sufficient to seize the exact user preferences using information stored in the user profile. First, the metadata might not be specified entirely in the e-learning systems where there is no service for recommendation feature which leads to the incorrect user profile. Second, the representation of user profiling cannot efficiently capture the relationship among the user items that have been accessed before. In addition to that, CBRS are not readily susceptible to the changes adopted by the user, and thus the content filtering system will undergo a new user and new item problem.

Knowledge Based Recommender Systems

Recommender System have a key role to play in e-learning while addressing the problem of information overload and help the learner to get relevant e-learning resources from a considerable collection both online as well as offline. In e-learning systems, Ontology-Based Recommender System (OBRS) added a new facet of ontology domain knowledge about e-learning resources in the process of recommendation while as conventional Recommender System still suggest items based on user ratings. By combining ontology with other recommendation methods will be helpful for recommending the resources in an e-learning system. Such hybridization overcomes the drawbacks associated with the individual recommenders like sparsity, cold start, new item problems, and can improve the overall quality and accuracy of the recommendations (Tarus, Niu & Mustafa, 2018).

Ontology-based Recommender System comes under the category of knowledge-based recommenders which utilize ontology for the representation of domain knowledge. In e-learning context domain ontology will helpful to model the knowledge about each learner and the resources about learning. Ontology-based recommendation Systems unlike, knowledge-based Recommender System do not experience the problems coupled with traditional Recommender System such as overspecialization, rating sparsity and cold-start problem, because ontology-based Recommender System rely mostly on domain knowledge rather than ratings given by the users (Zhao, Niu, Wang and Niu, 2015).

The ranking technique was brought in to limelight by (Gyeong et al, 2015) which was capable of delivering specific appraisal for the document relevance with respect to a specific query. The method employed was domain ontology to evaluate the linkage between the terms in the document. The Document semantics were exemplified in specified domain ontology with the help of Document Semantic Network (DSN) graph, and weighing approach based on the relationship was used to estimate the score of relevance in the document. Importance was given to the user interests and preferences for types of data to utilize the concept of personalization. Furthermore, the document semantics were depicted nicely in the form of a graph has emerged as the noteworthy aspect for the implausible improvement. A wonderful innovative idea by (Amir, 2014) with the help of Case-Based Reasoning (CBR) device launched for the personalization model for information retrieval based on ontology. The technique was committed to being user-friendly and scalable to understand the performance of information retrieval mechanism where results are ranked according to the user's interest. Two techniques were integrated together, CBR to customize the searching procedure and the ontology-based approach to exemplify the data to deliver users with alternate document recommendation. Recall and precision measure were carried out with the intent to assess and appraise the execution efficacy of the hybrid technique. Additionally, it was found that technique will improve with time in the itinerary domain for the transportation of metropolitan cargo.

Knowledge-based recommendation system using semantic web was advocated by (Zielinski, 2015) to illustrate the current status of the learner and the learning objects and learning material using knowledge pattern. The objective is to generate a student model and to track the progress of the student. For a specific student, the recommender was able to make the speculations regarding the objects that exist in a personalized learning path of the concerned learner. Furthermore, the main functions were also successfully implemented to assess the score for the best possible relevant learning object. An extension to Moodle in the form of ontology-based skill management was developed by (Rezgui, Hedia and Khaled, 2014) to check the growth, and assess the competency in student within a registered course. The ontology-based management of student competency design was developed in a course structure and certain attributes were integrated into Moodle. After integrated the attributes Moodle was competent enough to tackle the competencies along with some proof of instance. Also, they have created assorted categories of reports on competency according to profile such as faculty, administration and students.

Hybrid Recommender Systems

The Hybrid Recommender System is a multi-objective recommender system, which is a combination of subcomponents of single Recommender System like a combination of a Collaborative, Content-based approach, Knowledge-based, and Demography based approach. The Hybrid approach of recommendation was introduced to overcome the problems and the limitations of conventional Recommender System. In a hybrid approach, different methods are combined in together to optimize the prediction quality of recommendations and resolve the bottlenecks of conventional individual techniques. Combination of these recommendation approaches is done in different ways and can be classified as follows.

- Content-based and Collaborative methods are implemented separately and later their predictions are combined
- To incorporate a collaborative approach with some content-based characteristics
- The content-based approach is incorporated with some collaborative characteristics
- Construct a unified model that incorporates all approaches
- Incorporating keyword based on ontology of the knowledge-based approach
- Incorporating a knowledge-based approach with information retrieval techniques

The Hybrid techniques integrate multiple individual recommendation approaches to show better results and to mitigate the problems faced by individual systems. A hybrid approach can overcome the problems of scalability, sparsity, cold start, and overspecialization. A hybrid Recommendation system was proposed by (Heng-Ru, 2014) that were based on the interactive scenarios for user recommendations. The user recommender interaction is defined first and then the recommends N different Items to the user. The proposed system save the feedback or choices opted by the user them and if the recommended items are in favor, the user will be allowed browsing for a further search for recommendations till items do not favor her preferences. In addition to that K-Nearest Neighborhood (KNN) algorithm was also combined with the proposed to generate the nearest neighborhood. Finally, the scenario-based metrics were used to evaluate the system using diversity and recall feature.

Jose Aguilar et al (2017) marvelously brought a novel Intelligent Recommender System into light by extending the knowledge-based concept of Recommender System. The system has used fuzzy logic in combination with the cognitive maps and created five knowledge models about various facets that need to be considered during recommendations. The system uncovers new information, the preferences of the user, different learning methods and even criticism for exploiting the knowledge. The proposed system do not require knowledge engineering, user ratings and user information as its decisions are not dependent on individual preferences and are invulnerable to statistical errors. The aspects that guaranteed that the system is behaving intelligently are the reasoning capability and different representation of knowledge and learning. Recommender system exploits the extracted knowledge with the help of a learning mechanism which allows the system to update knowledge that was initially gathered in the form of domain and context information in initial inferences. The Proposed recommender system improved the recommendation quality because of knowledge representation and a different mechanism for reasoning and learning which traditional Recommender System do not possess simultaneously.

Another unique Recommender System approach which was systematically designed by (Ghazanfar and Prugel-Bennett, 2010) using the combination of different attributes like ratings, demographic information related to the items and features correlation. The system was based on cascading hybrid technique and it claims to outperform the traditional Recommender System and also overcome the recorded problem associated with RS. In order to allow the learner to have the utmost information for the purpose of learning, a splendid Hybrid Recommender System was formed by (Marouane et al, 2017) to suggest the content to the users on e-learning platforms for distance education. They have used the data mining techniques have divided the system into four parts to collect the information. The system assists to build the main centre of user's interest for accessing the material. The user information about their interest is collected in two modes explicit (collected from profile) and implicit (collected from the survey) mode. After a successful collection of information, they create a learner model and classify the content and the users also. Before recommending the new content and the content that has been already recommended, the system makes a similarity check between the content and the learners' and later create a log file of recommendations for learners'.

As the growth of e-learning material was mounted (Wei, Zhendong, Xiangyu and Yi, 2014) developed a Hybrid Recommendation system to recommend potential useful learning items to the users during their current learning process. The system was developed because the material was heterogeneous in nature and is available in different formats. So, the user with little knowledge about the domain and with a growing number of learning resources finds it difficult to choose courses for learning. The two methods were combined where CF was chosen to discover the items based on their content relationship and also Sequential Pattern Mining algorithm to filter the learning resources as per the common sequence of learning. The system was tested in the peer-to-peer online learning environment and in a centralized learning system where it has shown good performance.

Recommender Systems Using Other Approaches

Another important point is not to take care of the customization only, but also the delivery of the learning objects. Customization should not only be made about the choice of learning items, but also about their delivery. For example, sometimes a learner is recommended to go through certain survey papers before being recommended to go through some technical articles. It is because of the fact they these instructors believe that with this pattern learner will feel less intimidated and may prove effective for a learner to understand the papers. Conversely, in e-commerce, this pattern will not be taken care of and instead a list of unordered items is recommended to leave an impression of not being specific to any recommended item.

Farzan et al (2006) developed a recommender system namely course agent that focused on finding courses to match the user's career goals. The novel approach of this system was "do-it-your-self" that is to get feedback from the users and later providing the same to the system. So this system is mostly dependent on the student feedback rather than the system is choosing what can be the best for that particular student. Similarly (Cesar, 2009) with the help of data mining techniques constructed a recommendation system by classifying the courses "likely to succeed" and "not likely to succeed". These categories denote whether or not a student is going to score well or will achieve good grades, based on the history of his similar courses. This system also suffers from weakness, as they do not consider whether or not the course will be useful for the student, whether a student is likely to enjoy the course and classification of the courses are based on only yes or no scale without any course relation or course ranking. Maria et al (2015) came up with Recommender System which crunches the student's post-academic performance, the planned major courses and the data of similar fared students to arrive at a recommendation. The system is mostly used to arrive at grading students rather than what can best for him to study to affect his performance.

Tai D.W.S et al (2008) provide recommendations by searching learners' based on some attributes of a targeted learner. CF-based recommender system was developed to collect ratings from learners' and create a Vector Space Model (VSM). The rating of those learners' will be considered whose marks are above 80% of the total marks, which means that they might have studied the subject well. A learner with even 79.5% won't be considered for generating similar learner and in this way; the system will be induced with bias among the learners' who are genuinely well but didn't score 80% or above. Vinaya et al (2014) introduced the recommender system based on keyword to overcome the issues of ratings, scalability, and inadequacy during information overload and diverse user interest problems. They use specific keywords in order to signify items of user preference and the CF method to personalize the recommendations. The keywords extracted from the review are converted into negative keywords and positive keywords. The keywords are counted and the total number of keywords represents the weight of a particular keyword category. Then both the review weights are subjected to subtraction and if the result is positive the item will be recommended to the user and if the result is negative the item is not recommended. The system has shown improved accuracy over existing methods but it suffers heavy drawbacks in terms of negative keywords. There should be some algorithm that will create effective keyword categories otherwise the chances are that system will put positive keywords into the negative category.

Wang et al (2016) put forward an RS which was based on similarity categorization for detecting the query similarities to plan the execution of queries using machine languages. They employ association mining rule to ensure the similarities between the queries to be executed and also recommended an appropriate execution plan for newly formed queries. Zahir and Qadi (2016) justified that classification technique has been commonly used on queries in order to classify them into a set of a particular category. During information retrieval process user queries will create difficulties to fetch relevant information as it is difficult to interpret the queries that are ambiguous, having lesser number of relevant query words, and are noisy. The research practices have shown that evaluation of information retrieval is a big hitch and the challenging task is planning a dependable method which can measure the effectiveness of satisfying the information need of a learner.

It is difficult to take recommendations from one system and transfer to another due to lack of interoperability or domain dependency. The main challenge for RS is to recognize the purpose of a domain and to understand the interests of a learner in a much better way (Aleksandra, Vesin, Mirjana, Zoran and Lakhmi, 2017). Recommender system totally depends on ratings and interests of other users in the past, and then left it for a new user to respond to the choices that best match their requirements with respect to previous users. Instead of recommending courses at the initial stage most of the recommender system focuses only on recommending the learning material at a later stage. If a learner, at the beginning is suggested with the right courses to study the learning material will logically become more productive

Pedagogically items liked by the learners' may not be appropriate for them. Then it should be handled by the recommender system to help in customizing the learning items. The learners' at the college or university level may not be satisfied with the course advisers, and it is also possible that advisers could not devote enough time to students or may not have sufficient knowledge about all the courses offered in an institute. It has also been seen that while handling complex tasks humans tend to have a blind spot, and they try to give advice based on personal preferences. The basic aim of Recommendations is to open student's vision towards courses they are not aware of or might have skipped due to lack of knowledge.

DISCUSSION AND RECOMMENDATIONS

The chapter will help to assess the importance of the methodology used in the developing different types of Recommender System that will assist to personalize the items in an e-learning system. The study focused on information retrieval technique which is the backbone of any recommender system to overcome the problem of information overload. Recommender system aims to provide personalized information about courses, products or even services to users and alleviate the information retrieval challenges. The system will provide recommendations which are based on users' interest, preferences or information needs and thus personalization can be achieved by comparing user query and profiles with items in the repository.

In this study, it is highlighted that the problem encountered by individual recommendation approaches during the evaluation was mainly related to information retrieval. The performance of Recommender System using a particular technique may be affected by user queries, as the queries provided by the users may contain those relevant terms that are named with different vocabulary in the database, and this word mismatch makes it difficult to retrieve more relevant information. Further, it was shown that the hybrid system can handle the critical issue concerning the ambiguity, imperfection of query words and then an appropriate query transformation to retrieve more valid and related information. The study suggests that the performance of the hybrid technique is much better than other individual algorithms in retrieving the information for the recommendation. This study offers a motivation for basic algorithms to find new applications in the area of recommendation system to provide personalization to the learners' in an e-learning system. Ontology can also play a vital in the role in linking the items together with the help of certain relationships and can also provide a graphical view of different domains and the items to gain a better understanding of the domain.

With regard to the findings as discussed above, concerning this study, certain things that are recommended are as follows.

- This is a wakeup call for all administrators of higher educational institutes to act upon by introducing e-learning into their curriculum and for and researchers it is high time to provide modern means of technical support for these learning systems.
- It is recommended to avoid developing an individual recommender system. If the system is meant to provide the support for an online community a hybrid should be given preference instead, since it will contain all the advantages of individual systems by avoiding the features of limitations.
- There will be added advantage if the hybrid recommender system possesses some semantic features to create a relation between the courses being taught in institutes and offer learners' a complete overview of the interlinked relationship between them.
- The management of the institutes should provide facilities for their students and scholars to excel in creating a digital environment and support the institute in developing e-documents.
- The leaders of the educational technology should work together as collaborators to create a new opportunity for learners and not as missionaries.

- The use of technology should be encouraged in educational institutes and the faculty should be given sufficient time to learn the new evolutionary technology to master.
- The faculty should support the management in introducing these new learning methodologies since the new generation of learners is all based on mobile technology and it would be difficult to cope with the tech-based learners if modern means of education is not introduced.

CONCLUSION

This chapter offered a diligent survey on the recommender system and their importance in e-learning systems to provide personalization. The study provides an insight of the underlying algorithms which finds the latest applications in the area of recommendation systems for personalization in an e-learning system. Personalization is being acknowledged as the most challenging and important issue in current e-learning systems. Various methods were proposed to enhance the e-learning environment by taking learner characteristics or factors into account. The modern e-learning systems should take into account the requirements and needs of an individual learner. There were different approaches to personalize the items, and one such approach is of recommendation in which learner requirement are personalized in existing systems. The focus of this study was on different categories of recommendation approach for personalization and showcases various recommendation approaches in e-learning systems that have been developed using modern computational methodologies. Since most of these approaches suffer from a cold start, rating, sparsity, new user, new item and overspecialization problem. Hence a definite need for developing an effective recommender system that provides better and accurate suggestions resulting in the development of a hybrid recommender system that overcomes the drawbacks of existing individual systems and minimizes learner's efforts. After conducting a thorough review of the literature and other related works, it has been identified that hybridization of techniques enhanced the information retrieval and can improve the effectiveness of recommender systems. The study suggests that the performance of the hybrid technique is much enhanced as compared to other individual algorithms in retrieving the information for the personalization.

REFERENCES

Adomavicius, G., & Tuzhilin, A. (2005). Toward the Next Generation of Recommender Systems: A Survey of the State-of-the-Art and Possible Extensions. *IEEE Transactions on Knowledge and Data Engineering*, *17*(6), 734–749. doi:10.1109/TKDE.2005.99

Aleksandra, K. M., Vesin, B., Mirjana, I., Zoran, B., & Lakhmi, C. J. (2017). Recommender Systems in E-Learning Environments: E-Learning Systems:Intelligent Techniques for Personalization. *Springer International Publishing*, *112*, 51–75.

Alfadly, A. (2013). The Efficiency Of The (LMS) In AOU, Kuwait, As a Communication Tool in An E-Learning System. *International Journal of Educational Management*, *27*(2), 157–169. doi:10.1108/09513541311297577

Almahairi, A., Kastner, K., Cho, K., & Courville, A. (2015). Learning Distributed Representations from Reviews for Collaborative Filtering. In *Proceedings of the 9th ACM Conference on Recommender Systems*. Association for Computing Machinery. 10.1145/2792838.2800192

Amir, Z., Amna, B., Mourad, A., & Afef, F. (2014). An Ontology-Based Personalized Retrieval Model Using Case Base Reasoning. *Procedia Computer Science*, *35*, 213–222. doi:10.1016/j.procs.2014.08.101

Arunachalam, R. (2014). Bringing out the Effective Learning Process by Analyzing of E-learning Methodologies. *Indian Journal of Science and Technology*, *7*(5), 41–43.

Bobadilla, J., Ortega, F., Hernando, A., & Gutierrez, A. (2013). Recommender Systems Survey. *Knowledge-Based System, 46*, 109–132.

Burke, R. (2007). Hybrid Web Recommender Systems. In P. Brusilovsky, A. Kobsa, & W. Nejdl (Eds.), Lecture Notes in Computer Science: Vol. 4321. *The Adaptive Web* (pp. 377–408). Springer. doi:10.1007/978-3-540-72079-9_12

Cesar, V., Javier, B., Leila, S., & Alvaro, O. (2009). Recommendation. In *Higher Education Using Data Mining Techniques* (pp. 190–199). Educational Data Mining.

Fakoya, T., Adewale, S., & Oladoja, P.l. (2015). Ontology-Based Model for E-Learning Management System (O-Bmems). *International Journal of Computer Science Issues*, *12*(3), 118–126.

Farzan, R., & Brusilovsky, P. (2006). Social Navigation Support In A Course Recommendation System. In *Proceedings of International Conference on Adaptive Hypermedia and Adaptive Web-based Systems*, (pp. 91-100). Springer Verlag. 10.1007/11768012_11

Ghauth, K. I., & Aniza, A. N. (2010). Learning Materials Recommendation Using Good Learners Ratings and Content-Based Filtering. *Educational Technology Research and Development*, *58*(6), 711–727. doi:10.100711423-010-9155-4

Ghazanfar, M. A., & Prugel-Bennett, A. (2010). A Scalable, Accurate Hybrid Recommender System. *IEEE 2010 Third International Conference on Knowledge Discovery and Data Mining*, 94-98. 10.1109/WKDD.2010.117

Gyeong, J. H., Lee, J. H., & Hyo, W. S. (2015). Semantic Relation Based Personalized Ranking Approach for Engineering Document Retrieval. *Advanced Engineering Informatics*, *29*(3), 366–379. doi:10.1016/j.aei.2015.01.003

Heng-Ru, Z., Fan-Min, X. H., & Yuan-Yuan, X. (2015). A Hybrid Recommender System Based on User-Recommender Interaction. In *Mathematical Problems in Engineering* (pp. 1–11). HINDAWI.

Imran, H., Belghis, Z. M., & Ting-Wen, C. (2016). Kinshuk and Sabine, G. (2016). "PLORS: A Personalized Learning Object Recommender System. *Vietnam Journal of Computer Science*, *3*(1), 3–13. doi:10.100740595-015-0049-6

Ji-won, H., Jae-choon, J., Hye-sung, J., & Heui-seok, L. (2016). A Collaborative Recommender System for Learning Courses Considering the Relevance of a Learner's Learning Skills. *Journal of Cluster Computer.*, *19*(4), 2273–2284. doi:10.100710586-016-0670-x

Jieun, S., & Seoung, B. K. (2017). Content-Based Filtering For Recommendation Systems Using Multi attribute Networks. *Expert Systems with Applications*, *89*, 404–412. doi:10.1016/j.eswa.2017.08.008

Jose, A., Priscila, V., & Guido, R. (2017). A General Framework For Intelligent Recommender Systems. *Applied Computing and Informatics*, *13*(2), 147–160. doi:10.1016/j.aci.2016.08.002

Karasavvidis, I., & Kollias, V. (2014). Technology Integration in the Most Favorable Conditions: Findings from A Professional Development Training Program. In Research on e-learning and ICT in education. New York: Springer. doi:10.1007/978-1-4614-6501-0_14

Kyung-Yong, J., Dong-Hyun, P., & Jung-Hyun, L. (2004). Hybrid Collaborative Filtering and Content-Based Filtering for Improved Recommender System. In *Lecture Notes in Computer Science* (Vol. 3036, pp. 295–302). Springer.

Laurillard, D. (2013). *Teaching as a Design Science: Building Pedagogical Patterns for Learning and Technology* (2nd ed.). New York: Taylor & Francis Group. doi:10.4324/9780203125083

Lei, L. (2014). *Next Generation of Recommender Systems: Algorithms and Applications* (Doctoral dissertation). Florida International University Electronic Theses and Dissertations. Retrieved from http://digitalcommons.fiu.edu/etd/1446

Maria, G., Shade, K., & Nicolae, G. (2015). A Recommender for Improving the Student Academic Performance. *Procedia: Social and Behavioral Sciences, 180*, 1481–1488. doi:10.1016/j.sbspro.2015.02.296

Marouane, E. M., Salma, G., & Mohamed, K. R. (2017). Towards an Intelligent Hybrid Recommendation System for E-Learning Platforms Using Data Mining. *International Journal of Emerging Technologies in Learning, 12*(6), 52–76. doi:10.3991/ijet.v12i06.6610

Pei-Chann, C., Cheng-Hui, L., & Meng-Hui, C. (2016). A Hybrid Course Recommendation System by Integrating Collaborative Filtering and Artificial Immune Systems. *Algorithms, 9*(47), 2–18.

Rezgui, K., Hedia, M., & Khaled, G. (2014). Extending Moodle Functionalities With Ontology-Based Competency Management. *Proceeding of International Conference on Knowledge-Based and Intelligent Information & Engineering Systems, 35*, 570-579.

Ricci, F., Rokach, L., Shapira, B., & Kantor, P. B. (2011). *Recommender Systems Handbook* (1st ed.). Springer. doi:10.1007/978-0-387-85820-3

Robin, D. (2011). Web 3.0: Implications for Online Learning. *Tech Trends Springer, New York, 55*(1), 42–46. doi:10.100711528-011-0469-9

Tai, D. W. S., Wu, H. J., & Li, P. H. (2008). Effective E-Learning Recommendation System Based On Self-Organizing Maps and Association Mining. *The Electronic Library, 26*(3), 329–344. doi:10.1108/02640470810879482

Tarus, J. K., Niu, Z., & Mustafa, G. (2018). Knowledge-based Recommendation: A Review Of Ontology-Based Recommender Systems For E-Learning. *Artificial Intelligence Review, 50*(1), 21–48. doi:10.100710462-017-9539-5

Vinaya, B. S., & Pramod, B. G. (2014). Towards Keyword Based Recommendation System. *International Journal of Science and Research, 3*(11), 1318–1323.

Wang, F., Yang, Z., Li, Z., & Zhou, J. (2016). Query Classification by Leveraging Explicit Concept Information. *Lecture Notes in Computer Science, 10086*, 636–650. doi:10.1007/978-3-319-49586-6_45

Wang, H., Wang, N., & Yeung, D. Y. (2015). Collaborative Deep Learning for Recommender Systems. *Proceedings of the 21th ACM SIGKDD International Conference on Knowledge Discovery and Data Mining – KDD*. 10.1145/2783258.2783273

Wei, C., Zhendong, N., Xiangyu, Z., & Yi, L. (2014). A Hybrid Recommendation Algorithm Adapted In E-Learning Environments. *World Wide Web (Bussum)*, *17*(2), 271–284. doi:10.100711280-012-0187-z

Zahir, J., & Qadi, A. E. (2016). *Recommendation System for Execution Plans Using Machine Learning*. Mathematical and Computational Applications.

Zhao, X., Niu, Z., Wang, K., Niu, K., Liu, Z. (2015). Improving Top-N Recommendation Performance Using Missing Data. *Mathematical Problems in Engineering*, 1-14.

Zielinski, A. (2015). A Utility-based Semantic Recommender for Technology-Enhanced Learning. *Proceeding of IEEE International Conference on Advanced Learning Technologies*, 394-396. 10.1109/ICALT.2015.120

Chapter 4
Predicting the Academic Performance of Students Using Utility-Based Data Mining

Sidath R. Liyanage
University of Kelaniya, Sri Lanka

K. T. Sanvitha Kasthuriarachchi
University of Kelaniya, Sri Lanka

ABSTRACT

Data mining in education has become an important topic in the sphere of influence of data mining. Mining educational data encompasses developing models, plotting data, and utilizing machine learning algorithms to derive patterns on educational data by attempting to uncover hidden patterns, create information for hidden relationships using educational statistics, and perform many more operations that are unfeasible using traditional computational tools. This research aims to identify the main factors that influence the academic performance of learners in tertiary education system in Sri Lanka. A conceptual framework and an analytical framework on factors affecting the academic performance was constructed with this aim. The analytical framework was then validated with the data collected from technology learners in a tertiary educational institute.

DOI: 10.4018/978-1-7998-0010-1.ch004

INTRODUCTION

Data mining is devoted to examine high capacity data repositories to generate information and determine knowledge. Data mining techniques are applied to discover data patterns, organize information, discover relationships among data, and to structure association rules that are difficult to be carried out using classical search algorithms. Therefore, data mining is considered as a very beneficial technique to derive patterns and to make predictions in various real world settings including education.

Educational Data mining supports to find patterns in data and to make predictions in various aspects of education to support decision makers in the education industry (Alejandro Pena-Ayala, 2014). Modeling the learners' performance is an important application of educational data mining. The modeled results, patterns and the relationships can help educationalists to make important decisions pertaining to students' education. Data mining can be applied to identify factors that affects the performance of the learners and levels of the learner's performances. This knowledge can then be used to determine how the courses should be adapted to different learning styles of students while fulfilling the learning outcomes of the course. Discovered patterns can also be used to provide feedback to learners leading to improved performance by the students.

It has been found that the factors affecting the students' performance can be identified by applying proper learning analytic methods (Chatti, Dyckhoff, Schroeder and Ths, 2012). This potential has led to development of the new domain of Educational Data Mining (EDM). The main objective of using data mining in education is to enhance the process of educational practices and teaching and learning materials through more effective decision making with the insights produced by EDM. Identification of factors to determine the learning of students by analyzing their behaviors. Different interactive course materials can be used for conveying adaptive learning and facilitating personalized learning materials or practices. Analysis of educational records from different facets can recognize significant pointers for assessing the educational standings and for making important insights about the interactions of students', teachers and fellow students.

The educational data is gathered in many different manners, named, databases, online e-leaning data, Learning Management System (LMS) data of educational institutes and using survey instruments. The internet is allowing the students to corporate with the university and execute educational activities via the web. In distance learning or e-learning, students are able to perform collaborative learning by building relationships with learners' community, subject experts and educational facilitators.

Mining educational data can be useful for the analysis of students' data and derive predictions (Romero C, Ventura S, 2013), (Romero C, Ventura S., 2007), (Chatti, Dyckhoff, Schroeder and Ths, 2012). There are more studies which are based on building and modeling the students, visualizing students' data, students' groupings, social network usage analysis of the students, and analysis of students' distance learning data that makes decision making easier for course facilitators. Even though the prediction of students' performance is also another important application area of EDM, only a few studies has addressed this issue (Chatti, Dyckhoff, Schroeder and Ths, 2012). Many similar studies have used statistical methods rather than data mining for the analysis of performance data.

In predicting the students' performance by identifying the main factors affect to the performance using different data mining algorithms. In this study, Naive Bayes algorithm, Decision Tree, Support Vector Machine and Random Forest algorithm algorithms are used to perform the mining activities to derive the prediction models. Based on the model given by most accurate algorithm, the significant variables which can determine the performance of the students are identified. Then, the variables were tested for their impact to the target variable. The results of the prediction will be helpful in deriving important decisions in the education industry in many more ways.

Background

Educational system of Sri Lanka was considered in this study where the education system in Sri Lanka is divided into four levels: (1) pre-primary education (2) primary education (3) secondary education and (4) Tertiary education. The research problem was identified in the university students' records, which falls into tertiary education level. The research study has carried out by selecting several university students with their data and performing data mining methods to the selected data. In this section, a detail discussion about the tertiary education in Sri Lanka and the educational data mining is presented.

Tertiary Education in Sri Lanka

In Sri Lanka the education offers higher education facilities based on five major streams. Namely, Mathematics, Biology, Commerce, Arts and Technology. The performance at the Advanced Level (A/L) examination which completed under the above mentioned streams is the base for selecting the students for tertiary education by the government of Sri Lanka. The University Grant Commission in Sri Lanka (UGC) is mainly support to state universities by serving financial funds for the improvement of undergraduate studies, planning the academic activities and monitoring them, implementing policies in respect of university education in Sri Lanka. The z- score method determines the eligibility of the university admission under the guidelines given by UGC in Sri Lanka.

State universities in Sri Lanka provide various specializations for the education. Engineering, Physical Science, Mathematics programs can be selected by the students who completed the A/L examination in mathematics stream since they already grabbed the prerequisite knowledge in mathematics. Only the students who have done Biology in A/L examination will be selected for the Medical science, Biological science, Agricultural science degrees. This is same as the Commerce related, Art degree programs and Technology degree programs. Students of any stream who have achieved the required performance will be enrolled to technological degree programs. The state universities are conducting a selection test for the candidates prior to select the students. However, there is no such constraint for students to apply for technology degree programs such as IT degrees, Software Engineering degrees or computer networking degrees in degree awarding institutes. If the candidate is having minimum qualification of three passes for A/L examination will eligible to apply for technology degree programs. There are some institutes which allow the candidates to enroll even without meeting these minimum requirement as well.

Importance of Analysis and Educational Data Mining

Data mining plays a very significant step in Knowledge Discovery in Databases (KDD) which is used to discover novel and potentially important relationships between data, discover useful insight from huge datasets and make better and more intelligent decisions. The KDD process is illustrated in Figure 1. Utilization of data mining algorithms in different industries comprising education to analyze data about students to originate important knowledge areas, and derive prediction patterns are important advantages that can be gained by the decision makers. Mining the educational data to address important questions in education field is known as Educational Data Mining (Romero C, Ventura S., 2007). Application of data mining on educational data improves current educational practices and learning materials by supporting decision and policy makers.

Applications of educational data mining methods comprise several steps as shown in Figure 1. It includes (1) Selection of appropriate data for analysis, (2) Preprocess data, (3) Transform and integrate data, (4) Perform data mining and finally, (5) Interpretation of identified patterns.

Initially, an appropriate data set has to be selected in the related domain to carry out the study. This data set will be the sample which represents the whole population of the domain. This is named as raw data or the primary data. Once the

Figure 1. Educational knowledge discovery and data mining process

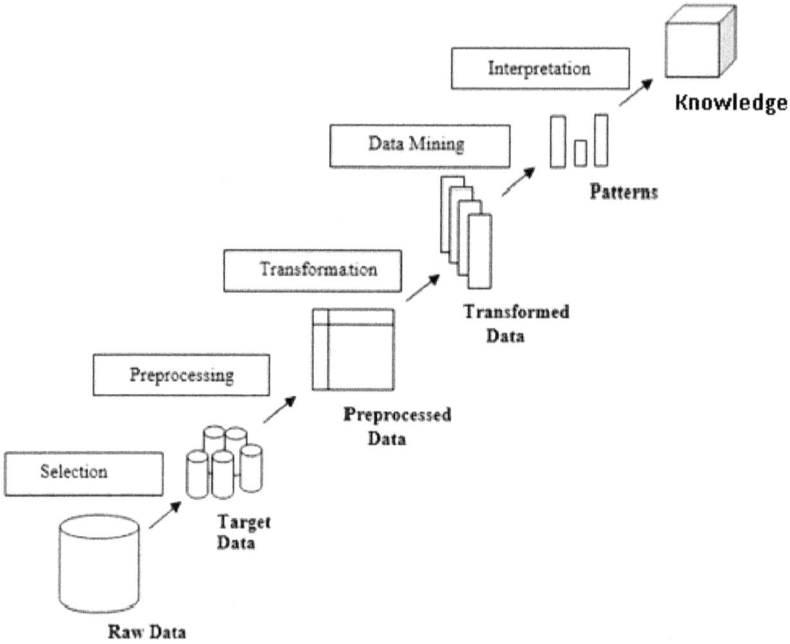

primary data is gathered, the inconsistencies have to be handled. Inconsistencies in the data set includes outlier values and noisy data; the data with errors. These data have to be cleaned in different steps; missing value handling, smoothing the noisy data and removing outliers (Dey, N. et. al. 2018). Next, the preprocessed data have to be integrated from multiple data sources to a single database. This may create redundant data. Before the data mining tasks are initiating, they also have to be handled. Next, data transformation has to be done to take the data into a format which is capable of performing mining tasks. Smoothing, generalization, aggregation, attribute construction, normalization and feature construction can be used to transform the data. Further, the data reduction methods; attribute selection, numerosity reduction, cube aggregation and dimensionality reduction have to be applied to the data. Then a suitable data mining method should be selected among predictive mining and descriptive mining. There are several educational data mining methods available such as prediction, outlier detection, clustering, Social Network Analysis, relationship mining, process mining, discovery of models, text mining, distillation of data for human judgment, and knowledge tracking (Romero C, Ventura S, 2013). Selection of the appropriate mining method has to be done based on the data and the data analysis task (Lan, Kun et. al., 2018). Finally, the analysis results should be interpreted. It's done in data interpretation and consolidation step. The knowledge discovered in the mining model has to be incorporated into a performance system and remove the conflict with previously believed knowledge.

Due to web based education, teachers and students are not restricted to a specific location. But, they can communicate via internet. Learning Management Systems (LMS) are installed in universities to add web technology to replace the traditional face-to- face education. Modular Object Oriented Developmental Learning Environment (MOODLE) is a freely available learning system to smooth management of powerful and flexible online courses.

E-learning systems generate massive information, log data about students' activities and communication with others for analyzing the performance and behavior (Bates, 2011). The e- learning data is used in finding the patterns by applying data mining algorithms to make decisions to improve teaching and learning of the institutes and also, to increase the revenue of the business in institutes.

Various Data Mining Algorithms

There are several data mining algorithms. Naïve Bayes classifier, K- nearest neighbor algorithm, Decision Tree algorithm, Support Vector Machine and Neural Networks are among them. They carry out the mining activities in many different forms depend on the mining tasks (Varlamis, I., 2017)

Naïve Bayes Classifier

Naïve Bayes algorithm is based on Bayes' Theorem. It uses strong assumptions which are independent. (Heide Brücher, Gerhard Knolmayer, Marc-André Mittermayer, 2002). This classifier can train with a relatively slight amount of training data for the estimation of the parameters for classification tasks. The classifier is often work in different complex real-world circumstances.

K-Nearest Neighbor (KNN)

The k-nearest neighbor algorithm is a learning algorithm that characterized objects built on closest feature space in the training set (Eui-Hong et. al., 1999). A measure call Euclidean Distance is typically used in this algorithm in making the prediction model. This algorithm is effective to use when a large data set is available for the analysis task but, a higher computational cost has to be paid.

Decision Tree

The Decision tree algorithm is a more powerful and popular technique for classification and prediction tasks in data mining. It represents rules, which can be used by humans and used in databases. The results known as prediction rules generated by the algorithm are more understandable and it uses less computation for the classification activities. However, the training the data is computationally expensive since all splitting field have to be sorted by searching the optimal and the pruning is also expensive since different sub-trees must be designed and compared.

Neural Networks

Neural network as a mining algorithm requires vastly parallel and adaptive processing in many circumstances such as prediction of future behaviour, pattern classification, clustering and time series analysis as well (Hwee-Tou Ng, et. al., 1997). The main advantage of this algorithm is its powerfulness of modeling complex functions, eeasiness, and very little user expertise requirement. The drawbacks of neural networks is its high computing cost which consumes high CPU and physical memory usage (Miguel E. Ruiz, Padmini Srinivasan, 1998).

Support Vector Machines

Support Vector Machine is a famous classification method which is based on the Structural Risk Minimization theory (Vladimir N. Vapnik, 1995). Unlike Decision Tree and Neural network the training the model is relatively less expensive in this method. However, the major drawback of the algorithm is it takes high time and require considerable memory consumptions in the training and classifying stages.

Educational Data Mining Tools

For mining the educational data various open source and commercial tools are available as:

TADA-Ed

This is a Tool for "Advanced Data Analysis in Education". It's able to visualize and mine the students' online web based exercise and use to derive pedagogically important patterns. This tool pre- process the data into a format which is capable of easily generates meaningful results during the mining process.

LOCO- Analyst

This tool is using to provide feedback on the activities the students have performed during the learning process and the social interaction among the other learners via the virtual learning environment. LOCO- Analyst is able to help the teachers to advance the content and the configuration of web based courses.

O3R

Ontology – based Rules Retrieval and Rummaging is a tool which uses to retrieve and analyze patterns in educational environment.

BNT- SM

Bayes Net Tool for Student Modeling is well suited for the modeling of the students' changing knowledge state during the learning process. The tool will describe the relationships among students' knowledge and the behavior when the data set with a condensed XML specification for Bayes net is inputted.

EDM Vis Tool

This is a visualization tool which graphically represents the tutor log data to improve the understanding of students' problem solving and to provide understandings about how to improve teaching and learning.

DBMiner

This is an interactive data mining and OLAP tool which applies to large data sets. It consists of data summarization, comparison, association, classification and prediction techniques to perform Knowledge discovery, pattern matching and identification of hidden relationships.

Value of Prediction in Education

A researcher known as Baker, suggested four significant areas of applications of data mining in education (Romero C, Ventura S., 2010). Improve student models, improve domain models, scientific research and studying the support of learning software. There are more research studies have been conducted under these categories such as;

1. Analysis and visualization of data
2. Providing feedback for supporting instructors
3. Recommendations for students
4. Predicting students' performance
5. Modeling the students
6. Detecting students' behaviors
7. Student grouping
8. Social network analysis
9. Developing concept maps
10. Constructing courseware

Data mining has been used in many industries including banking, marketing, transportation, telecommunication and health. Mainly this is used to analyze financial data in banking industry for classification of customers, detection of financial crimes and loan payment prediction. Identification of the buying patterns of the customers', their retention in the business and satisfaction of the business activities, the mining algorithms are widely used. Not only these industries the education industry is also getting benefits of data mining in many aspects such as students' performance prediction, grouping students based on various characteristics of themselves and their learning patterns, modeling the students, giving support for course creators to content development, analysis of distance learning data, visualization of students' data, analyzing the student usage patterns of social network and etc.

A special consideration is given in the review of literature on the application of mining tasks to predict the academic performance. The review of the existing literature on Educational Data mining tools, it could be used for facilitating effective use for mining educational data for decision making. However, it was revealed that there are few studies carried out in investigating the major reasons which affect negatively towards the performance of learners in Sri Lanka. Not only that, the studies were not validated the interestingness of the patterns to the academic performance also.

Evaluating the Interestingness of Patterns

Data mining derives patterns which are more trivial as well as patterns which are novel. The actual usefulness of the trivial patterns can be identified by measuring the interestingness of the patterns. These measures afford a standard filtering and ranking based on the execution of algorithms. Interestingness measures are used in three circumstances; (1) Used in the pattern extraction process to identify the attribute/ objective and value pairs in the patterns. (2) Used in measuring the weight of goodness of patterns. (3) Identify the patterns which are different from the rule set (Jabez J. Christoper, et. al., 2016). There are several criteria for measuring the interestingness of patterns. They are; coverage, conciseness, peculiarity, reliability, surprisingness, diversity, actionability, utility and novelty (Liqiang Geng, Howard J. Hamilton, 2006).

Further, they categorized into three sub groups: (1) objective, (2) subjective and (3) semantics- based. A measure which depends on the raw data is known as an objective measure. Objective measures depend upon probability theory, information theory or statistics. Coverage, conciseness, peculiarity, reliability and diversity are known as objective measures. Subjective measurement depends on the knowledge of user and the data that has to be known to measure the interestingness. Surprisingness and are novelty are subjective measures. If a measure is considered as the semantics, it falls into semantic category. A utility function is used to accomplish the goal of the users. Actionability and utility are in semantic measurement group.

Considering all the interestingness measures, the utility based interestingness measurement is applied for the study. This is not restricted only into statistical trait of data, but also the utility of derived patterns. Therefore, this is highly important since it's focused on the users' specific objectives and the utility of the derived patterns (Shen, Y.D., et. al., 2002). Several utility based measures are available with minor differences between each other. (1) Weighted item set mining; a weight value will be assigned for each item in the derived patterns by ranking them according to their importance. (2) Normalized weighted support method can be used for an instance where more data items exist in the patterns. (3) Vertical weighted support is another method which assigns weights for transactions based on the significance of them. (4) Vertical and the horizontal weights together is known as mixed weighted support method. (5) Objective oriented utility based approach sets objectives for mining to care a given objective statistically as well as semantically (Shen, Y.D., et. al., 2002). These attributes are partitioned into two categories as target attributes and non target attributes. In this approach, how interestingly the non target attributes are supporting the target attributes is measured.

In objective oriented utility (OOU) based method, the user will set an objective to mine the data. The target attributes/ objects and non target attributes/ non target objects are the two types of attributes/ objects in OOU. The target attributes are appeared in the consequent of the rule. Non target attributes are placed in the antecedent of the rules (Shen, Y.D., et. al., 2002).

The support values, confidence values and utility values of each rule could be calculated using the formula given below.

Support:

$$s\% = \frac{count\left(\left\{I_1,\ldots,\ I_m,\ obj\right\},\ DB\right)}{\left|DB\right|} * 100 \qquad (1)$$

where, *count* ({*I*1, ... I_m, *obj*}, *DB*) denotes the count of the records in dataset which consists of the value in the rule apart from obj and |*DB*| *is* for the total count of records in the dataset.

Confidence:

$$s\% = \frac{count\left(\left\{I_1,\ldots,\ I_m,\ obj\right\},\ DB\right)}{\left|DB\right|} * 100 \qquad (2)$$

where, *count* ({*I*1,..., *Im*}, *DB*) denotes the count of the records in dataset which consists of the value in the rule apart from obj.

Utility:

The total **of all** the positive utilities and all negative utilities of each attribute which are fulfilling the object (obj) are calculated and obtain the highest utilized attributes.

The usage and the validity of the rule and the attributes involve in the rule are measured based on the support value, confidence value and the utility value of each rule.

Factors That Affect to Academic Performance of Learners

According to the existing studies in modeling the performance factors of students, some factors were identified as important features to hold by learners. They are (1) Prior domain knowledge: Prior domain knowledge is obtained before a certain learning task. It contains conceptual as well as metacognitive knowledge components (Dochy, De Rijdt, & Dyck, 2002). This is measured using the grades obtained in examinations. This study, considered the Mathematical and English knowledge of students as the most valuable prerequisite courses for technology learners from the facts found in literature. (2) Prior achievement; the prior achievement refers to a student's performance during school, cumulative GPA in the university and the grade the student earned in a different course. On the one hand, prior achievement related to the prior knowledge and it affects to the academic performance. Non- cognitive variables, personality traits such as involvement to the social activities are considered as other influencing factors as predictors of student academic performance. The (3) support of family, (4) demographic factors such as gender and race and the (5) organization of the course modules, the teaching and learning process of the institute are also has a direct involvement to the performance of students (Delavari, N., et. al., 2004).

Proposed Methods

The data collection has conducted using database data and a survey. A questionnaire has been prepared by including a set of related questions to gather the data from selected research sample. Students in tertiary education in Sri Lanka includes to the population. The random probability sampling method is used to select the sample. The sample of this study consisted of 3794 learners who have sat for their final examination of an institute which offers degrees in Information Technology in Sri Lanka. A printed copy of the questionnaire is distributed among the sample to gather the responses and then completed responses are collected on the spot. The performance records of these learners such as the semester GPAs and grades are collected by compiling various queries in the student data repository of the selected institute.

Based on the extensive literature and the data collected from the survey and database, 24 independent/ predictor variables are selected. They are; Age of the learner (Age), Gender of the learner (Gender), Location of the learner (Location), Father's occupation (Fjob), Mother's occupation (Mjob), Average Family Income (AverageFamilyIncome), A/L Stream of the learner (A/LStream), Grade for A/L English (A/LenglishGrade), Grade for O/L English (O/LenglishGrade), Lecture Attendance (LectureAttendance), Hours Spend for Studies Per Day (HoursSpend), Participation to extracurricular activities (ExtraActivities), Use of social network (SocialNetworkUsage), Political involvement (InvolvementforPolitics), Memberships of societies in the institute (membershipsofSocieties), Is learner won scholarships during study period? (WonScholarships), learners' satisfaction about the teaching in the institute (SatisfactionofTeaching), is learner having previous fail modules? (FailModules), GPA of semester 1 (GPAS1), GPA of semester 2 (GPAS2), GPA of semester 3 (GPAS3), GPA of semester 4 (GPAS4), GPA of semester 5 (GPAS5) and GPA of semester 6 GPAS6. Age, Gender, Hometown cover the demographic factors, ExtraActivities, SocialNetworkUsage, InvolvementforPolitics and membershipsofSocieties are selected to test the involvement of social factors. The involvement to academic activities are considered in two aspects. (1)Secondary education details and (2) Tertiary education details. Secondary education details covered by A/LStream, A/LenglishGrade and O/LenglishGrade. The institute conducts academic activities in English medium. Therefore a better fluency level in English is important to bear by learners to successful in their studies. FrequencyofAttendancetoLectures, HoursSpendforStudiesPerDay, FailModules, GPAS1, GPAS2, GPAS3, GPAS4, GPAS5 and GPAS6 are used to cover the tertiary education details. Occupation of the learner's father, Occupation of learner's mother, AverageFamilyIncome of the learner cover the family commitment and institutional contribution checks by WonScholarships and SatisfactionofTeaching variables. The grade (Grade) of the learner in the end of the three years degree program is considered as the dependent variable in the study.

Next, the missing values and the incomplete data in the data set are controlled by performing the steps of median imputation. Case deletion has been applied to some records to remove them from data set. Then integrated the records into a Comma Separated Value file (CSV file) for the analysis using data mining algorithms.

The CSV file which contains the data set is preprocessed, transformed and integrated. As the first step of preliminary data analysis of this research, the general information/ descriptive statistics of respondents is summarized using tables and graphs. This would helpful for understanding the characteristics of the sample.

Next, five hypotheses are defined as follows.

Hypothesis One: The social factors are affected to the academic performance of learners.

In this hypothesis, the affect of Social network usage, attendance to the academic activities, average study hours allocated per week, and extracurricular activities towards the academic performance of students are determined.

Hypothesis Two: The demographic factors are affected to the academic performance of learners.

The hypothesis determines whether the age, gender and hometown of the student affect for the academic performance of the students.

Hypothesis Three: The academic activities are affected to the academic performance of learners.

In this hypothesis, the affect of prior knowledge, prior achievements and current performance of students to their academic performance is determined based on

Marks for assignments, quizzes, class tests, lab activities, final examination, results for O/L examination, results for A/L examination and A/L study stream.

Hypothesis Four: The family commitment is affected to the academic performance of learners.

Occupation of parents and average monthly income of the family are included into the family commitment factor of the students in this hypothesis.

Hypothesis Five: The institutional contribution is affected to the academic performance of learners.

This hypothesis determines whether the course fee for a semester, number of credits per semester, interaction of the students with instructor in the teaching and learning process and motivation given through financial scholarships are affecting to the academic performance of the students.

The conceptual framework of the study is illustrated in Figure 2.

Figure 2. Conceptual Framework

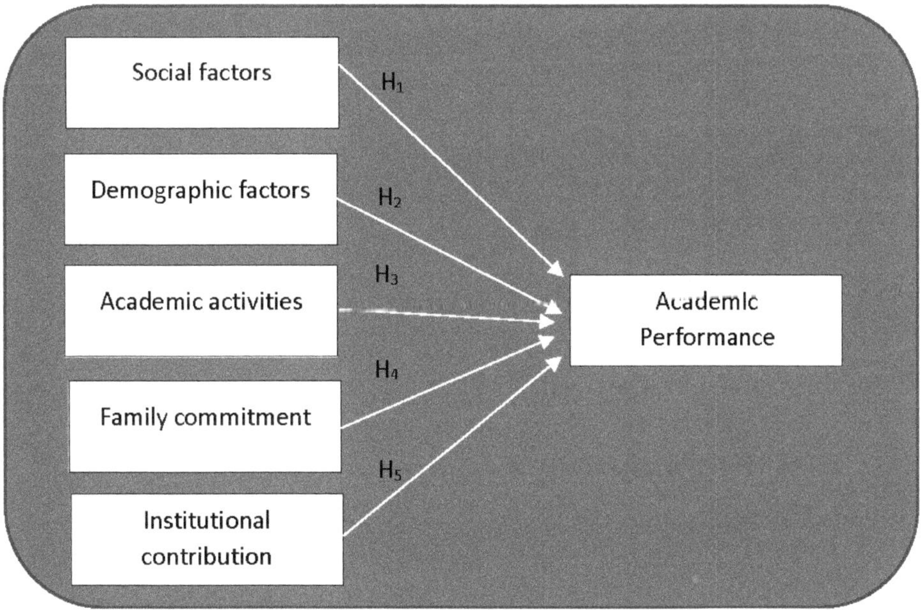

Analysis and Experimental Results

After an extensive analysis of data using the selected data mining algorithms, the results are collated. The distribution of age of the students in the sample is represented using the histogram in Figure 3.

According to the Age of the respondents, 33% of students are of age 19. 24% of students are of age 20. 11% of students are of age 21. The percentage of students of age 22 is the 22%. 6% of students are of age 23. 2% of age 24 students are in the data set. The remaining 2% are of age 25 and above.

Pie chart generated for gender representation by R Studio is illustrated in Figure 4.

61% of male students and 39% of female students are included into the sample.

The grade distribution is illustrated in Figure 5. Accordingly, the scale used in representing data items in the dataset, 1 denotes A pass, 2 denotes A-, 3 denotes B+, B denoted by 4, 5 denotes B-, 6 denotes C+, 7 for C, 8 for C-, 9 denotes D+, 10 denotes D, 11 denotes D- and E denoted by 12.Accordingly, the count and percentage of grade obtained by each student is illustrated in following Table 1.

Figure 3. Age Distribution

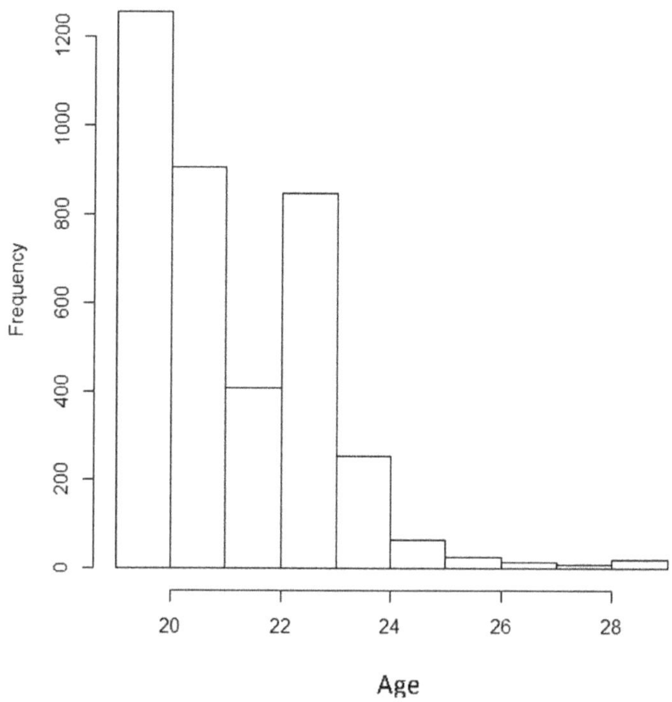

Figure 4. Gender Distribution

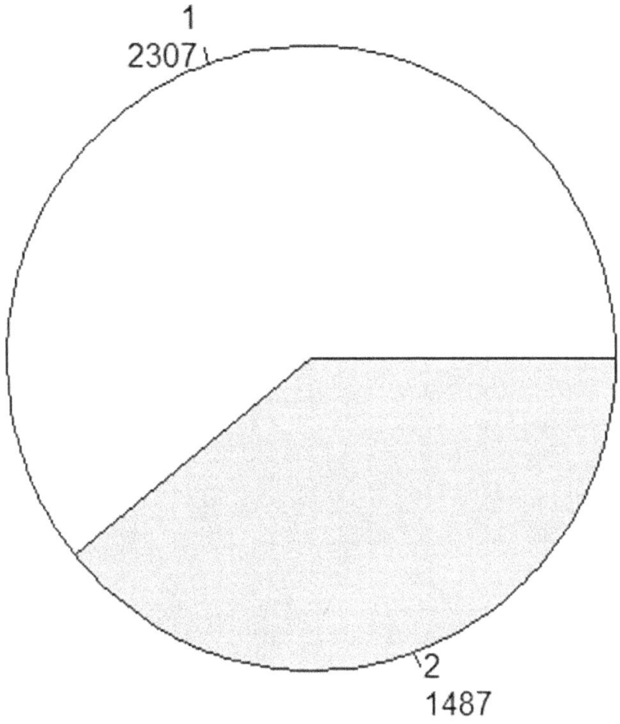

The descriptive statistical details of each independent variable is represented in following Table 2.

The descriptive statistical details of the dependent variable is represented in following Table 3.

Data Mining Prediction Model

Next, a selected set of mining algorithms are used to build up the prediction model. Preprocessed data set is fed into NB algorithm, DT algorithm, RF algorithm and SVM algorithm. R studio package consists of various libraries and methods to support for data mining tasks.

In order to initiate the analysis, 50% of data in the data collection is considered as the training set. Next 50% of data is considered as testing data set. Training data set is for model training. The model will learn from the training set. Testing data set measures how much the model is learnt using the trained data.

Training and testing data sets are fed to R Studio software to perform the analysis using the above mentioned algorithms and performed 10 fold cross validation to

Figure 5. Grade Distribution

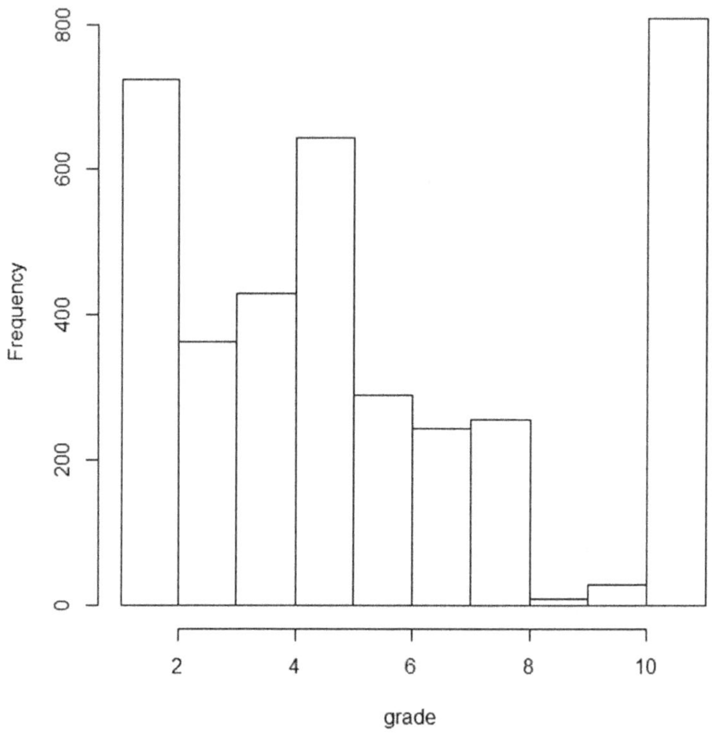

Table 1. Grade Distribution of the Sample

Grade	Count	Percentage
A	725	19%
A-	363	9%
B+	428	11%
B	644	17%
B-	290	8&
C+	243	6%
C	256	8%
C-	9	0.3%
D+	28	0.7%
D	772	20%
D-	36	0.9%

Table 2. Statistics of Independent Variables

Variable	Min	Max	Mean	Median
Gender	1	3	1.39	1
Age	19	29	20.6	20
Location	1	2	1.293	1
PreviousFailures	0	1	0.028	0
Father's occupation	1	9	5.938	6
Mother's occupation	1	9	1.498	1
AverageIncome	1	7	5.929	6
A/LStream	1	6	2.007	2
A/LEnglishGrade	1	5	1.344	1
O/LEnglishGrade	1	5	1.039	1
FrequencyofAttendance	1	4	3.858	4
HoursSpendForStudy	1	6	3.406	3
ExtraActivities	1	1	1	1
SocialNetworkUsage	1	1	1	1
InvolvementforPolitics	2	2	2	2
MembershipsofSocieties	1	2	1.998	2
wonScholarships	1	2	1.99	2
SatisfoactionofTeching	1	1	1	1
GPAS1	0	4	2.143	2
GPAS2	0	4	2.170	2
GPAS3	0	4	2.001	2
GPAS4	0	4	2.148	2
GPAS5	0	4	2.143	2
GPAS6	0	4	2.123	2

Table 3. Statistics of Dependent Variable

Variable	Min	Max	Mean	Median
Grade	1	11	4.863	4

Table 4. Performance of Mining Models

Criteria	NB Model	DT Model	RF Model	SVM Model
Correct Classified Instances	1153	1220	1200	1149
Incorrect Classified Instances	111	44	64	115
Accuracy of the Prediction	92.17%	97.1%	96.78%	92.05%
Kappa Statistics	81.91%	93.57%	93.27%	80.58%
Precision	89.403%	94.85%	94.56%	89.24%
Recall	99.75%	98.71%	98.41%	98.86%
F-Measure	87.5%	95.79%	95.52%	86.95%

record the accuracies. The 3 times repeated cross validation is done and the results are recorded in each time. The results are organized as in Table 4. Based on the results, the best algorithm has identified to obtain the predication model.

Table 4 illustrates the performance of models derived by each mining algorithm.

As per the results depicted in the above table, it's clear that all mining algorithms produced good results which are having closer accuracies to each other. However, the Decision Tree algorithm has shown the best accuracy level. Therefore, the model derived by it has selected to continue in making results of the study. The selected model consists of thirteen independent variables which affect to the performance of Sri Lankan students.

Figure 6 shows the tree generated by the model.

According to the data mining model, Lecture Attendance, Age, Occupation of Mother, Grade for O/L English, Occupation of Father, Average Income of the Family (per month), A/L study stream, GPA of semester 1, GPA of semester 2, GPA of semester 3, GPA of semester 4, GPA of semester 5 and GPA of semester 6 are selected as the most influencing factors to determine the academic performance of learners.

Next, the importance of independent variables extracted by the Decision Tree model is measured by ranking the feature importance under feature selection method.

According to the Figure 7, all predictor variables are containing a relatively good variable importance which is varying between 0.65 and 0.79. Based on this model, thirteen rules are built as listed below.

Rule 1: If Frequency of Attendance to Lectures is above 50%, then the overall grade of the student is above C+.

Rule 2: If Age of the student is between 19 and 25, then the overall grade of the student is above C+.

Rule 3: If Mother is doing a job, then the overall grade of the student is above C+.

Figure 6. Tree Generated by the Model

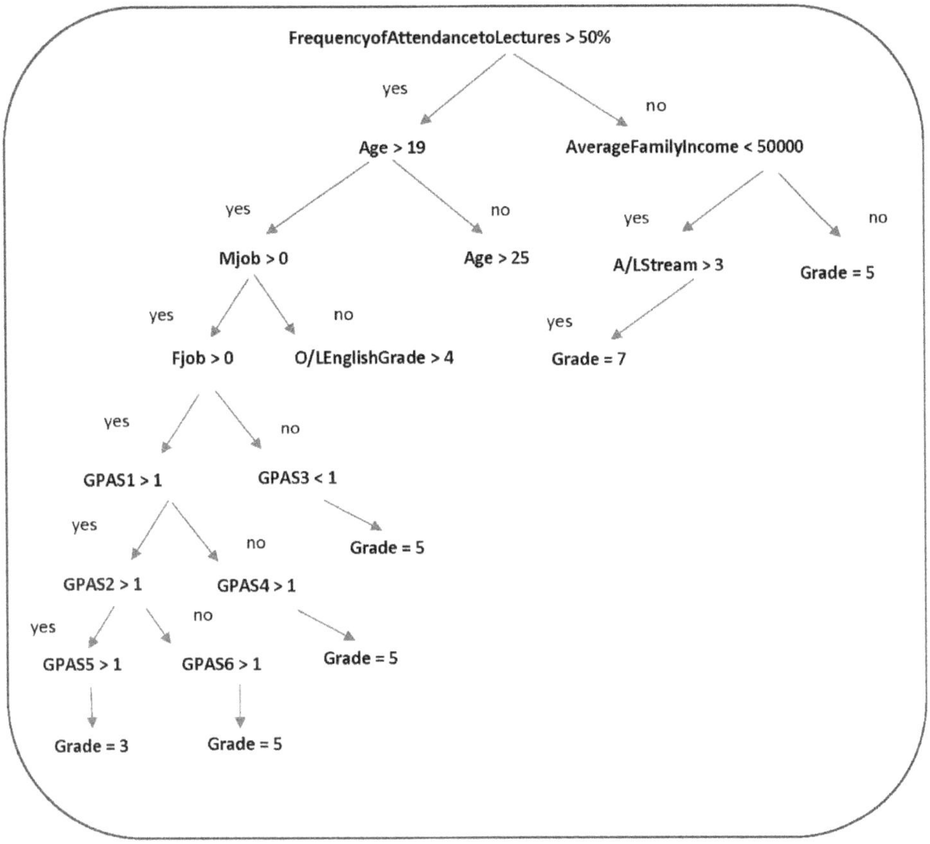

Rule 4: If, the O/L English Grade is above 'S', then the overall grade of the student is above C+.

Rule 5: If Father is doing a job, then the overall grade of the student is above C+.

Rule 6: If Average Family Income is above 50000, then the overall grade of the student is above C+.

Rule 7: If the A/L Stream is Biology | Mathematics | Commerce, then the overall grade of the student is above C+.

Rule 8: If GPAS1 is above 2, then the overall grade of the student is above C+.

Rule 9: If GPAS2 is above 2, then the overall grade of the student is above C+.

Rule 10: If GPAS3 is above 2, then the overall grade of the student is above C+.

Rule 11: If GPAS4 is above 2, then the overall grade of the student is above C+.

Rule 12: If GPAS5 is above 2, then the overall grade of the student is above C+.

Rule 13: If GPAS6 is above 2, then the overall grade of the student is above C+.

Figure 7. Representation of Variable Importance in Decision Tree Model

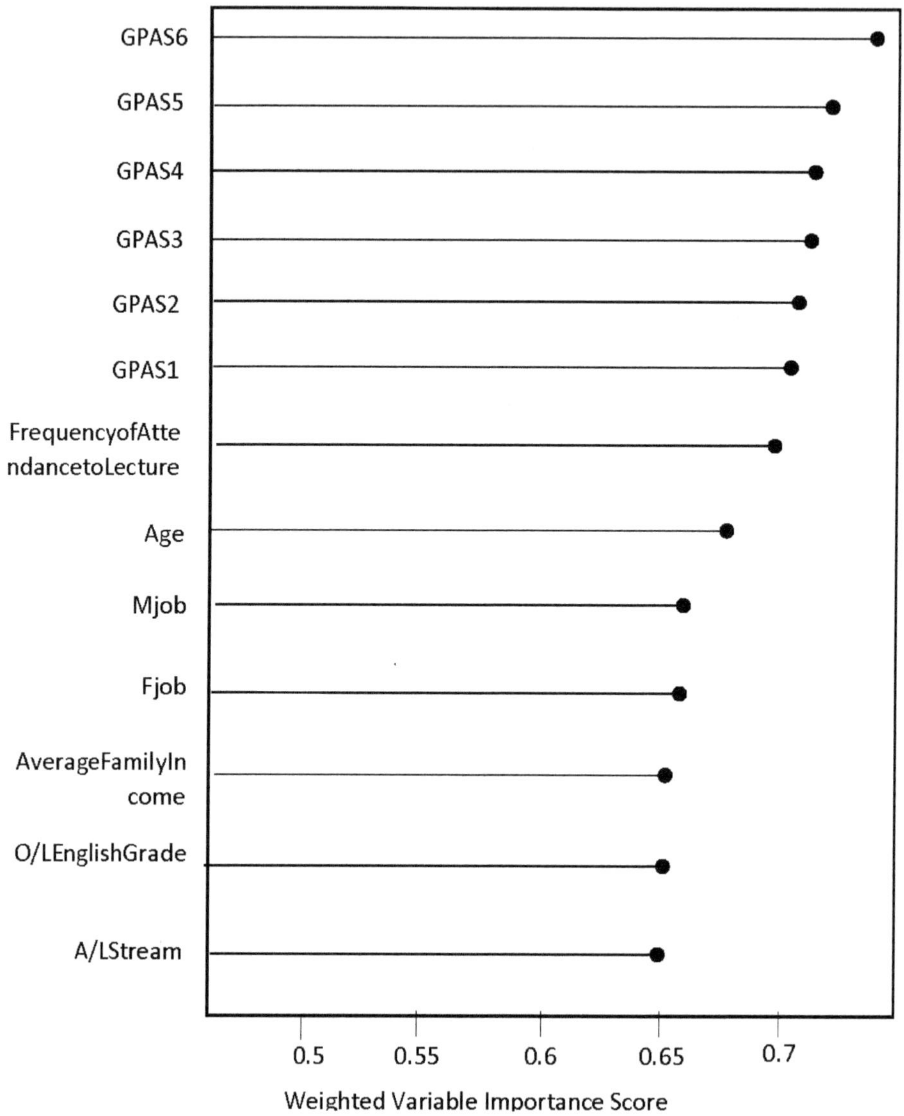

Measurement of Interestingness of Rules

These rules are generated by the Decision Tree algorithm using the model derived in the analysis. However, the rules from rule number 8- 13 are considered as more general since, they are about the Grade Point Average (GPA) value of the students which directly affects to the final grade or the performance of the student. Therefore, except the rule number 8 to 13, the other rules are considered and measured the interestingness of the predictor variables involve in the rules.

The OOU based method is used to evaluate the interestingness of rules in the selected mining model. Firstly, the non- target and target attributes of the rules are identified. Secondly, to each possible individual value of target attributes, a weight value is assigned. Thirdly, the confidence, support and the utility of item sets in the rules are calculated to select the most interesting item set to predict the performance of students.

LectureAttendance, Age, Mother's occupation (Mjob), O/LEnglishGrade, Father's occupation (Fjob), AverageFamilyIncome and A/LsubjectStream are selected as non target attributes. The grade obtained the end of degree program is highlighted as the target attribute. The target attribute also known as the object (*obj*). The objective (*obj*) is selected to grade on or above C+ (Grade >= C+) since the pass grade level is C+. Then weight values for each grade associated into the object is assigned as shown in Table 5. This weight assignment is done based on the credits offered for the degree in the institute.

The non- target attributes in the rules are separated as classes and calculated the utility of each of them in the dataset. The support values, confidence and utility values of these non- target attributes in order to achieve the target, are measured and Table 6 illustrates them.

Accordingly, the item sets with the highest support, confidence, and the utility values to support to the object (*obj:* Grade >= C+) are selected and concluded as the

Table 5. Weights of Obj.

Grade	Weight Value
A+	1.6
A	1.4
A-	1.2
B+	1.0
B	0.8
B-	0.6
C+	0.4
C	0.2
C-	0
D+	-0.2
D	-0.4
E	-0.6

Table 6. Support, Confidence and Utility of Item Sets of rules

Item Set	Support (%)	Confidence (%)	Utility
Lecture Attendance < 50%	0	0	-1.4
Lecture Attendance 51% - 74%	0.05	45.8	3
Lecture Attendance 75% - 94%	27	93	4.6
Lecture Attendance 95% - 100%	36	63	78.4
Age = 19	0.98	50	0.4
Age = 20	13.8	62	27.8
Age = 21	11.3	40.3	10.8
Age = 22	0.98	25	8.8
Age = 23	0.98	25	0.2
Age = 24	0.98	50	2.2
Age = 25	0.98	50	2
Age = 26	0	0	-0.4
Age = 27	0	0	-0.4
Age = 29	0	0	-0.8
Mother's Job = house wife	26.1	53	33.6
Mother's Job = teacher	17.7	59	33.8
Mother's Job = doctor	0.49	25	0.2
Mother's Job = Nurse	1.97	80	-0.2
Mother's Job = Government Job Holder	2.94	46.66	1.2
Mother's Job = Job holder of the private sector	5.4	50	1.8
Mother's Job = business lady	0.98	100	2.2
Mother's Job = Work at Overseas	0.49	100	1
Mother's Job = Retired	1.48	75	2.2
O/L English Grade = 'A'	33.9	54	46
O/L English Grade = 'B'	9.8	51.3	15
O/L English Grade = 'C'	6.4	50	10.2
O/L English Grade = 'S'	3.9	72.7	5.8
O/L English Grade = 'W'	2.4	52.4	1.3
Father's Job = teacher	4.9	55.6	12.6
Father's Job = forces	0.98	50	1
Father's Job = doctor	1.48	50	3
Father's Job = Government Job Holder	6.34	50	1.6
Father's Job = Job holder of the private sector	1.96	80	-0.6
Father's Job = business man	52.7	73.3	54.4
Father's Job = Work at Overseas	0.98	50	1
Average Family Income between 25000- 30000	0.49	100	0.8
Average Family Income between 30000- 50000	6.4	44.8	5.6

continued on the following page

Table 6. Continued

Item Set	Support (%)	Confidence (%)	Utility
Average Family Income between 50000- 80000	10.8	51.1	18.4
Average Family Income between 80000- 100000	5.6	35.8	2.3
Average Family Income between 100000- 200000	11.8	66.66	22.8
Average Family Income between 200000- 300000	24.13	53.8	36
Average Family Income between 300000- 400000	0	0	-0.8
A/L Stream = Arts	5.4	61.1	11
A/L Stream = Biology	13.79	50.9	21
A/L Stream = Commerce	6.4	59	10.6
A/L Stream = IT	0.49	100	1.4
A/L Stream = Mathematics	27	53.9	39.4
A/L Stream = Other	0.98	40	1.2

Obj: Grade >= C+

most influencing factors to determine the performance of tertiary level students in Sri Lanka. Table 7 illustrates the interesting patterns derived by Objective Oriented Utility based method.

Education enables learning, obtains new knowledge, improves various skills and qualities, generates beliefs, and propensities. Strategies in education incorporate narrating, exchanging, instructing, preparing, and coordinating research. This is mostly takes place under the direction of instructors, even though some students might prefer self-study. Several motivational factors play behind utilizing Data Mining in the education industry. In the analysis stage of this study, the attributes which are the most critical in predicting the performance of the students in tertiary education system are identified through Decision Tree data mining algorithm.

Table 7. Interesting Rules

Rules	Support (S%)	Confidence (C%)	Utility (U)
LectureAttendance 95% - 100%	36	63	78.4
Age = 20	13.8	62	27.8
Mother's Job = teacher	17.7	59	33.8
Mother's Job = house wife	26.1	53	33.6
O/L English Grade = 'A'	33.9	54	46
Average Family Income between 200000- 300000	24.13	53.8	36
Father's Job = business man	52.7	73.3	54.4
A/L Stream = Mathematics	27	53.9	39.4

After validating the model using interestingness measurements, the factors which affect to the academic performance of tertiary level learners in Sri Lanka are identified (see figure 8).

Accordingly, the learners' attendance to academic activities, age, occupation of parents, income of the family, fluency of English, performance for Mathematics, and past performance are affecting to the academic performance of the learners in tertiary education system in Sri Lanka.

Attendance to academic activities which is identified as a social factor of learners is included to the mining model. The students who kept a better attendance level for lectures and other academic activities in an average of 95-100% were emphasized as good performers. This proves that the hypothesis one can be accepted. Most of these high performers are of age 20. In Sri Lanka, most of the fresh school leavers are of age 20. They prefer to explore new things and technologies and do various technological innovations. In this study the attribute age is considered as a demographic factor of students, it proves that the hypothesis two can be accepted. Next, if a student passed the O/L English examination in Sri Lanka with an 'A' grade

Figure 8. Factors affect to Academic Success of Learners

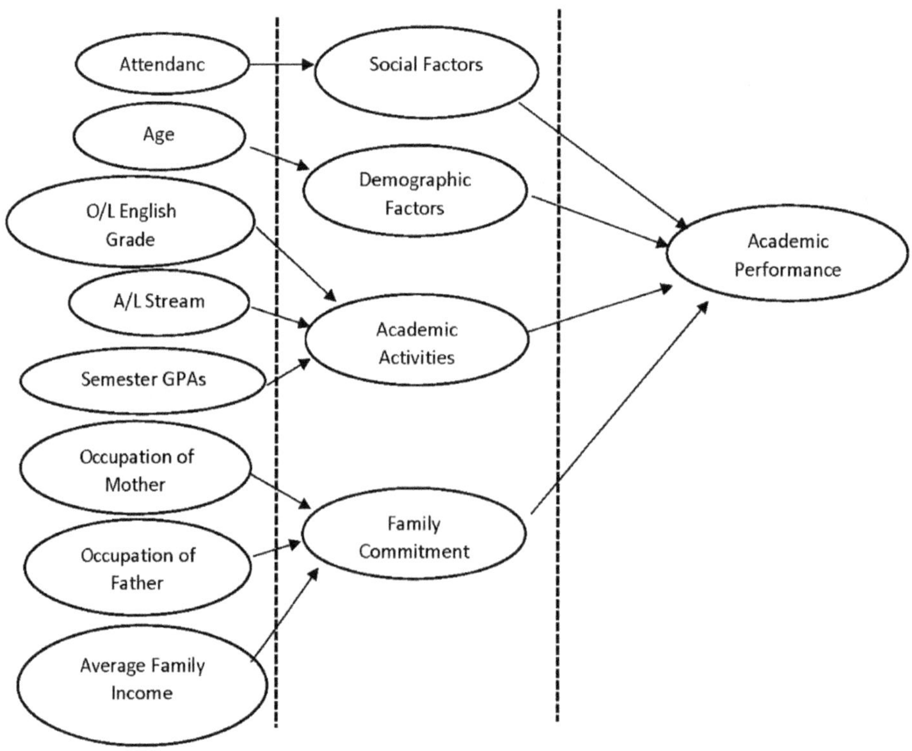

and followed Mathematics stream at the A/L examination in Sri Lanka which, is the university entrance examination, are most likely to perform better.

The students are required to have a perfect communication in English since the tertiary education is mostly based on English medium. Since majority of the students in Sri Lanka complete their secondary education in their mother language, fluency in English will be an added advantage for them. A good mathematical knowledge, good in analytical thinking and problem solving skills are another sets of skills which these students must improve to obtain a better performance level in the tertiary education. Not only have that, the GPA obtained in previous semesters also influenced for the academic success of the learners. GPA of previous semesters, Grade for O/L English, and Stream of A/L studies are representing the academic factor. Therefore, the hypothesis three can be accepted. Learners whose mothers are teachers and housewives, and fathers are business men are visualizing better performance in the education. When mother is a teacher or a housewife, they would have time to spend for the education of their children and guide them. Even for fathers who are running businesses are flexible in investing money for the education of their children. Majority of the high performers have already shown an average income of the family between 200000 to 300000 Sri Lankan rupees, which means their parents are well capable in buying the necessary technological equipment for them as well as providing economical support to their education. By including occupation of parents and the family income level, the hypothesis four can also be accepted. As mentioned above, the motivation provided by the institute, number of credits given to complete the studies, the fee for the studies and the teaching and learning in the institute are not included to the final model derived in the study. This implies that the hypothesis five has to be rejected.

CONCLUSION

The social factors (Lecture Attendance), demographic factors (Age), family commitment (Occupation of Mother, Occupation of Father, Average Family Income per month), Past performance for academic activities (Grade for O/L English, A/L study stream, GPA of semester 1, GPA of semester 2, GPA of semester 3, GPA of semester 4, GPA of semester 5 and GPA of semester 6) are involving in determining the grade of the student. Therefore, these factors can be used to predict the students' academic performance.

The optimistic aspect of these types of result is that the management will be able to select candidates who has required competent level to the degree programs in the institute/ university. Not only that, the educators have sufficient time to look into the factors and make appropriate adjustments to the course content, delivery methods, preparation of assessments and other important things such as maintaining students' attendance to lectures, motivating them to do self-studies to improve performance prior to start a new semester. However, the selection of the performance/ GPA of the past semesters would not do a change in prediction results since, the GPA is a noticeable measurement for the performance of the students. However, even the main intention of this research study is to identify the influences affect to the academic performance of the students, the results of the model would help the educators, learners and their parents to determine the level of their performance and whether they are academically at-risk.

This research contributes to society in different aspects; especially in the educational decision making process by educators, educational providers and also for parents. Since the performance of the module correlates to the attendance of the students, educators/ lecturers can implement practical methods to attain a higher percentage of attendance for their module and revise their module curricular to engage the students in more self-learning and assess the progress in the classroom. It is advisable for institutes to introduce new modules related to Mathematics and English to enhance their knowledge in order for them to complete their technological modules in English language successfully. Institutional management can provide loan schemes or scholar-ships as financial support to students from low income families. Further, the parents need to be involved in continuous monitoring of the progress of their children despite time constraints owing to their busy lifestyles as negligence may affect their children's progress negatively. These factors will provide a concrete baseline in the process of making critical decisions in the educational industry.

FUTURE WORK

The modeling techniques can be further enhanced by collecting several other institutes who provide tertiary level technology education in Sri Lanka. The, text mining approaches can be used to analyze the textual data of the dataset instead of converting text data to numeric for the analysis.

REFERENCES

Bates. (2011). *Technology e-learning and distance education*. London: Routledge.

Brücher, H., Knolmayer, G., & Mittermayer, M.-A. (2002). Document Classification Methods for Organizing Explicit Knowledge. Engineering, Institute of Information Systems, University of Bern.

Chatti. (2012). A reference model for learning analytics. *International Journal of Technology Enhanced Learning,* 318–331.

Christoper, J. J., Nehemiah, K. H., & Arputharaj, K. (2016). Knowledge- based Systems and Interestingness Measures: Analysis with Clinical Datasets. *CIT. Journal of Computing and Information Technology*, *24*(1), 65–78. doi:10.20532/cit.2016.1002500

Delavari, N., Shirazi, M. R. A., & Beikzadeh, M. R. (2004). A New Model for Using Data Minig Technology in Higher Education Systems. *Information Technology Based Proceedings of the Fifth International Conference on Higher Education and Training - ITHET 2004,* 319-324.

Dey, N., Hassanien, A. E., Bhatt, C., Ashour, A., & Satapathy, S. C. (Eds.). (2018). *Internet of things and big data analytics toward next-generation intelligence*. Berlin: Springer. doi:10.1007/978-3-319-60435-0

Dochy, F., Segers, M., & Buehl, M. M. (1999). The relation between assessment practices and outcomes of studies: The case of research on prior knowledge. *Review of Educational Research*, *69*(2), 145–186. doi:10.3102/00346543069002145

Eui-Hong, H., Karypis, G., & Kumar, V. (1999). Text Categorization Using Weighted Adjusted k-Nearest Neighbor Classification, Department of Computer Science and Engineering. Army HPC Research Centre, University of Minnesota.

Lan, K., Wang, D., Fong, S., Liu, L., Wong, K. K. L., & Dey, N. (2018). A survey of data mining and deep learning in bioinformatics. *Journal of Medical Systems*, *42*(8), 139. doi:10.100710916-018-1003-9 PMID:29956014

Ng, H.-T., Goh, W.-B., & Low, K.-L. (1997). Feature Selection, Perceptron Learning, and a Usability Case Study for Text Categorization. *Proceedings of the 20th Annual International ACM-SIGIR Conference on Research and Development in Information Retrieval*, 67-73.

Pena-Ayala. (2014). Educational Data Mining: A survey and a data mining- based analysis of recent works. *Journal of Expert Systems with Applications*, 1432-1462.

Romero C, Ventura S., (2007). Educational data mining: a survey from 1995 to 2005. *Journal of Expert Systems with Applications*, 135–146.

Romero, C., & Ventura, S. (2010). Educational data mining: A review of the state-of-the-art. *IEEE Transactions on Systems Management and Cybernetics- Part C. Applications and Reviews*, *40*(6), 601–618.

Romero, C., & Ventura, S. (2013). Data Mining in Education. *WIREs. Data Mining and Knowledge Discovery*, *3*(1), 12–27. doi:10.1002/widm.1075

Ruiz, M. E., & Srinivasan, P. (1998). Automatic Text Categorization Using Neural Network. *Proceedings of the 8th ASIS SIG/CR Workshop on Classification Research*, 59-72.

Shen, Y. D., Zhang, Z., & Yang, Q. (2002). Objective- oriented utility based association mining. *Proceeding of the 2002 IEEE International Conference on Data Mining*, 426-433.

Geng & Hamilton. (2006). Interestingness Measures for Data Mining: ASurvey. *ACM Computing Surveys*, *38*(3), 9.

Vapnik, V. N. (1995). *The Nature of Statistical Learning Theory*. New York: Springer. doi:10.1007/978-1-4757-2440-0

Varlamis, I., Apostolakis, I., Sifaki-Pistolla, D., Dey, N., Georgoulias, V., & Lionis, C. (2017). Application of data mining techniques and data analysis methods to measure cancer morbidity and mortality data in a regional cancer registry: The case of the island of Crete, Greece. *Computer Methods and Programs in Biomedicine*, *145*, 73–83. doi:10.1016/j.cmpb.2017.04.011 PMID:28552128

KEY TERMS AND DEFINITIONS

Attribute Selection: The process of selecting a subset of attributes for building a model.

Case Deletion: This is a method of imputation in when all cases with a missing value are deleted.

Classification: The process in which the objects are understood and group into classes.

Cluster: Grouping a set of objects into objects in the same group are similar.

Cross Validation: Division of data set into training and testing set and validate the results of them.

Data Interpretation: The process of doing collection, analysis and present the data.

Data Mining: Collection of methods use for analysis of data.

Educational Data Mining: Application of data mining techniques on educational data.

K Means Algorithm: A mining algorithm for clustering.

Kappa Statistic: This measures inter-rater agreement for qualitative attributes.

Knowledge Discovery in Databases: An iterative process of extracting knowledge from raw data.

Outliers: Are values that stays in an abnormal distance from other values in a random sample from a population.

Precision: Positive predictive values.

Chapter 5
Data Mining in Global Higher Education:
Opportunities and Challenges for Learning

Evan G. Mense
Southeastern Louisiana University, USA

Pamela A. Lemoine
Troy University, USA

Michael D. Richardson
Columbus State University, USA

ABSTRACT

Historically, educators in higher education have searched for reliable means and methods to increase student learning. Many techniques and strategies have been used and even some have taken the form of laws to incorporate certain approaches to learning. However, there has not been one method proved effective in all situations for all students. One of the biggest challenges that global educational institutions face is the explosive growth of educational data and how to use this data to improve the quality of instructional and managerial decisions. Global higher education leaders embraced data-driven practices as an opportunity to improve efficiency, objectivity, transparency, and innovation. As a result, global higher education institutions are producing a large amount of student related data every year. Technology has given educators in higher education access to methods for assessing learning and engagement. Educational data mining is a relatively new process in global higher education that provides a tool to analyze this data and extract valuable information.

DOI: 10.4018/978-1-7998-0010-1.ch005

INTRODUCTION

Education is an essential element for the improvement and progress of a country (Martin, 2017). For years, higher education institutions have been expected to demonstrate that students were learning and achieving success by outcomes attainment, retention and/or graduation, and career occupation (Altbach, 2016). The increasing use of technology has led to tremendous change in the way global higher education institutions modify and adapt to satisfy societal and governmental demands for accountability (Mu-azu, 2019). Educators are experiencing a new world of higher education; the nature of learners and learning is changing dramatically because of the development and wide availability of the new technologies in this global world (DiCerbo, & Behrens, 2014). The increased use of technology-based learning systems has also amplified the amount of data available (Clichici, Moagar-Poladian, & Dragoi, 2017).

Lack of adequate knowledge in higher education institutions about how to use data may prevent the achievement of the quality objectives and demands (Aldowah, Al-Samarraie, & Fauzy, 2019). One technique that is now readily available to institutions is data mining methodologies that can help bridge knowledge gaps in higher education (Goyal, & Vohra, 2012). Data mining in education can provide new methods to discover knowledge from educational databases in order to analyze student's performance and assist in their learning (Manek, Vijay, & Kamthania, 2016).

Extracting knowledge from collected data offers many new opportunities and guides the higher education institutions to make decisions based on student needs (Jindal & Borah, 2013). Data mining is known for its powerful role in uncovering hidden information, parsing out data patterns, organizing information about hidden relationships, and revealing many findings that are not easily produced by manual manipulation of data or even classic computer-based information systems (Slater, Joksimović, Kovanovic, Baker, & Gasevic, 2017). Data mining has huge transformational potential for global higher education: discovering how people learn, predicting learning, and understanding real learning behavior (Chaurasia, Kodwani, Lachhwani, & Ketkar, 2018). By achieving these goals, educational data mining can be used to design better and smarter types of learning technologies and to better inform learners and educators (Wise, 2019). Noteworthy emerging data mining applications include student needs assessment, retention management, enrollment management, performance prediction and improvement of placement tests (Dhekankar & Datar, 2015).

Globalization

Global higher education institutions are interested in predicting the paths of students, identifying student course programs and which students will require remediation (Ali, 2013). Data mining techniques are analytical tools that can be used to extract meaningful knowledge from large data sets. The quality of global higher education institutions necessitates services most likely to meet the needs of students, academic staff, and other stakeholders (Marginson, 2016). Global higher education institutions are facing decreased funding during a time of scarce resources yet increased accountability for productivity in the development and articulation of knowledge (Martins, Miguéis, Fonseca, & Alves, 2019). The concept of globalization refers to the increasing economic interdependence of national economies across the world through a rapid increase in cross-border movement of goods, service, technology and capital. Global higher education today faces its greatest combinations of challenges: economic uncertainty, accountability and massification overlaid by emerging technologies that are changing the culture of higher education (Richardson, Jenkins, & Lemoine, 2017). Consequently, global higher education institutions are attempting to develop the capacity to adapt and modify to the new models of knowledge and information (Lane, Lemoine, Tinney, & Richardson, 2014).

Higher education in the future will be much less class-based, and much more topic-based. This model is already being explored with the idea that learning is not paced so much by the faculty as it is by the student's own capacity to acquire the material. Additionally, the topic selection for an individual's education will be based on an individual student's need and interests, not the preselected curriculum for a particular class or degree (Gorodilov & Chuchulina, 2018).

Many higher education theorists speculate that universities of tomorrow will be structured more as a network of specialists, similar to a group of performing actors. If this is the future, higher education must produce a viable, robust, adapting organization that can survive and prosper in a variety of future environments (Bourn, 2018). Thus, the focus needs to be on learning and development of new knowledge instead of specific solutions to current problems. Global higher education will have to develop new learning and teaching strategies, to differentiate by offering different products and services, to add more value to the student and teaching, and to focus more on the user (Verger, Steiner-Khamsi, & Lubienski, 2017) as the higher education sector adjusts to the new global environments that are characterized by flexibility, diversity, increased competition and unpredictable change (Marshall, 2018).

What are Data and Information?

Data are considered one of the most valuable assets available to universities. Global universities store data about their students, resources and activities. Data mining can leverage these data resources for information about students and learning (Kumar & Chadha, 2011). Educational data sources can be analyzed to detect students at-risk to increase retention and graduation (Baepler & Murdoch, 2010). Globally, there is currently an overwhelming demand for higher education (Sarantinos, 2019). Students expectations are increasing which demands that higher education needs to change for the future (Na & Tasir, 2017). Additionally, resources are scarce globally, and universities are faced with the challenge to continuously increase their capabilities and performance for students and society (Bhise, Thorat, & Supekar, 2013).

The situation forces universities to become entrepreneurial to stay efficient, competitive and attractive. Data and the information obtained by the institution are resources that should be developed and used to help the institution demonstrate competence (Calvard, 2016). Each term data are collected (e.g. applicant and student data) but remain a widely untapped potential. Data mining can be used to analyze large amounts of data generated by the university. Universities can detect patterns and gain insights from the data resources and focus on student related analysis with the objective to better understand the teaching and learning culture (Elbadrawy, Polyzou, Ren, Sweeney, Karypis, & Rangwala, 2016).

Data are "the raw facts or details that represent some type of transaction or activity within an organization" (Lewis, Goodman & Fandt, 2001, p. 571). Data are numerical forms that can be digitally transmitted or processed; data are the points of contact between the organization and the environment; they are the objective measures of interaction and not solutions themselves. In contrast, information "is the result of the process of transforming data into a meaningful and useful form for a specific purpose" (Lewis, et al., p. 571). Stated in another form, information is designed to inform and create knowledge. Raw data are simply numbers and by itself yields no information. Data are the raw material for information, and information is the raw material for knowledge (Kennedy, 2019). Information is data that has been processed into a form that is meaningful to the recipient. Data are facts and statistics that can be quantified, measured, counted, and stored. Information is data that has been categorized, counted, and thus given meaning, relevance, or purpose. Information is the aggregation of data to make coherent explanations implying an increased usefulness. Consequently, information ultimately provides meaning to data giving meaning by way of relational connection (Mislevy, Behrens, Dicerbo, & Levy, 2012).

As the saying goes, 'information is power' and this is especially so in global higher education. The world is shifting into an information revolution making the industrial revolution obsolete. With this change comes an explosion of data which educators are left to assimilate into useful information (Mense, Lemoine, Garretson, & Richardson, 2018). However, the ability to interpret this avalanche of data, to extract meaning from artificial fields of data, has expanded much more slowly (Thille, Schneider, Kizilcec, Piech, Halawa, & Greene, 2014). Global higher education is experiencing a social and economic change that is evolving from an industrial focus at a national level, to an information focus at a global level. Data are collected because people believe that it is a potential source of valuable knowledge, providing a competitive advantage. Finding the valuable information hidden in the data, however, is a difficult task (Badia, 2014).

Today the cascade of educational data is increasingly augmented by digital technology that make the power of the data even more persuasive. The past 20 years have seen the increased recording, storage, manipulation and distribution of data in digital form (Kuhnel, Seiler, Honal, & Ifenthaler, 2018). In this sense, digital forms of data are now being generated and processed on an unprecedented scale (Fatima, Fatima, & Prasad, 2015). This shift is often described in terms of 'three Vs' of volume, velocity and variety – i.e., increases in the amount of data that is now being produced; the speed in which this data can be produced and processed and the range of data types and sources that now exist (Kasemsap, 2016).

What is Data Mining?

Data mining is a computational method of processing data which can be applied to collect information. Researchers use data mining techniques to sort through data for implicit relationships and identifies patterns and establishes relationships between different data sets provided in a database (Natek & Zwilling, 2014). It is a process that analyses huge amounts of data for useful information to reveal trends and patterns which otherwise may be undetected (Kumarapathirana, 2018). Data mining may not provide causality, but in many instances, correlation might still yield interesting and powerful results. The aim of data mining is to extract information from datasets and convert it to easy to understand materials and information (Martins, Migueis, & Fonseca, 2018).

Advantages of Data Mining

Data mining involves procedures that search for new and generalizable relationships and findings. Educational data mining attempts to mine and determine helpful patterns and valuable learning information from educational data frameworks, for example, admissions frameworks, registration frameworks, course administration, and other frameworks managing student data (Nithya, Umamaheswari, & Umadevi, 2016). Educational data is incremental in nature but due to the exponential growth of data maintaining the data is difficult. Data mining techniques can be applied with students' data to obtain knowledge which can be used to predict the student's performance (Oskouei & Askari, 2014). This knowledge will help improve the educational quality, students' performance and to decrease failure rates. Increasingly, very large data sets are available from students' interactions with online learning and other sources and from interactions with other students (Preethi & Goswami, 2015). Data mining methods have become very effective data analysis tools, primarily because of their ability to deal with large volumes of structured and unstructured data and their ability to discover relevant and valuable information (Şengür, & Karabatak, 2018).

Data mining is about transforming data into information, information into knowledge and knowledge into value for global higher education institutions. This new knowledge offers tremendous promise for increasing the effectiveness of teaching and learning. Data mining enhances the education process and improves its outcomes, operational efficiency, and effectiveness. One of the educational problems that are solved with data mining is the prediction of students' academic performances, a goal is to predict an outcome that can improve student performance (Shingari, Kumar, & Khetan, 2017).

Data can be collected from different educational systems where the data reside in databases. The data can be personal records or academic records that can be used to understand students' learning behavior and to assist instructors in improving teaching and learning. Data mining is utilized to reinforce understanding of learning methods associated with increasing the learning opportunities for students (Tegegne & Alemu, 2018). Data mining applications can analyze large amounts of data to create information about previously unknown patterns to support objective instructional decisions and the long-term success of an organization by using existing resource data (Wagner & Yaskin, 2015).

Data mining methods are implemented at most advanced global universities today for analyzing available data and extracting information for enhanced decision making, particularly about learning (Ayesha, Mustafa, Sattar, & Khan, 2010). Possible target areas for data mining include: high and low yielding programs of study, enrollment targets and marketing, planning for university growth and sustainability, and student systems which include registration, study records, time to graduation, retention, graduation rates, and improved quality of instruction (Algarni, 2016). Data mining tools can predict future trends and behaviors, allowing institutions to make proactive, knowledge-driven decisions. Data mining can answer questions that traditionally were too time consuming to resolve. Data miners search databases for hidden patterns, finding predictive information that will assist with improved teaching and learning (Baker, 2010).

Data mining software allows the user to analyze data from different dimensions categorize it and summarize the relationship which improves quality, efficiency, and achievement. Data mining is also utilized to determine the impact of pedagogical strategies on students, and how students understand courses. The academic performance of students is based on several factors such as previous academic records, economic status, family background, and demographic data (Cheslock, Hughes, & Umbricht, 2014).

Data mining supports higher education institutions in making timely and informed decisions in the prediction of dropouts, forecasting for admissions, courses preferred by the students, and recruiting strategies preferred by potential students (Ahmad, Ismail, & Aziz, 2015). While global higher education institutions have collected volumes of data for years, the data were never analyzed to help students or the institutions, leading some to proclaim higher educational institutions as data-rich but information poor (Huang, Huang, & Chuang, 2016).

The analysis of data collected from the interaction of users with educational and information technology has attracted much attention recently with the objective of improving the learning processes though use by faculty (Dahiya, 2017). Throughout the world, faculty are expected to use student data to guide their instruction. The common refrain of faculty being "data driven" is not only an expectation, but also increasingly a formal criterion used in faculty evaluations. Yet, many faculty often struggle to use data due to a lack of skills and knowledge to develop instructional responses (Colvin, 2017).

Education Data Mining

Baker and Yacef (2009) described the following four goals of EDM: (1) Predicting student's future learning behavior, (2) Discovering or improving models of assessment, (3) Studying the effects of educational support, and (4) Advancing scientific knowledge about learning and learners.

Educational data mining is concerned with methods for exploring the unique types of data that come from educational settings, and using those methods to better understand students, and the settings in which they learn (Gašević, Dawson, Rogers, & Gašević, 2016). Educational data mining applies techniques relating for learning analytics and quantitative observation methods in order to understand how students respond to the higher education learning system and how it impacts their learning. Educational data mining is important to understand student learning behavior during the learning process and to understand learners' and faculty challenges (Khan & Choi, 2014).

Education data mining is used to evaluate the performance of students in the higher education environment by mining to measure the performance of the students (Hegazi & Abugroon, 2016). The analysis of student performance is a key task performed by the higher education institution to maintain the record of a student's performance, efficiency and effectiveness during the learning process (Ikbal, Tamhane, Sengupta, Chetlur, Ghosh, & Appleton, 2015). For evaluating the performance of the students, universities have to maintain their records in various activities for data mining to construct useful and meaningful information from large datasets or a database of the student's information (Kowalczyk & Buxmann, 2014). Obviously, students are the primary assets of the higher education institution because in higher education a student's performance quality can lead to competent graduates (Simon & Bugusa, 2018). Educational data mining is an ever-evolving process that continually progresses towards the formation and development of core values of the institution. These values are mostly to nurture the talent and capabilities of the students and to address student learning with proactive expertise to meet learning objectives (Peña-Ayala, 2014).

Educational data mining is an attractive interdisciplinary process that deals with the development of methods to utilize data originating from an educational context (Wardrip & Shapiro, 2016). It is concerned with developing, researching, and applying methods to detect patterns in large collections of educational data that would otherwise be hard or impossible to analyze. As such, disclosed knowledge is highly useful to better understand how students learn and effects of different settings on their achievement (Thakar, Mehta, & Manisha, 2015). This can help to improve educational outcomes and to gain insights into various educational phenomena about learning. Data collected from higher education institutions can be aggregated over large numbers of students and can contain many variables. It has been speculated that educational data mining methods are frequently unique in relation to standard data mining methods, because of the need to absolutely account for the multi-level chain of command and non-independence in educational data (Hamza & Kommers, 2018).

Educational data mining is concerned with developing approaches for discovering relationships in the unique and increasingly large-scale data that come from educational spheres and using such approaches to better understand student behavior and learning outcomes (Kashyap & Chauhan, 2015). Higher education increasingly plans to capture and store data that can be analyzed to make predictions that exemplify learner behavior and achievement. Educational data mining makes use of both highly detailed and limited data to discover meaningful information about different types of learners, how they learn, and the effect of instructional strategies embedded within various learning environments (Kumar, Singh, & Handa, 2017).

One general goal of educational data mining is to better understand how students learn and to make use of data to present appropriate tasks, learner activities, and resources aimed at optimizing student learning (Kunjir, 2015). For faculty the primary objective is to obtain feedback on the content, delivery, and structure of learning. Hence, educational data mining techniques can help in enhancing student performance, course selection, and increase the retention rate of an institution and decrease the dropout possibility (Abu-Oda & El-Halees, 2015).

Learning

The main objective of higher education institutions is to provide a quality education to its students. One way to achieve the highest level of quality in higher education is by using data to build predictive knowledge for prediction regarding enrollment of students, participation in particular courses and prediction about students' performance. This knowledge is typically hidden among the educational data sets and it is extractable through data mining techniques (Bhushan & Deshmukh, 2014).

Global higher education is a vast and important subject. In recent years the amount of data stored in educational databases has grown rapidly and contains hidden information about how to improve student performance and learning. The ability to predict student performance is very important in higher education because funding can be determined by the success of students, often by retention and/or graduation rates (Kelchen, 2018). Data mining can be used to enhance understanding of learning to identify, extract and evaluate variables related to the learning process and progress of students. The activities of learning are larger and more complex than ever (Pradnya, 2015). The data are also larger because of mechanisms to collect evidence of learning that can be embedded within technology-mediated learning environments. Consequently, everyone becomes to some extent a data analyst—learners using analytics to become increasingly self-aware of their own learning and faculty as they acquire a level of data literacy required to interpret a student's progress and calibrate their instruction (Papamitsiou & Economides, 2014).

As students are involved recipients of the process of learning, different learning tasks can be formulated with different groups of students based on their needs. Data mining can assist students with personalized education and can increase the interest of students towards their own learning (Shahiri, Husain, & Rashid, 2015). Data mining can also provide an insight into the methods and techniques students use to learn. Faculty can analyze the data and determine the most commonly made errors and to detect if students require extra support during the process of learning (Saa, 2016).

Digitally-mediated information and electronically distributed data have transformed, and will continue to transform, how instruction in higher education is designed and delivered. Today's students will experience several major career changes during their lifetimes, with many of those careers being nonexistent at present. Faculty must comprehend that learning is truly a life-long process, for them just as much as for their students. They must be willing to change and use new forms of technology to reach learners (Sumitha & Vinothkumar, 2016).

Learning Analytics

Learning analytics, an outgrowth of data mining, is defined as the "measurement, collection, analysis, and reporting of data about learners and their contexts, for the purposes of understanding and optimizing learning and the environments in which it occurs" (Hui & Kwok, 2019, p. 198). Essentially, learning analytics employs data to improve learning contexts and help learners succeed. To accomplish these goals, learning analytics systems input data from a variety of sources and output descriptive information about student populations (Larose & Larose, 2015). The information is employed to discover behaviors, characteristics, or other attributes that appear to lead to student difficulties or successes (Viberg, Hatakka, Bälter, & Mavroudi, 2018). Learning analytics systems attempt to predict, based on known attributes, which students are "at risk" so that educators can intervene quickly (Jayaprakash, Moody, Eitel, Regan, & Baron, 2014). Interventions emanating from learning analytics systems include notifications to students, advisors, or faculty; requirements for students to meet with support services, changes to institutional processes or policies or other actions intended to support improved student outcomes (Nunn, Avella, Kanai, & Kebritchi, 2016).

Learning analytics have become a well-considered aspect of modern digital learning environments (Gasevic Dawson, & Siemens, 2014) where the use of learning process data provides faculty the opportunity to analyze students' learning progression as well as to identify obstacles and risks (da Cunha, Moura, & Analide, 2016). Higher education institutions are increasingly turning to learning analytics to identify and intervene with students at risk of underperformance or dropping out (Baker, & Siemens, 2014). Higher education institutions worldwide are expanding their use of learning analytics to answer long-standing calls for accountability and act on genuine concerns for students' ability to learn and succeed (Rubel & Jones, 2017).

The pervasive collection of data has opened the possibility for higher education institutions to use learning analytics methods to improve the quality of the student experience (Ray & Saeed, 2018). Other outcomes include the improvement of student retention, timely feedback and intervention, support for informed decision-making and personalized assistance to students (Wong, Li, & Choi, 2018). However, the adoption of these methods faces multiple challenges (Stewart, 2017), particularly at the course level where instructors are not familiar with the methodology or unwilling to change their methods of instruction (Hemaid & Halees, 2015).

Learning analytics systems come in a variety of forms and draw from a wide range of data sources (Ifenthaler, 2016). Many are "home grown" by individual higher education institutions (Flanagan & Ogata, 2018), and even more are offered by vendors either as single offerings or suites of learning analytics solutions (Xing, Guo, Petakovic, & Goggins, 2015). The learning analytics landscape is growing and fast changing; it is difficult to obtain a census of all the options (Finnie, Fricker, Bozkurt, Poirier, & Pavlic, 2017). In general, learning analytic tools tend to be aggregated in the following system categories: enrollment management, relationship management, learning management system activity and/or achievement monitoring, integrated advising, early-alert warning for students, and degree mapping (Avella, Kebritchi, Nunn, & Kanai, 2016). Typically, the data used by learning analytics systems comes from student information systems and learning management systems (Mustafina, Galiullin, Al-Jumeily, Petrov, Alloghani, & Kaky, 2018).

Opportunities in Data Mining for Learning

Data mining is a dynamic technology to analyze and extract the hidden potential data to be converted to useful information. It discovers information within the data that manual reports cannot efficiently and effectively reveal (Bogarín, Cerezo, & Romero, 2018). Educational data mining provides better understanding of student behavior and knowledge, as well as new information on student behaviors in learning (Hegazi, Alhawaat, & Hilal, 2016). This knowledge can be used to inform decisions related to course development and pedagogy, and further engage students. This strategy can also lead to more rigorous, higher-quality evaluation of teaching methods and techniques (Klasen & Ifenthaler, 2019).

Educational data mining is raising expectations to extract the data that come from educational settings and by using those techniques for greater prediction of students' behavior, academic performance, and subject area interest (Bousbia & Belamri, 2014). As the development of online learning is growing, a large amount of log data on student activity is available and accumulated in Learning Management Systems (LMS) (Ghadge, 2019). This massive volume of data can be analyzed in order to discover hidden information about students and their learning progress (Baker, Lindrum, Lindrum, & Perkowski, 2015).

The primary goal of higher education institutions is to give quality education to their students (Liu, Bartimote-Aufflick, Pardo, & Bridgeman, 2017). Data mining improves their capability by extracting knowledge and patterns from the student database and study factors that will affect their education and learning capabilities (Reich, Tingley, Leder-Luis, Roberts, & Stewart, 2014). These learning patterns can help faculty understand their students better to help in reducing failure rates and improving the quality of teaching (Monjurul Alom & Courtney, 2018). Data mining can provide immediate feedback to students and faculty about academic performance in order to predict student outcomes and it can identify pedagogic approaches that seem most effective with particular students (Sønderlund, Hughes, & Smith, 2018).

Institutions of higher education are very focused on their students' academic performance (McCoy & Byrne, 2017). Not only is this an accreditation and evaluation criterion, but it is also at the heart of the institution's contribution to successfully preparing the next generation for their future (Casey & Azcona, 2017). Given the importance of academic performance and success, a higher education institution benefits from predicting students' academic performance (Thakar, 2016). Many higher education institutions using data mining to predict academic performance (Peña-Ayala, 2014). The early knowledge of university students according to their potential academic performance can be a useful to mitigating failure and increase achievement (Barrett, 2017).

Enrollment

Enrollment management is frequently used in higher education to facilitate students to meet planned goals. Enrollment management is a systematic set of activities designed to exert more influence over student enrollment preferences (Yadav & Pal, 2012). Enrollment management will often include marketing, financial aid and admission policies. The explanation and prediction of enrollment in higher education institutions is one of the most debated topics in higher education. Predicting student enrollment in higher education institutions is a complex decision-making process that is more than merely relying on test scores (Pucciarelli & Kaplan, 2016). Previous research indicates that student enrollment depends on diverse factors such as personal, socio-economic, family and other institutional variables. To ascertain the relationships among these variables demands the capabilities demonstrated by data mining to help predict which students will enroll and their reasons for enrollment (Asif, Merceron, & Pathan, 2014).

Student Retention

Student retention is an area of active research and study demanded by many policy making bodies who control budgets and funding (Beer & Lawson, 2017). Higher education institutions have used various methods to increase retention and student engagement (Meedech, Iam-On, & Boongoen, 2016). Most responses are in two broad categories; reactive—faculty and staff respond to specific cases and causes, or preventative--action designed to target large groups of students to provide detailed and personalized information to improve student achievement (Villano, Harrison, Lynch, & Chen, 2018).

The attempts to find all plausible causes for student departure has been inconsistent; however, there is broad agreement that student engagement in a course usually leads to higher achievement (Mayra & Mauricio, 2018). Attendance has also been shown through data mining to increase retention such that attendance is also a strong indicator of a student's final grade (Espinoza & Genna, 2018).

In a societal sense, students who opt to end their college career without obtaining a degree often accumulate large debts, which they tend to have a hard time repaying as their income is drastically lower than a college graduate (Freitas, Gibson, Du Plessis, Halloran, Williams, Ambrose, Dunwell, & Arnab, 2015). Society makes a direct investment by permitting students access to higher education because this investment comes from taxes paid by the majority of the population (Dwyer, Williams, & Pribesh, 2019).

Some students who leave a given institution are simply enrolling at another institution, but more often than desired many students leave due to factors that institutions can control (Mittal, 2017). There are many causes for attrition, which can range from under preparation before college to lack of class attendance (Delen, 2011). To help alleviate this problem data mining systems have been designed to examine targeted advising, lengthy course sequences, early alerts, and students at risk (Jones, 2019).

Students at Risk

As higher education continues to adapt to the constantly changing requirements demanded by society, student attrition continues to distress universities (Lawson, Beer, Rossi, Moore, & Fleming, 2016). Effective data mining has provided early alerts for students who are at-risk academically (Sarra, Fontanella, & Di Zio, 2018). Early alert systems are designed to provide students who are academically at-risk a rapid indication to alter their performance (Umer, Susnjak, Mathrani, & Suriadi, 2018). Early alert systems use various techniques for identifying students that may be at-risk (Sneyers & De Witte, 2018). These techniques range from using data mining to identify students who could become at-risk to more manual methods where the professors are responsible for notifying students of concern (Palacios-Pacheco, Villegas-Ch, & Luján-Mora, 2018).

Predicting students who are at-risk is a very challenging task if it is done manually (Kenekayoro, 2018). Data mining plays a major role in analyzing the weak areas of students and focusing on the key areas of poor performance (Arunabh, & Anant, 2017). Data mining involves extracting information from various subjects and the gathered information is processed to determine areas of concern (Ashenafi, 2017). Data mining can provide significant information so that a student's performance evaluation becomes easier for faculty (Durairaj & Vijitha, 2014).

As stated earlier, attendance is a significant contributor to students at risk and for retention. To aid with both retention and identifying students at-risk, attendance monitoring systems are important data mining systems used to monitor student attendance and interest in a given course or courses (Brabazon, 2017). The expected benefits of attendance monitoring systems are to improve student engagement, performance, and retention (Almarabeh, 2017).

Attainment Gap

The widespread gap between those who enroll in higher education and those who graduate has been described as the attainment gap (Jones, 2015). Many factors impinge on the attainment gap from the admission of under prepared students admitted and the infrastructure of the institution. The disparities in educational attainment indicate that many longstanding structures, policies, and processes within universities are inadequate to meet the needs of the new majority of students because they are relatively disengaged from the university infrastructure (Koprinska, Stretton, & Yacef, 2015). Globally many countries and policy organizations are concerned about low-attainment rates and are ready for leaders to take action to close the attainment gap (Shingari, Kumar, & Khetan, 2017).

Data and information are critical components in transforming institutions to focus on learning and attainment for all students (Meghji & Mahoto, 2016). It is difficult to increase student success and close the attainment gap if institutional leaders, faculty, and policymakers do not have the data and information they need (Bhushan & Deshmukh, 2014). Answers to questions about how, and how well, students are moving into and through higher education are often lacking--particularly information regarding low-income and first-generation students, students of color, and working adults (Posselt, Abdelkafi, Fischer, & Tangour, 2019). The demands for increased institutional performance and student educational attainment result from factors that include decreased higher education funding, changing student demographics, labor market expectations, and public perceptions concerning the necessity and value of higher education (Dahiya, 2017). There is increasing pressure to provide outcomes-based evidence from higher education that can be assessed and reported by the use of data mining student data (Dietz-Uhler & Hurn, 2013).

Globally, many universities are concerned with the attainment gap and its influence on student performance; therefore, early identification of students at risk is of great importance to students and the university (Lemoine, Hackett, & Richardson, 2017). The student attainment gap is considered a key performance indicator for global higher education institutions (Kelchen, 2018). As a consequence, universities invest resources to reduce the attainment gap between good and poor performing students (Jones, 2015). Progression and retention are commonly regarded as the primary indicators of institutional performance meaning that the attainment gap is considered as one of the factors that contribute either positively or negatively to institutional performance (Al-Barrak & Al-Razgan, 2016).

Identifying students at-risk and providing interventions to provide useful supports to those students is necessary. One approach to addressing this problem is the use of predictive statistical models (Finnie, Fricker, Bozkurt, Poirier & Pavlic, 2017). Predictive modelling is the application of statistical and informational modelling techniques to make predictions based on previously recorded observations. Predictive modelling makes use of data from learning management systems, student information systems and student surveys (Borden & Coates, 2017).

Grouping

Grouping students is created according to their customized features, personal characteristics, etc. These groups of students can be used by the instructor to build a personalized learning system which can promote effective group learning accompanying personal learning (Wagner & Yaskin, 2015). Data mining can help faculty to identify the demographic, geographic and psychographic characteristics of students based on information provided by the students at the time of admission (Preethi & Goswami, 2015). Grouping students with similar aspirations is done automatically through course selection, but by using grouping within courses, faculty can increase the learning opportunities for students (Elbadrawy, Polyzou, Ren, Sweeney, Karypis, & Rangwala, 2016).

Predicting Student Performance

Researchers use different data mining techniques to predict student performance. Learning is an individual behavior as well as a social phenomenon. Data mining techniques can develop an evaluation system which can help faculty and students to know the characteristics of teaching and learning (Shahiri, Husain, Rashid, 2015). These techniques can also help students understand the rapidly developing real-life environment and adapt to current realities (Thille & Zimmaro, 2017).

Predicting student's overall performance is a difficult task (Sumitha & Vinothkumar, 2016). Data mining is a critical component of investigating and successfully developing models for evaluating learning efforts (Xing, Guo, Petakovic, & Goggins, 2015). Student learning is addressed in some goals and outcomes related to the development of overall student knowledge, skill, and dispositions (Ahmad, Ismail, & Aziz, 2015).

Challenges of Data Mining for Learning

Data mining can generate large amounts of information for faculty. Unfortunately, these data can be problematic in three main ways: data can be (1) too imprecise, (2) completely unavailable, or (3) inaccessible due to institutional silos (Oakleaf, Whyte, Lynema, & Brown, 2017). Developing methods and practices for handling these issues appropriately has been a significant ongoing challenge for researchers in this area. Another important recent development for educational data mining is the growing realization that not all key information is stored in one data stream (Calvard, 2016). Many projects have leveraged outcome data of various types, from college enrollment data and standardized exam data, to human coding of student engagement integrated with data streams where collecting representative data becomes essential (Wilson, Watson, Thompson, Drew, & Doyle, 2017). Typically, datasets provide very little information on cognitive skills other than certain measures of achievement and attainment, or social and behavioral skills, such as standardized test scores, attendance, and demographic data. One other highly important issue with using data is security and confidentiality concerns, because they cannot be made available publicly (Gašević, Dawson, & Jovanović, 2016).

Limitations of Data Mining

The trend of educational data mining shows that maximum research focuses only on academic objectives. There is also the issue of the alignment and interpretation of the incremental data. Also, with the presence of uncertain errors, no model can accurately give a prediction of one hundred percent accuracy. Dealing with very large databases (big data) is also problematic (Liñán & Pérez, 2015).

Educational data mining has an impact on many aspects of student success in higher education institutions. It is extremely beneficial for predicting student performance, grouping of students, predicting student profiles, and planning for teaching (Pradnya, 2015). Despite being an extremely beneficial activity, there are challenges in educational data mining. The first and the foremost is that educational data derived from various sources, which are evolutionary in nature and the amount and variety of data are always increasing. Secondly, the storage and the maintenance of the data becomes challenging for the institution (Rubel & Jones, 2017).

Critics of data mining speculate about issues such as student privacy, the effects of profiling learners, the intensification of certain pedagogies, test-driven teaching, and invasive faculty accountability regimes (Heath, 2014). As such, the practicalities of data mining present considerable challenges for higher education, three in particular: data access, data modeling, and data privacy (Ifenthaler & Tracey, 2016). A primary concern for many in higher education is student privacy. Data can be mined without student identification but to give assistance to at-risk students requires student identification (Bennett & Raab, 2017). Several countries have instituted laws and regulations regarding the use of identifiable student data (Zwitter, 2014). It could be assumed that this will be an expanding area of controversy in coming years.

Data Mining With Big Data

Big data mining is considered a natural outgrowth of typical data mining because higher education institutions have large data sets (Lumbantoruan, 2017). Mining big data has the capability of providing new useful information in complex massive datasets, that may be continuously changing (Daniel, 2015). Big data promises teachers and learners a new era of personalized instruction, responsive assessment, and enhanced learning (Daniel, 2017). Higher education institutions have large data sets which demand big data mining (Baker, 2015). Big data is helpful only when it is transformed into knowledge or useful information (Kitchin, 2014). Educational data is growing exponentially every year and the size of the data sets have been exceeded by the human ability for comprehension without the use of powerful data analysis tools (Kowalczyk & Buxmann, 2014). By applying the statistical and data mining techniques, much useful information and knowledge can be produced for higher educational institution to use for improving student learning (Calvard, 2016). Analysis of the huge amount of educational data involves data that is a mix of structured as well as unstructured data collected from simple as well as complex sources. When collected from various mechanized sources, this will generate big data (Chaurasia, Kodwani, Lachhwani, & Ketkar, 2018).

Future Research

1. How can more faculty become involved in the application of data to improve learning?
2. What are the priority areas for investigation?
3. How can data applications be more effectively used in the online environment?
4. To what extent should students be involved in analyzing their personal data?
5. How can privacy be protected?
6. What are the future applications of big data?
7. How can data mining be used more effectively by more clients to improve teaching and learning

CONCLUDING THOUGHTS

Global higher education institutions need to be more receptive and adaptable to new markets of independent learners, and learners from non-traditional pathways and be prepared to alter their infrastructure and practices to provide open access, technology-enhanced, personalized learning and support services to meet the demands for universal higher education. These universities will also need to focus upon ensuring that the quality of their teaching and learning services is maintained and improved upon in order to increase student success and satisfaction. However, institutions are overburdened with the complexity of managing and analyzing the data generated from education resources efficiently and effectively. Computing advancements have enabled real-time automatic gathering, processing, storage, and analysis of massive amounts of data. Despite significant opportunities for global higher education to improve decision making and expand student learning, several challenges remain regarding its full implementation such as security, privacy, ethics, lack of skilled professionals, data processing, storage, and interoperability.

REFERENCES

Abu-Oda, G. S., & El-Halees, A. M. (2015). Data mining in higher education: University student dropout case study. *International Journal of Data Mining & Knowledge Management Process*, *5*(1), 15–27. doi:10.5121/ijdkp.2015.5102

Adejo, O., & Connolly, T. (2017). An integrated system framework for predicting students' performance in higher education institution. *International Journal of Computer Science and Information Technology*, *9*(3), 149–157. doi:10.5121/ijcsit.2017.93013

Ahmad, F., Ismail, N. H., & Aziz, A. A. (2015). The prediction of students' academic performance using classification data mining techniques. *Applied Mathematical Sciences*, *9*(129), 6415–6426. doi:10.12988/ams.2015.53289

Al-Barrak, M. A., & Al-Razgan, M. (2016). Predicting student's final GPA using decision trees: A case study. *International Journal of Information and Education Technology (IJIET)*, *6*(7), 528–533. doi:10.7763/IJIET.2016.V6.745

Aldowah, H., Al-Samarraie, H., & Fauzy, W. M. (2019). Educational data mining and learning analytics for 21st century higher education: A review and synthesis. *Telematics and Informatics*, *37*, 13–49. doi:10.1016/j.tele.2019.01.007

Algarni, A. (2016). Data mining in education. *International Journal of Advanced Computer Science and Applications*, *7*(6), 456–461. doi:10.14569/IJACSA.2016.070659

Ali, M. (2013). Role of data mining in education sector. *International Journal of Computer Science and Mobile Computing*, *2*(4).

Almarabeh, H. (2017). Analysis of students' performance by using different data mining classifiers. *International Journal of Modern Education and Computer Science*, *9*(8), 9–15. doi:10.5815/ijmecs.2017.08.02

Altbach, P. G. (2016). *Global perspectives on higher education*. Baltimore, MD: JHU Press.

Arunabh, T., & Anant, P. (2017). Post hoc comparison in survival analysis: An easy approach. *The Journal of Bioscience and Medicine*, *5*(03), 112–119. doi:10.4236/jbm.2017.53012

Ashenafi, M. M. (2017). A comparative analysis of selected studies in student performance prediction. *International Journal of Data Mining & Knowledge Management Process*, *7*(4), 17–32. doi:10.5121/ijdkp.2017.7402

Asif, R., Merceron, A., & Pathan, M. K. (2014). Predicting student academic performance at degree level: A case study. *International Journal of Intelligent Systems and Applications*, *7*(1), 49–61. doi:10.5815/ijisa.2015.01.05

Avella, J. T., Kebritchi, M., Nunn, S. G., & Kanai, T. (2016). Learning analytics methods, benefits, and challenges in higher education: A systematic literature review. *Online Learning*, *20*(2), 13–29.

Ayesha, S., Mustafa, T., Sattar, A. R., & Khan, M. I. (2010). Data mining model for higher education system. *European Journal of Scientific Research*, *43*(1), 24–29.

Badia, A. (2014). Data, information, knowledge: An information science analysis. *Journal of the Association for Information Science and Technology*, *65*(6), 1279–1287. doi:10.1002/asi.23043

Baepler, P., & Murdoch, C. J. (2010). Academic analytics and data mining in higher education. *International Journal for the Scholarship of Teaching and Learning*, *4*(2), 17. doi:10.20429/ijsotl.2010.040217

Baker, R. (2010). Data mining for education. In B. McGaw, P. Peterson, & E. Baker (Eds.), *International encyclopedia of education* (3rd ed.). Oxford, UK: Elsevier. doi:10.1016/B978-0-08-044894-7.01318-X

Baker, R. S. (2015). *Big data and education* (2nd ed.). New York, NY: Teachers College, Columbia University.

Baker, R. S., Lindrum, D., Lindrum, M. J., & Perkowski, D. (2015, June). Analyzing early at-risk factors in higher education e-learning courses. In *Proceedings of the 8th International Conference on Educational Data Mining*, (pp. 150-155). Madrid, Spain: Academic Press.

Baker, R. S., & Siemens, G. (2014). Educational data mining and learning analytics. In K. Sawyer (Ed.), *Cambridge handbook of the learning sciences* (2nd ed.; pp. 253–274). New York, NY: Cambridge University Press. doi:10.1017/CBO9781139519526.016

Baker, R. S., & Yacef, K. (2009). The state of educational data mining in 2009: A review and future visions. *Journal of Educational Data Mining*, *1*(1), 3–16.

Barrett, B. (2017). The dual roles of higher education institutions in the knowledge economy. In B. Barrett (Ed.), *Globalization and change in higher education* (pp. 57–73). Cham, Switzerland: Palgrave Macmillan. doi:10.1007/978-3-319-52368-2_4

Beer, C., & Lawson, C. (2017). The problem of student attrition in higher education: An alternative perspective. *Journal of Further and Higher Education*, *41*(6), 773–784. doi:10.1080/0309877X.2016.1177171

Bennett, C. J., & Raab, C. D. (2017). *The governance of privacy: Policy instruments in global perspective*. New York, NY: Routledge. doi:10.4324/9781315199269

Bhise, R. B., Thorat, S. S., & Supekar, A. K. (2013). Importance of data mining in higher education system. *IOSR Journal of Humanities and Social Science*, *6*(6), 18–21. doi:10.9790/0837-0661821

Bhushan, S., & Deshmukh, V. (2014). Application of data mining technique for prediction of academic performance of student: A literature survey. *International Journal on Recent and Innovation Trends in Computing and Communication*, *2*(12), 3962–3965.

Bogarín, A., Cerezo, R., & Romero, C. (2018). A survey on educational process mining. *Wiley Interdisciplinary Reviews. Data Mining and Knowledge Discovery*, *8*(1), e1230. doi:10.1002/widm.1230

Borden, V. M. H., & Coates, H. (2017). Learning analytics as a counterpart to surveys of student experience. *New Directions for Higher Education*, *179*(179), 89–102. doi:10.1002/he.20246

Bourn, D. (2018). Globalisation, education and skills. In *Understanding global skills for 21st Century professions* (pp. 17–35). Cham, Switzerland: Palgrave Macmillan. doi:10.1007/978-3-319-97655-6_2

Bousbia, N., & Belamri, I. (2014). Which contribution does EDM provide to computer-based learning environments? In A. Peña-Ayala (Ed.), *Educational data mining: applications and trends*. Cham, Switzerland: Springer. doi:10.1007/978-3-319-02738-8_1

Brabazon, T. (2017). From digital disruption to educational excellence: Teaching and learning in the knowledge economy. *International Journal of Social Sciences & Educational Studies*, *3*(3), 188–203. doi:10.23918/ijsses.v3i3p188

Calvard, T. S. (2016). Big data, organizational learning, and sensemaking: Theorizing interpretive challenges under conditions of dynamic complexity. *Management Learning*, *47*(1), 65–82. doi:10.1177/1350507615592113

Casey, K., & Azcona, D. (2017). Utilizing student activity patterns to predict performance. *International Journal of Educational Technology in Higher Education*, *14*(1), 1. doi:10.118641239-017-0044-3

Chaurasia, S. S., Kodwani, D., Lachhwani, H., & Ketkar, M. A. (2018). Big data academic and learning analytics: Connecting the dots for academic excellence in higher education. *International Journal of Educational Management*, *32*(6), 1099–1117. doi:10.1108/IJEM-08-2017-0199

Cheslock, J., Hughes, R. P., & Umbricht, M. (2014). The opportunities, challenges, and strategies associated with the use of operations-oriented (big) data to support decision making within universities. In J. E. Lane (Ed.), *Building a smarter university: Big data, innovation, and analytics* (pp. 211–238). Albany, NY: State University of New York Press.

Clichici, D., Moagar-Poladian, S., & Dragoi, A. E. (2017). The tech-based economic development and the future of jobs. *Global Economic Observer*, *5*(1), 90.

Colvin, C., Dawson, S., Wade, A., & Gaevic, D. (2017). Addressing the challenges of institutional adoption. In C. Lang, G. Siemens, A. F. Wise, & D. Gaevic (Eds.), The handbook of learning analytics, (pp. 281–289). Alberta, Canada: Society for Learning Analytics Research (SoLAR). doi:10.18608/hla17.024

da Cunha, J. A., Moura, E., & Analide, C. (2016). Data mining in academic databases to detect behaviors of students related to school dropout and disapproval. In *New advances in information systems and technologies* (pp. 189–198). Cham, Switzerland: Springer. doi:10.1007/978-3-319-31307-8_19

Dahiya, V. (2017). Improving teaching and learning outcomes: An outlook on data analytics in education. *Universal Research Reports*, *4*(7), 146–151.

Daniel, B. (2015). Big data and analytics in higher education: Opportunities and challenges. *British Journal of Educational Technology*, *46*(5), 904–920. doi:10.1111/bjet.12230

Daniel, B. K. (2017). Big data in higher education: The big picture. In B. K. Daniel (Ed.), *Big data and learning analytics in higher education* (pp. 19–28). Cham, Switzerland: Springer. doi:10.1007/978-3-319-06520-5_3

Delen, D. (2011). Predicting student attrition with data mining methods. *Journal of College Student Retention*, *13*(1), 17–35. doi:10.2190/CS.13.1.b

Dhekankar, P. M., & Datar, D. D. (2015). Analysis of student performance by using data mining concept. *International Journal on Recent and Innovation Trends in Computing and Communication*, *3*(5), 2942–2944.

DiCerbo, K. E., & Behrens, J. T. (2014). *Impacts of the digital ocean on education*. London, UK: Pearson.

Dietz-Uhler, B., & Hurn, J. E. (2013). Using learning analytics to predict (and improve) student success: A faculty perspective. *Journal of Interactive Online Learning*, *12*(1), 17–26.

Durairaj, M., & Vijitha, C. (2014). Educational data mining for prediction of student performance using clustering algorithms. *International Journal of Computer Science and Information Technologies*, *5*(4), 5987–5991.

Dwyer, L. J., Williams, M. R., & Pribesh, S. (2019). Impact of early alert on community college student persistence in Virginia. *Community College Journal of Research and Practice*, *43*(3), 228–231. doi:10.1080/10668926.2018.1449034

Elbadrawy, A., Polyzou, A., Ren, Z., Sweeney, M., Karypis, G., & Rangwala, H. (2016). Predicting student performance using personalized analytics. *Computer*, *49*(4), 61–69. doi:10.1109/MC.2016.119

Espinoza, P., & Genna, G. M. (2018). Hi, I want to talk to you about your progress: A large course intervention for at-risk college students. *Journal of College Student Retention*. doi:10.1177/1521025118790054

Fatima, D., Fatima, S., & Prasad, A. V. K. (2015). A survey on research work in educational data mining. *IOSR Journal of Computer Engineering*, *17*(2), 43–49.

Finnie, R., Fricker, T., Bozkurt, E., Poirier, W., & Pavlic, D. (2017). *Using predictive modelling to inform early alert and intrusive advising interventions and improve retention*. Toronto: Higher Education Quality Council of Ontario.

Flanagan, B., & Ogata, H. (2018). Learning analytics platform in higher education in Japan. *Knowledge Management & E-Learning: An International Journal, 10*(4), 469–484.

Freitas, S., Gibson, D., Du Plessis, C., Halloran, P., Williams, E., Ambrose, M., ... Arnab, S. (2015). Foundations of dynamic learning analytics: Using university student data to increase retention. *British Journal of Educational Technology, 46*(6), 1175–1188. doi:10.1111/bjet.12212

Gašević, D., Dawson, S., & Jovanović, J. (2016). Ethics and privacy as enablers of learning analytics. *Journal of Learning Analytics, 3*(1), 1–4. doi:10.18608/jla.2016.31.1

Gašević, D., Dawson, S., Rogers, T., & Gašević, D. (2016). Learning analytics should not promote one size fits all: The effects of course-specific technology use in predicting academic success. *The Internet and Higher Education, 28*, 68–84. doi:10.1016/j.iheduc.2015.10.002

Gasevic, D., Dawson, S., & Siemens, G. (2014). Let's not forget: Learning analytics are about learning. *TechTrends, 59*(1), 64–71. doi:10.100711528-014-0822-x

Ghadge, J. (2019). Impact of e-learning environment on student performance using data mining classification techniques. *International Journal of Innovative Knowledge Concepts, 7*(1), 220–223.

Gorodilov, M., & Chuchulina, E. (2018). Internalization of the university as a factor in improving the quality of education. *Managerial Challenges of the Contemporary Society. Proceedings, 11*(2), 119.

Goyal, M., & Vohra, R. (2012). Applications of data mining in higher education. *International Journal of Computer Science Issues, 9*(2).

Hamza, H. A. A., & Kommers, P. (2018). A review of educational data mining tools & techniques. *International Journal of Educational Technology and Learning, 3*(1), 17–23. doi:10.20448/2003.31.17.23

Heath, J. (2014). Contemporary privacy theory contributions to learning analytics. *Journal of Learning Analytics, 1*(1), 140–149. doi:10.18608/jla.2014.11.8

Hegazi, M. O., & Abugroon, M. A. (2016). The state of the art on educational data mining in higher education. *International Journal of Computer Trends and Technology, 31*(1), 46–56. doi:10.14445/22312803/IJCTT-V31P109

Hegazi, M. O., Alhawaat, M., & Hilal, A. (2016). An approach for integrating data mining with Saudi universities database systems: Case study. *International Journal of Advanced Computer Science and Applications, 7*(6), 213–218.

Hemaid, R. K., & Halees, A. M. (2015). Improving teacher performance using data mining. *International Journal of Advanced Research in Computer and Communication Engineering, 4*(2), 407–412. doi:10.17148/IJARCCE.2015.4292

Huang, T. C. K., Huang, C. H., & Chuang, Y. T. (2016). Change discovery of learning performance in dynamic educational environments. *Telematics and Informatics, 33*(3), 773–792. doi:10.1016/j.tele.2015.10.005

Hui, Y. K., & Kwok, L. F. (2019). A review on learning analytics. *International Journal of Innovation and Learning, 25*(2), 197–222. doi:10.1504/IJIL.2019.097673

Ifenthaler, D. (2016). Are higher education institutions prepared for learning analytics? *TechTrends, 61*(4), 366–371. doi:10.100711528-016-0154-0

Ifenthaler, D., & Tracey, M. W. (2016). Exploring the relationship of ethics and privacy in learning analytics and design: Implications for the field of educational technology. *Educational Technology Research and Development, 64*(5), 877–880. doi:10.100711423-016-9480-3

Ikbal, S., Tamhane, A., Sengupta, B., Chetlur, M., Ghosh, S., & Appleton, J. (2015). On early prediction of risks in academic performance for students. *IBM Journal of Research and Development, 59*(6), 5–1. doi:10.1147/JRD.2015.2458631

Jayaprakash, S. M., Moody, E. W., Eitel, J. M. L., Regan, J. R., & Baron, J. D. (2014). Early alert of academically at-risk students: An open source analytics initiative. *Journal of Learning Analytics, 1*(1), 6–47. doi:10.18608/jla.2014.11.3

Jindal, R., & Borah, M. D. (2013). A survey on educational data mining and research trends. *International Journal of Database Management Systems, 5*(3), 53–73. doi:10.5121/ijdms.2013.5304

Jones, K. M. (2019). Advising the whole student: eAdvising analytics and the contextual suppression of advisor values. *Education and Information Technologies, 24*(1), 437–458. doi:10.100710639-018-9781-8

Jones, S. (2015). The game changers: Strategies to boost college completion and close attainment gaps. *Change: The Magazine of Higher Learning*, *47*(2), 24–29. doi:10.1080/00091383.2015.1018085

Kasemsap, K. (2016). The role of learning analytics in global higher education. In *Developing effective educational experiences through learning analytics* (pp. 282–307). Hershey, PA: IGI Global. doi:10.4018/978-1-4666-9983-0.ch012

Kashyap, G., & Chauhan, E. (2015). Review on educational data mining techniques. *International Journal of Advanced Technology in Engineering and Science*, *3*(11), 308–316.

Kelchen, R. (2018). Do performance-based funding policies affect underrepresented student enrollment? *The Journal of Higher Education*, *89*(5), 702–727. doi:10.1080/00221546.2018.1434282

Kenekayoro, P. (2018). An exploratory study on the use of machine learning to predict student academic performance. *International Journal of Knowledge-Based Organizations*, *8*(4), 67–79. doi:10.4018/IJKBO.2018100104

Kennedy, K. (2019). Why is data so hard? Challenges, solutions, and future directions. In *Technology leadership for innovation in higher education* (pp. 268–290). Hershey, PA: IGI Global. doi:10.4018/978-1-5225-7769-0.ch011

Khan, I. A., & Choi, J. T. (2014). An application of educational data mining (EDM) technique for scholarship prediction. *International Journal of Software Engineering and Its Applications*, *8*(12), 31–42.

Kitchin, R. (2014). Big data, new epistemologies and paradigm shifts. *Big Data and Society*, *1*(1), 1–12. doi:10.1177/2053951714528481

Klasen, D., & Ifenthaler, D. (2019). Implementing learning analytics into existing higher education legacy systems. In D. Ifenthaler, D. K. Mah, & J. K. Yau (Eds.), *Utilizing learning analytics to support study success*. Cham, Switzerland: Springer. doi:10.1007/978-3-319-64792-0_4

Koprinska, I., Stretton, J., & Yacef, K. (2015). Predicting student performance from multiple data sources. In C. Conati, N. Heffernan, A. Mitrovic, & M. F. Verdejo (Eds.), *Artificial intelligence in education* (Vol. 9112, pp. 678–681). New York, NY: Springer International. doi:10.1007/978-3-319-19773-9_90

Kowalczyk, M., & Buxmann, P. (2014). Big data and information processing in organizational decision processes. *Business & Information Systems Engineering*, *6*(5), 267–278. doi:10.100712599-014-0341-5

Kuhnel, M., Seiler, L., Honal, A., & Ifenthaler, D. (2018). Mobile learning analytics in higher education: Usability testing and evaluation of an app prototype. *Interactive Technology and Smart Education*, *15*(4), 332–347. doi:10.1108/ITSE-04-2018-0024

Kumar, M., Singh, A. J., & Handa, D. (2017). Literature survey on student's performance prediction in education using data mining techniques. *International Journal of Education and Management Engineering*, *7*(6), 42–49. doi:10.5815/ijeme.2017.06.05

Kumar, V., & Chadha, A. (2011). An empirical study of the applications of data mining techniques in higher education. *International Journal of Advanced Computer Science and Applications*, *2*(3).

Kumarapathirana, K. P. S. D. (2018). Using data mining for improving education of university students–A survey. *International Journal for Innovation Education and Research*, *6*(9), 78–83. doi:10.31686/ijier.Vol6.Iss9.1155

Kunjir, A. (2015). Recommendation of data mining technique in higher education. *International Journal of Computational Engineering Research*, *5*(3), 29–35.

Lane, K. E., Lemoine, P. A., Tinney, T. M., & Richardson, M. D. (2014). Modify and adapt: Global higher education in a changing economy. *International Journal of Innovation in the Digital Economy*, *5*(2), 24–36. doi:10.4018/ijide.2014040103

Larose, D. T., & Larose, C. D. (2015). *Data mining and predictive analytics* (1st ed.). Hoboken, NJ: John Wiley & Sons, Inc.

Lawson, C., Beer, C., Rossi, D., Moore, T., & Fleming, J. (2016). Identification of 'at risk' students using learning analytics: The ethical dilemmas of intervention strategies in a higher education institution. *Educational Technology Research and Development*, *64*(5), 957–968. doi:10.100711423-016-9459-0

Lemoine, P. A., Hackett, P. T., & Richardson, M. D. (2017). Global higher education and VUCA–Volatility, uncertainty, complexity, ambiguity. In *Handbook of Research on Administration, Policy, and Leadership in Higher Education* (pp. 549–568). Hershey, PA: IGI Global. doi:10.4018/978-1-5225-0672-0.ch022

Lewis, P., Goodman, S., & Fandt, P. (2001). *Management: Challenges in the 21st century*. Cincinnati, OH: South-Western College Publishing.

Liñán, L. C., & Pérez, Á. A. J. (2015). Educational data mining and learning analytics: Differences, similarities, and time evolution. *International Journal of Educational Technology in Higher Education*, *12*(3), 98–112.

Liu, D. Y. T., Bartimote-Aufflick, K., Pardo, A., & Bridgeman, A. J. (2017). Data-driven personalization of student learning support in higher education. In A. Peña-Ayala (Ed.), *Learning analytics: Fundaments, applications, and trends*. Cham, Switzerland: Springer. doi:10.1007/978-3-319-52977-6_5

Lumbantoruan, R. (2017). Big data, academic data university. *Fundamental Management Journal*, *2*(1), 57–66.

Macfadyen, L., Dawson, S., Pardo, A., & Gašević, D. (2014). The learning analytics imperative and the sociotechnical challenge: Policy for complex systems. *Research & Practice in Assessment*, *9*(2), 17–28.

Manek, S., Vijay, S., & Kamthania, D. (2016). Educational data mining-A case study. *International Journal of Information and Decision Sciences*, *8*(2), 187–201. doi:10.1504/IJIDS.2016.076517

Marginson, S. (2016). Global stratification in higher education. In *Higher education, stratification, and workforce development* (pp. 13–34). Cham: Springer. doi:10.1007/978-3-319-21512-9_2

Marshall, S. J. (2018). *Shaping the university of the future: Using technology to catalyse change in university learning and teaching*. New York, NY: Springer. doi:10.1007/978-981-10-7620-6

Martin, W. J. (2017). *The global information society*. New York, NY: Taylor & Francis. doi:10.4324/9781315239385

Martins, M. P., Migueis, V. L., & Fonseca, D. S. B. (2018, June). Educational data mining: A literature review. In *2018 13th Iberian Conference on Information Systems and Technologies (CISTI)* (pp. 1-6). IEEE. 10.23919/CISTI.2018.8399281

Martins, M. P., Miguéis, V. L., Fonseca, D. S. B., & Alves, A. (2019, February). A data mining approach for predicting academic success–A case study. In *International Conference on Information Technology & Systems* (pp. 45-56). Cham, Switzerland: Springer. 10.1007/978-3-030-11890-7_5

Mayra, A., & Mauricio, D. (2018, April). Factors to predict dropout at the universities: A case of study in Ecuador. In *Global Engineering Education Conference (EDUCON)*, 2018 *IEEE* (pp. 1238-1242). IEEE. 10.1109/EDUCON.2018.8363371

McCoy, S., & Byrne, D. (2017). Student retention in higher education. In *Economic insights on higher education policy in Ireland* (pp. 111–141). Cham, Switzerland: Springer. doi:10.1007/978-3-319-48553-9_5

Meedech, P., Iam-On, N., & Boongoen, T. (2016). Prediction of student dropout using personal profile and data mining approach. In *Intelligent and evolutionary systems* (pp. 143–155). Cham, Switzerland: Springer. doi:10.1007/978-3-319-27000-5_12

Meghji, A. F., & Mahoto, N. A. (2016). Using big data to improve the educational infrastructure and learning paradigm. In *Effective big data management and opportunities for implementation* (pp. 158–181). Hershey, PA: IGI Global. doi:10.4018/978-1-5225-0182-4.ch011

Mense, E. G., Lemoine, P. A., Garretson, C. J., & Richardson, M. D. (2018). The development of global higher education in a world of transformation. *Journal of Education and Development*, *2*(3), 47. doi:10.20849/jed.v2i3.529

Mislevy, R. J., Behrens, J. T., Dicerbo, K. E., & Levy, R. (2012). Design and discovery in educational assessment: Evidence centered design, psychometrics, and educational data mining. *Journal of Educational Data Mining*, *4*(1), 11–48.

Mittal, V. (2017). A real time data mining model to predict academic attrition. *International Journal for Research in Science Engineering & Technology*, *4*(8), 46–54.

Monjurul Alom, B. M., & Courtney, M. (2018). Educational data mining: A case study perspectives from primary to university education in Australia. *International Journal of Information Technology and Computer Science*, *10*(2), 1–9. doi:10.5815/ijitcs.2018.02.01

Mu-azu, I. A. (2019). The search for academic excellence: The hard facts and bitter truths. *Journal of Applied and Advanced Research*, *4*(1), 1–5. doi:10.21839/jaar.2019.v4i1.259

Mustafina, J., Galiullin, L., Al-Jumeily, D., Petrov, E., Alloghani, M., & Kaky, A. (2018, September). Application of learning analytics in higher educational institutions. In *2018 11th International Conference on Developments in eSystems Engineering (DeSE)* (pp. 163-168). IEEE. 10.1109/DeSE.2018.00039

Na, K. S., & Tasir, Z. (2017, November). Identifying at-risk students in online learning by analysing learning behaviour: A systematic review. In *2017 IEEE Conference on Big Data and Analytics (ICBDA)* (pp. 118-123). IEEE. 10.1109/ICBDAA.2017.8284117

Natek, S., & Zwilling, M. (2014). Student data mining solution–knowledge management system related to higher education institution. *Expert Systems with Applications*, *41*(14), 6400–6407. doi:10.1016/j.eswa.2014.04.024

Nithya, P., Umamaheswari, B., & Umadevi, A. (2016). A survey on educational data mining in field of education. *International Journal of Advanced Research in Computer Engineering & Technology*, *5*(1), 69–78.

Nunn, S., Avella, J. T., Kanai, T., & Kebritchi, M. (2016). Learning analytics methods, benefits, and challenges in higher education: A systematic literature review. Online Learning, 20(2).

Oakleaf, M., Whyte, A., Lynema, E., & Brown, M. (2017). Academic libraries & institutional learning analytics: One path to integration. *Journal of Academic Librarianship*, *43*(5), 454–461. doi:10.1016/j.acalib.2017.08.008

Oskouei, R. J., & Askari, M. (2014). Predicting academic performance with applying data mining techniques. *Computer Engineering and Applications Journal*, *3*(2), 79–88. doi:10.18495/comengapp.v3i2.81

Palacios-Pacheco, X., Villegas-Ch, W., & Luján-Mora, S. (2018, August). Application of data mining for the detection of variables that cause university desertion. In *International Conference on Technology Trends* (pp. 510-520). Cham, Switzerland: Springer.

Papamitsiou, Z., & Economides, A. A. (2014). Learning analytics and educational data mining in practice: A systematic literature review of empirical evidence. *Journal of Educational Technology & Society*, *17*(4).

Peña-Ayala, A. (2014). Educational data mining: A survey and a data mining-based analysis of recent works. *Expert Systems with Applications*, *41*(4), 1432–1462. doi:10.1016/j.eswa.2013.08.042

Posselt, T., Abdelkafi, N., Fischer, L., & Tangour, C. (2019). Opportunities and challenges of higher education institutions in Europe: An analysis from a business model perspective. *Higher Education Quarterly*, *73*(1), 100–115.

Pradnya, P. S. (2015). Overview of predictive and descriptive data mining techniques. *International Journal of Advanced Research in Computer Science and Software Engineering*, *5*(4).

Preethi, N., & Goswami, D. (2015). A review on role of data mining techniques in enhancing educational data to analyze student's performance. *International Journal of Computer Science and Information Technology Research*, *3*(1), 123–129.

Pucciarelli, F., & Kaplan, A. (2016). Competition and strategy in higher education: Managing complexity and uncertainty. *Business Horizons*, *59*(3), 311–320. doi:10.1016/j.bushor.2016.01.003

Ray, S., & Saeed, M. (2018). Applications of educational data mining and learning analytics tools in handling big data in higher education. In *Applications of big data analytics* (pp. 135–160). Cham, Switzerland: Springer. doi:10.1007/978-3-319-76472-6_7

Reich, J., Tingley, D., Leder-Luis, J., Roberts, M. E., & Stewart, B. (2014). Computer assisted reading and discovery for student generated text in massive open online courses. *Journal of Learning Analytics*, *2*(1), 156–184. doi:10.18608/jla.2015.21.8

Richardson, M. D., Jenkins, W. M., & Lemoine, P. A. (2017). Planning for innovation and disruption in a global environment. *Educational Planning*, *23*(3), 11–24.

Rubel, A., & Jones, K. (2017). Data analytics in higher education: Key concerns and open questions. *University of St. Thomas Journal of Law and Public Policy*, *11*(1), 25–44.

Saa, A. A. (2016). Educational data mining & students' performance prediction. *International Journal of Advanced Computer Science and Applications*, *7*(5), 212–220.

Sarantinos, V. (2019). Examining the factors shaping the debate around the globalization of higher education: Key factors and influences. In *Higher education and the evolution of management, applied sciences, and engineering curricula* (pp. 1–26). Hershey, PA: IGI Global. doi:10.4018/978-1-5225-7259-6.ch001

Sarra, A., Fontanella, L., & Di Zio, S. (2018). Identifying students at risk of academic failure within the educational data mining framework. *Social Indicators Research*, 1–20. doi:10.100711205-018-1901-8

Selwyn, N. (2015). Data entry: Towards the critical study of digital data and education. *Learning, Media and Technology*, *40*(1), 64–82. doi:10.1080/17439884.2014.921628

Şengür, D., & Karabatak, S. (2018). Data mining techniques based students achievements analysis. *Turkish Journal of Science & Technology*, *13*(2), 53–59.

Shahiri, A., Husain, W., & Rashid, N. (2015). A review on predicting student's performance using data mining techniques. *Procedia Computer Science*, *72*, 414–422. doi:10.1016/j.procs.2015.12.157

Shingari, I., Kumar, D., & Khetan, M. (2017). A review of applications of data mining techniques for prediction of students' performance in higher education. *Journal of Statistics and Management Systems*, *20*(4), 713–722. doi:10.1080/09720510.2017.1395191

Shukora, N. A., Tasira, Z., & Vander Meijden, H. (2015). An examination of online learning effectiveness using data mining. *Procedia: Social and Behavioral Sciences, 172*, 555–562. doi:10.1016/j.sbspro.2015.01.402

Simon, C., & Bugusa, Y. (2018). Survey on data mining approach for analysis and prediction of student performance. International Journal of Engineering & Technology, 7(4.5), 467-470.

Slater, S., Joksimović, S., Kovanovic, V., Baker, R. S., & Gasevic, D. (2017). Tools for educational data mining: A review. *Journal of Educational and Behavioral Statistics*, *42*(1), 85–106. doi:10.3102/1076998616666808

Sneyers, E., & De Witte, K. (2018). Interventions in higher education and their effect on student success: A meta-analysis. *Educational Review*, *70*(2), 208–228. doi:10.1080/00131911.2017.1300874

Sønderlund, A. L., Hughes, E., & Smith, J. (2018). The efficacy of learning analytics interventions in higher education: A systematic review. *British Journal of Educational Technology*. doi:10.1111/bjet.12720

Stewart, C. (2017). Learning analytics: Shifting from theory to practice. *Journal on Empowering Teaching Excellence*, *1*(1), 10.

Sumitha, R., & Vinothkumar, E. S. (2016). Prediction of students outcome using data mining techniques. *International Journal of Scientific Engineering and Applied Science*, *2*(6), 8.

Tegegne, A. K., & Alemu, T. A. (2018). Educational data mining for students' academic performance analysis in selected Ethiopian universities. *Information Impact: Journal of Information and Knowledge Management*, *9*(2), 1–15.

Thakar, P. (2016). Performance analysis and prediction in educational data mining: A research travelogue. *International Journal of Computers and Applications*, *110*(15), 60–68.

Thakar, P., & Mehta, A., & Manisha. (2015). Performance analysis and prediction in educational data mining: A research travelogue. *International Journal of Computers and Applications*, *110*(15), 60–68.

Thille, C., Schneider, E., Kizilcec, R. F., Piech, C., Halawa, S. A., & Greene, D. K. (2014). The future of data-enriched assessment. *Research and Practice in Assessment*, *9*, 5–16.

Thille, C., & Zimmaro, D. (2017). Incorporating learning analytics in the classroom. *New Directions for Higher Education*, *2017*(179), 19–31. doi:10.1002/he.20240

Umer, R., Susnjak, T., Mathrani, A., & Suriadi, S. (2018, November). A learning analytics approach: Using online weekly student engagement data to make predictions on student performance. In *2018 International Conference on Computing, Electronic and Electrical Engineering (ICE Cube)* (pp. 1-5). IEEE. 10.1109/ICECUBE.2018.8610959

Verger, A., Steiner-Khamsi, G., & Lubienski, C. (2017). The emerging global education industry: Analysing market-making in education through market sociology. *Globalisation, Societies and Education, 15*(3), 325–340. doi:10.1080/14767724.2017.1330141

Viberg, O., Hatakka, M., Bälter, O., & Mavroudi, A. (2018). The current landscape of learning analytics in higher education. *Computers in Human Behavior, 89*, 98–110. doi:10.1016/j.chb.2018.07.027

Villano, R., Harrison, S., Lynch, G., & Chen, G. (2018). Linking early alert systems and student retention: A survival analysis approach. *Higher Education, 76*(5), 903–920. doi:10.100710734-018-0249-y

Wagner, E., & Yaskin, D. (2015). Predictive models based on behavioral patterns in higher education. In C. Dede (Ed.), *Data intensive research in education: Current work and next steps* (pp. 23–31). Washington, DC: Computing Research Association.

Wardrip, P. S., & Shapiro, R. B. (2016). Digital media and data: Using and designing technologies to support learning in practice. *Learning, Media and Technology, 41*(2), 187–192. doi:10.1080/17439884.2016.1160929

Wilson, A., Watson, C., Thompson, T. L., Drew, V., & Doyle, S. (2017). Learning analytics: Challenges and limitations. *Teaching in Higher Education, 22*(8), 991–1007. doi:10.1080/13562517.2017.1332026

Wise, A. F. (2019). Learning analytics: Using data-informed decision-making to improve teaching and learning. In *Contemporary technologies in education* (pp. 119–143). Cham, Switzerland: Palgrave Macmillan. doi:10.1007/978-3-319-89680-9_7

Wong, B. T.-W., Li, K. C., & Choi, S. P.-M. (2018). Trends in learning analytics practices: A review of higher education institutions. *Interactive Technology and Smart Education, 15*(2), 132–154. doi:10.1108/ITSE-12-2017-0065

Xing, W., Guo, R., Petakovic, E., & Goggins, S. (2015). Participation-based student final performance prediction model through interpretable genetic programming: Integrating learning analytics, educational data mining and theory. *Computers in Human Behavior, 47*, 168–181. doi:10.1016/j.chb.2014.09.034

Yadav, S. K., & Pal, S. (2012). Data mining application in enrollment management: A case study. *International Journal of Computers and Applications*, *41*(5).

Yukselturk, E., Ozekes, S., & Turel, Y. K. (2014). Predicting dropout student: An application of data mining methods in an online education program. *European Journal of Open, Distance and E-learning*, *17*(1), 118–133. doi:10.2478/eurodl-2014-0008

Zwitter, A. (2014). Big data ethics. *Big Data and Society*, *1*(2), 1–6. doi:10.1177/2053951714559253

ADDITIONAL READING

Cohen, A. (2017). Analysis of student activity in web-supported courses as a tool for predicting dropout. *Educational Technology Research and Development*, *65*(5), 1285–1304. doi:10.100711423-017-9524-3

Cole, A. W., & Weber, N. L. (2019). The use of emerging technology exploration projects to guide instructional innovation. In *Technology leadership for innovation in higher education* (pp. 165–184). Hershey, PA: IGI Global. doi:10.4018/978-1-5225-7769-0.ch007

de Wit, H. (2017). Global: Internationalization of higher education: Nine misconceptions. In *Understanding higher education internationalization* (pp. 9–12). Rotterdam, Netherlands: Sense Publishers. doi:10.1007/978-94-6351-161-2_2

Gallardo-Exhenique, E. E., Marques-Molias, L., Bullen, M., & Stribos, J. (2015). Let's talk about digital learners in the digital era. *International Review of Research in Open and Distance Learning*, *16*(3), 156–187.

Gursoy, M. E., Inan, A., Nergiz, M. E., & Saygin, Y. (2017). Privacy-preserving learning analytics: Challenges and techniques. *IEEE Transactions on Learning Technologies*, *10*(1), 68–81. doi:10.1109/TLT.2016.2607747

Jo, I. H., Yu, T., Lee, H., & Kim, Y. (2015). Relations between student online learning behavior and academic achievement in higher education: A learning analytics approach. In *Emerging issues in smart learning* (pp. 275–287). Berlin, Heidelberg: Springer. doi:10.1007/978-3-662-44188-6_38

Klašnja-Milicevic, A., & Ivanovic, M. (2018). Learning analytics--New flavor and benefits for educational environments. *Informatics in Education*, *17*(2), 285–300. doi:10.15388/infedu.2018.15

Leitner, P., Khalil, M., & Ebner, M. (2017). Learning analytics in higher education—a literature review. In *Learning analytics: Fundaments, applications, and trends* (pp. 1–23). Cham, Switzerland: Springer. doi:10.1007/978-3-319-52977-6_1

Long, P., & Siemens, G. (2011). Penetrating the fog: Analytics in learning and education. *EDUCAUSE Review*, *48*(5), 1–40.

Pardo, A., & Siemens, G. (2014). Ethical and privacy principles for learning analytics. *British Journal of Educational Technology*, *45*(3), 438–450. doi:10.1111/bjet.12152

Pistilli, M. D., Willis, J. E., & Campbell, J. P. (2014). Analytics through an institutional lens: definition, theory, design and impact. In J. A. Larusson & B. White (Eds.), *Learning analytics: From research to practice* (pp. 79–102). New York, NY: Springer.

Reyes, J. A. (2015). The skinny on big data in education: Learning analytics simplified. *TechTrends*, *59*(2), 75–80. doi:10.100711528-015-0842-1

Roberts, L. D., Chang, V., & Gibson, D. (2017). Ethical considerations in adopting a university-and system-wide approach to data and learning analytics. In *Big data and learning analytics in higher education* (pp. 89–108). Cham, Switzerland: Springer. doi:10.1007/978-3-319-06520-5_7

Shum, S. B., Aberer, K., Schmidt, A., Bishop, S., Lukowicz, P., Anderson, S., ... Edmonds, B. (2012). Towards a global participatory platform: Democratising open data, complexity science and collective intelligence. *The European Physical Journal. Special Topics*, *214*(1), 109–152. doi:10.1140/epjst/e2012-01690-3

Singh, R. P. (2018). Learning analytics: Potential, protection, and privacy in the educational system. In *Impact of learning analytics on curriculum design and student performance* (pp. 1–18). Hershey, PA: IGI Global. doi:10.4018/978-1-5225-5369-4.ch001

Uddin, M. F., & Lee, J. (2016). Utilizing relevant academic and personality features from big unstructured data to identify good and bad fit students. *Procedia Computer Science*, *95*, 383–391. doi:10.1016/j.procs.2016.09.349

Wang, Y. (2016). Big opportunities and big concerns of big data in education. *TechTrends*, *60*(4), 381–384. doi:10.100711528-016-0072-1

West, D., Huijser, H., & Heath, D. (2016). Putting an ethical lens on learning analytics. *Educational Technology Research and Development*, *64*(5), 903–922. doi:10.100711423-016-9464-3

Wong, B. T. M. (2017). Learning analytics in higher education: An analysis of case studies. *Asian Association of Open Universities Journal*, *12*(1), 21–40. doi:10.1108/AAOUJ-01-2017-0009

Zhong, L. (2015). A systematic overview of learning analytics in higher education. *Journal of Educational Technology Development and Exchange*, *8*(2), 3. doi:10.18785/jetde.0802.03

Chapter 6
Intelligent Tutoring System

Abhishek Singh Rathore
Shri Vaishnav Vidyapeeth Vishwavidyalaya, India

Siddhartha Kumar Arjaria
Rajkiya Engineering College, India

ABSTRACT

With digitization, a rapid growth is seen in educational technology. Different formal and informal learning contents are available on the internet. Intelligent tutoring system provides personalized e-learning to the learners. Different attributes like historical data, real-time data, behavioral, and cognitive are usually used for personalization. Based on the personalization, the intelligent tutoring system aims to provide easy and effective understanding. Recent research highlights the effect of learner's behavior and emotions on effective teaching-learning process. This chapter provides a brief description of the intelligent tutoring system, current developments, instructional techniques, proposed solution, and future recommendations. The emphasis of the study is to provide insights on self-regulated learning.

DOI: 10.4018/978-1-7998-0010-1.ch006

INTRODUCTION

In the modern era, the use of technology changes the method of learning. Now learners are equipped with various electronic gadgets. These gadgets are not only used for entertainment, but also for the learning. Learning objects are available on the internet that can be accessed from anywhere and anytime. Such type of learning is regarded as E-Learning and quite helpful in industry and education sector for all types of learners. The interest of the users is continuously increasing in this type of new learning method. It is considered as a basic building block of learning in the twenty-first century.

With the advancement of internet and communication technology, more innovative techniques will appear to support e-learning. With the huge amount of information available, the internet is considered as best learning material for the learner. Problem with this huge data is finding relevant material for learning and recommending what to read next. When a different number of learners are available with different knowledge level and learning styles, the recommendation becomes more difficult. Problem with such type of systems is that they are general, means not specific for the individual learner. Such systems cannot monitor the performance of the learner and could not personalize lesson according to the users' style learning and adapt accordingly. Personalization in the teaching-learning process is an important issue and need is to provide flexibility in the teaching-learning process so that individual learner gets personal attention (Chen, 2008). Thus, a tutoring system is needed for learners that can intelligently recommend relevant learning materials individually. To understand the learner's need and make an adaptation, Artificial Intelligence techniques are added in the learning systems and such systems are known as Intelligent Tutoring Systems (ITS). The Intelligent Tutoring System (ITS) is an expert system model one to one student-teacher learning process by improving understanding and perception (Noh, Ahmed, Halim, & Ali, 2011).

Intelligent Tutoring System

The Intelligent Tutoring System, a computer-based system tries to model a personalized human tutor for the learners. It tracks the student's progress and provides individual guidance in an interactive environment.

Based on the learner's capability ITS recommends what to read next. Different types of recommendation system that's available in the text are Collaborative filtering, Content-based, Knowledge-based, Ontology-based, Hybrid, Demographic-based, Utility-based, Context aware-based, Trust aware-based, Fuzzy-based and Group recommender (Taraus, Niu, & Mustafa, 2018). The basic architecture of the ITS is depicted in Figure 1. ITS consists of four main models, namely: Expert model, Test model, Learner model, and User Interface model. Each model has a specific role and interacts with each other.

1. **Expert Model:** It is also known as a domain model or Knowledge-base. This comprises of knowledge-base for the predefined domain and/or sub-domain. Usually, the domain knowledge is defined in structured files like in XML or in ontology form. Content organization and structure are the keys to ITS, often based on content hierarchy, metadata, and sequencing. A strong hierarchical relationship between concept nodes provides hyperlinks that help in curriculum sequencing for the individual learner. The personalized recommendations are based on learner's activity log and pedagogical patterns.
2. **Test Model:** Its job is continuous evaluation of learner's progress throughout learning. An online examination is conducted after the completion of every concept. Assignments, practice sets, exams, and other evaluation techniques are used to define the learning styles of the learner. Learner's strength and weakness are recorded for further recommendations. Different sets and levels of questions basic measure for identifying strength and weakness. Time elapsed and user behavior is also modeled for defining learning styles. All this information helps in creating a learner's profile.
3. **Learner Model:** It stores all the information on learner right from her registration. In addition to personal details, learning styles, knowledge-level and domain are the most critical issues for the ITS. The main aim of the learning is to improve the knowledge-level of the learner, a continuous process is used to record the knowledge level of the user throughout the learning process.

Figure 1. Basic architecture of intelligent tutoring system

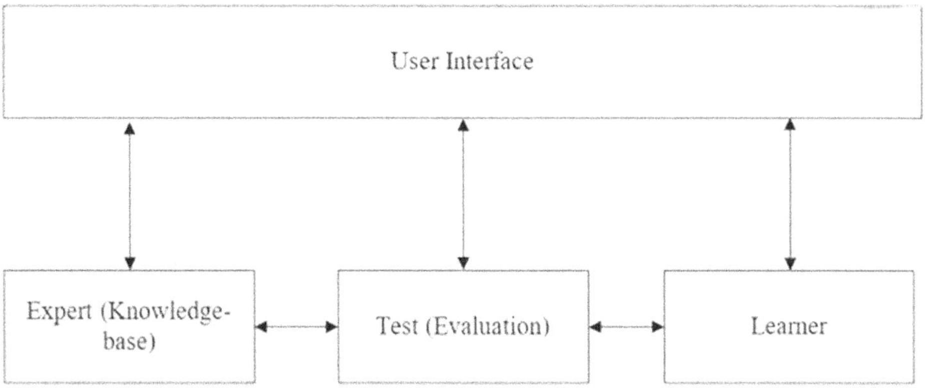

Few learner model record learner's behavior, attitude, and activities through behavioral modeling, while conversational agents are used for learners' feedback. When predicting learner's domain, it can lead to better personalization and recommendation.

4. **User Interface:** It is responsible for retrieving content from the knowledge-base. It provides the realization of all the models. It displays the information to the users and sends information forthe processing of the previous three models. For more interactive learning, virtual reality and audio-visual contents are augmented in the interfaces.

The goal of the ITS is to simulate the learner behavior, the education process, **effective** evaluation of user of her response and make the learning easy and smart. The objective of this study is to:

- Provide flexible and adaptive learning
- Provide immediate and customized instructions.
- Minimize human interventions
- Effective evaluation system

Background

In recent year, lots of approaches have been proposed in the area of e-learning and intelligent tutoring system for the better-personalized learning model for the learners. This section includes different models provided by various researchers. Generally, the authors divided the intelligent tutoring system into an expert, learner, test and user interface models. In addition to these models, adaptive hypermedia (Brusilovsky, 1996) are added for navigation hyperspace that observes browsing behavior of the learner. Adaptive hypermedia-based models adapt users' behavior and personalized accordingly (Brusilvosky, 2001). A combined system of adaptive hypermedia with adaptive navigation and presentation of the Expert model (Phobun & Vicheanpanya, 2010) is proposed for personalized learning style and teaching strategy.

The ITS continuously tries to learn learner's behavior and adapt accordingly (Samuelis, 2007) to provide learning contents with examples and problems for practice. A rule-based and case-based artificial intelligence approached are used to infer learner's teaching style for better adaptation. (Noh, Ahmed, Halim, & Ali, 2011). Cognitive and motivational states of the learner are focused while developing the learner's model (Pavlik Jr., Brawner, Olney, & Mitrovic, 2013). A rule-based adaptive ITS based on mastery learning technique improves the accuracy of the expert model by student profiling (Kularbphettong, Kedsiribut, & Roonrakwit, 2015). A sensory preference based Adaptive learning model is proposed to assess learner's knowledge. A virtual teacher is integrated with it for versatility (Bradac & Kostolanyova, 2017).

In addition to learner model, an interactive simulation learning approach is combined in the domain model to get stability and accuracy for ITS (Huertas & Juarez-Ramirez, 2013). A Bayesian network is employed in ITS for inferring prior probabilities (Butz, Hua, & Maguire, 2006) while the agent-based approach is used for trainer model (El-Khouly, Far, & Koono, 2000). A Bayesian-based inference engine is used in the test model of ITS for decision making. Question are selected according to posterior probability and thus helpful for assessing learner's cognitive levels (Ramírez-Noriega, Juárez-Ramírez, & Martínez-Ramírez, 2017).

SCORM SN (Jesukiewicz, 2009) based pedagogical strategies with software agents is proposed for mature and stable architecture (Marciniak, 2014). The WordNet-based ontology is created for domain-based knowledge. Learner's emotion detection from his facial expression in addition to learner's knowledge track is employed in ITS for improved teaching and learning process (KHALFALLAH & SLAMA, 2015). For effective determination of affective state (Petrovica, Anohina-Naumeca, & Ekenel, 2017), a sensor free approach (Baker, et al., 2012) Self-assessment Manikin is applied for fundamental emotions (Bradley & Lang, 1994). However, mood types are not included in the proposed approach. Another sensor-free approach considers emotional factors based on Self-assessed Manikins is proposed for personalization without using specific emotion detection system (Arevalillo-Herraez, Marco-Gim´enez, Arnau, & Gonz´alez Calero, 2017).

Use of natural language processing is often seemed in a conversational dialog based ITS. The AutoTutor (Al Emran & Shaalan, 2014) applied LSA with pattern matching for dimension reduction. Why2-Atlas (Vanlehn, et al., 2002) is an iterative approach, works on explanation and essays submitted by the learner. Bettle II (Dzikovska, et al., 2010) utilizes the capabilities of NLP to examine the self-explanation given by learners as feedback. Natural-K, an authoring system utilizes the power of natural language to define domain knowledge in ITS (Jung & VenLehn, 2010). The system performs well, but issues related to paraphrasing are not considered. OSCAR conversational ITS determines the learner's learning style from the natural language for automatic curriculum sequencing (Latham, Crockett, McLean, & Edmonds, A conversational intelligent tutoring system to automatically predict learning styles, 2012). Selecting one learning-style for a learner might be inappropriate and results in poor prediction, therefore an adaptation algorithm is employed on OSCAR conversational ITS on learning-style dimensions to improve learning experiences (Latham, Crockett, & McLean, An adaptation algorithm for an intelligent natural language tutoring system, 2014). AG_Tutor (Mahmoud &

El-Hamayed, 2016) utilizes the power of NLP in the expert model to define feature words that can appear in practice exercise. Usually, uncertainty exists in learning styles and sometimes, conversational ITS does not consider behavioral variables that lead to incorrect predictions. A fuzzy decision tree combines the behavioral variables of all learning styles to provide a better prediction with coherent learning styles (Crockett, Latham, & Whitton, 2017).

Case-based reasoning, the multi-agent system is applied in learner's model for better co-operation. Each learner is described as a case having domain specific and domain independent information. The multi-agent system extracts relevant features of different learners and retains the same cases for another learner if having a higher similarity (González, Burguillo, & Llamas, 2007). A rule-based inference engine is employed in an expert model of web-based ITS to imitate real classroom teaching-learning process (Keles, Ocak, Keles, & Gulcu, 2009)

Preference-based teaching (Gao, Ries, Simon, & Zilles, 2017) adapted the idea "valid teacher/learner pair" (Goldman & Mathias, 1996) along with complexity parameter of recursive teaching (Zilles, Lange, Holte, & Zinkevich, 2011). A complexity parameter is proposed to teach any concept from an infinite number of classes including closed-sets.

A data mining framework (Amela, Diez, & Valles, 2011) clusters four dimensions (processing, perception, input and understanding) to assess different learning styles (Felder & Silverman, 1988), while students' classification on knowledge level is based on Blooms Taxonomy (Bloom, 1956) and collaborative competence (Baldiris, et al., 2008). A trinomial graph based on Fridman's notation is used for knowledge representation and XML based inference engine is used to support ITS for learning algebra (Arevalillo-Herráez, Arnau, & Marco-Giménez, 2013). Domain knowledge of topological properties is used to create a bipartite graph for link prediction that consequences in learning recommendations for the end user (Lia, Zhang, Meng, & Lia, 2014).

A neural network based formalization of ITS interface is proposed to a model natural way of decision making. Didactic Ergonomy concepts are employed as a computational model for better personalization (Curilem, Barbosa, & de Azevedo, 2007). The image recognition technique is applied to classify images with the augmented reality to design an interactive learning system (Lee, Choi, & Park, 2009). Augmented learning model founded over inquiry-based technique for interactive learning (Creane, Crotty, & Farren, 2015).

A conceptual map model with n-gram ($1< n <6$) is employed automatically to create learning material for the learner (Gunel & Asliyan, 2010). The probabilistic models are used to create a conceptual model, the use of generative probabilistic models might be more accurate. Learner feedback is important and it helps to advance in the learning cycle, the Support Vector Machine and Conditional Random Fields models are employed in ITS to collect learner's feedback (Gutierrez & Atkinson, 2011).

The impact of high-level sustainability requirements, for longer life of the system; is thoroughly studied and classified into five dimensions. These five dimensions are highly correlated and have a strong impact on each other (Alharthi, Spichkova, & Hamilton, 2018).

The dependency of learner's domain always is a critical issue in the design of ITS. Fuzzy cognitive maps (FCM) are employed to identify the learner's domain and knowledge level for personalization (Chrysafiadi & Virvou, Fuzzy logic for adaptive instruction in an e-learning environment for computer programming, 2015). FCM is used to identify the dependencies between various domains. Speech interface and virtual reality contents are used with FCM for learner's domain knowledge prediction. A hybrid approach of discrete wavelet transform and wavelet packet decomposition is used to extract features from speech signals. Hybrid approach nullifies the drawbacks of individual approach (Sathia Bhama, Hariharasubramanian, Mythili, & Ramachandran, 2017).

Behavior intention based activity index model to predict the learner's attitude is suggested in the self-regulated learning environment (Kim & Moon, 2018). Temporal modeling is employed in a self-regulated learning environment to predict learner's long-term success (Gardner & Brooks, 2018). Concept extraction and knowledge tracing techniques are applied to analyze multi-source data for personalized learning recommendation in the self-regulated learning environment (Zhang, Zhu, Wang, & Chen, 2018).

Curriculum sequencing is another dimension of ITS, which provides personalized and flexible learning path (Al-Muhaideb & Menai, 2011). Bayesian network is used to find user preference for extracting shortest learning path for the learners (Anh, Ha, & Dam, 2008), while learner's profile is utilized by Neural network (Kwasnicka, Szul, Markowska Kaczmar, & Myszkowski, 2008), Apriori algorithm (Hsich & Wang, 2010) and variable length genetic algorithm (Dwivedi, Kant, & Bhardwaj, 2018) are used to generate learning path.

In collaborative learning domain, individual learner interacts with other members to complete predefined goals. Here, members are interdependent for collective success. A shared mental model is taken into consideration for collective training (Rouse & Morris, 1986). This shared modeling process is augmented with ITS to improve the learning performance of interdependent members with adaptive instructions (Fletcher & Sottilare, 2018).

The comparative study of different Intelligent Tutoring System (ITS) is shown in *Table 1*.

Table 1. Comparative Study of different Intelligent Tutoring System (ITS)

Model Name	Technique Used	Target Model	Features
Adaptive ITS (Phobun & Vicheanpanya, 2010)	Adaptive Hypermedia	Expert Model	Knowledge Relationships and Prerequisite Knowledge Relationships
Rule-Based and Case-Based ITS	Rule-Based And Case-Based Reasoning	Expert Model	Knowledge Representation, Learning, Search Strategy Effectiveness, User Feedback, Incomplete Input and Knowledge Base Expansion
ITS for Vehicle Dynamics (Huertas & Juarez-Ramirez, 2013)	Cognitive Task Analysis	Expert Model, Domain Model	Knowledge representation
Adaptive Web-Based ITS (Kularbphettong, Kedsiribut, & Roonrakwit, 2015)	Mastery Learning Technique	Expert and Learner Model	Student Profiling
Remote Laboratory (KHALFALLAH & SLAMA, 2015)	Facial Expression	Learner Model	Student Emotions (Anger, Happiness, Surprise, Sadness)
Affective Tutoring Systems (Petrovica, Anohina-Naumeca, & Ekenel, 2017)	Self-assessment Manikin	Learner Model	Student Emotions
AG_Tutor (Mahmoud & El-Hamayed, 2016)	Adaptive Learning	Expert Model, Learner Model	Curriculum Sequencing
ITS (Vélez-Langs & Argüello, 2007)	Instructional Cognitive Theory	Expert and Domain Model	Personality Aspects
Cooperative Intelligent Tutoring System (González, Burguillo, & Llamas, 2007)	Case-based Reasoning, Multi-agent system	Learner Model	Domain Independent Information, Domain Specific Information
ITS (Arevalillo-Herráez, Arnau, & Marco-Giménez, 2013)	Intention-Based Affective Learning	Learner Model	Affective States
Conversational Intelligent Tutoring Systems (Crockett, Latham, & Whitton, 2017)	Fuzzy Decision Trees	Expert Model	Student's Learning Style
ITS (Ramírez-Noriega, Juárez-Ramírez, & Martínez-Ramírez, 2017)	Bayesian Network	Test Model	Knowledge Level Complexity: Bloom's Taxonomy
ELaCv2 (Chrysafiadi, Virvou, & Sakkopoulos, Optimizing Programming Language Learning Through Student Modeling in an Adaptive Web-Based Educational Environment, 2020)	Adaptive Learning	Learner Model	Prior Knowledge, Domain Knowledge, Knowledge Level
ITS (Troussas, Krouska, & Virvou, 2020)	Multi Module Model	Learner Model	Cognitive States, Tailored Learning Pathways

Issues and Problems With Current Techniques

Based on the previous section, it is observed that different ITS provides a solution for at least one of the four basic models of the ITS. A general-purpose teaching-learning model with personalized recommendations is considered as standard ITS. To deal with factors such as scalability, flexibility, and reusability of different models are still a challenge. Affective, cognitive and behavioral states of learner are considered as the best learning in current ITS techniques (Tomar & Nielson, 2013), still, precise modeling of these states is still an issue. This section covers the issues and problems related to current ITS techniques.

1. Initially, the learner model is too simple. But when we are looking for personalization, it has to accommodate all the variables that record history and can predict the future. Since learning is a continuous process where all the variables are updated continuously; accommodation of all the variables for the learner model in a universal set is an expensive task. With continuous updates of variables, consistency might be an issue.
2. Another issue with the learning model is that they are standalone and designed for predetermined sets of knowledge-base. Interoperability/flexibility/reusability between different knowledge-base can reduce cost. Lack of standardization of expert and learner model.
3. In the expert model, knowledge is represented in different ways, still, the structure remains independent of any domain whereas concepts are domain dependent.
4. In the self-regulated learning environment, learning strategy dictates overall learning procedure, the issue arises with personalization. Every learner is different from another learner, how can ITS defined a standard strategy for learning.
5. How to map learner's model with the expert model. In addition to that learning should be easy and realistic?
6. Most ITS could not make the correct sequence of learning with the goal of personalization. If the correct sequence is available, learner models are not optimized with respect to time for individual learners.
7. Most ITS are built for academics, no standard empirical evaluation techniques are available to measure the correctness of the system. How accurately ITS can model knowledge and other attributes to get better personalization?
8. If the user is continuously working on the ITS her behavior can be modeled easily. But, if the learner engaged with another application of the computer like net-surfing or games, how can ITS model off-task behavior of the learner (Baker & Rossi, 2013) ? How to reduce this behavioral disengagement?

9. Conversational-based ITS usually works on natural language processing techniques. In fully automated text processing, usually, the paraphrase is ignored. Such inconsistencies do not consider behavioral variables that lead to incorrect predictions for learning style.
10. For effective teaching-learning process, the learner's domain of interest is the first input. Another task is to identify her expertise level. Usually, learners could not rate themselves so accurately on the expertise level. The over-confident one rate themselves high on the other hand, few learners underestimate themselves and rate very low. A key challenge is how to predict learner's domain and expertise-level accurately and how to recommend new concepts from different domains to her?
11. Learners who are emotionally unstable, can't deal well with learning information (Goleman, 1995). To optimize the learning process, emotional intelligence is also included in ITSs. A cognitive disequilibrium is calculated as a confusion (D'Mello & Graesser, Dynamics of affective states during complex learning, 2012). Efforts have been made, still, classifiers accuracy of emotional intelligence introduce an error of ~27% (Sottilare, Ragusa, Hoffman, & Goldberg, 2013).
12. While learning, a learner's emotions can be momentary or prolonged. When a leaner stuck in something, can have negative emotions. On the other hand, she can feel pride or delighted when solving a problem or getting everything right (D'Mello, Blanchard, Baker, Ocumpaugh, & Brawner, 2014). A learner with negative emotions needs special attention (Fiedler, 2001) while with positive emotions, a learner can try to solve a complex problem (Clore & Huntsinger, 2007). In ITSs, the impact of these positive and negative emotions are still not considered.

SOLUTIONS AND RECOMMENDATIONS

This section covers the solutions and proposed recommendations for the ITS. The main focus is to provide recommendations in the learner, test, and expert/domain model. The learner model consists of attitude, behavior, and knowledge-level of the user and can be regarded as a part of the domain model. The initial task is to identify and extract variables that can provide more relevant information for personalization. These variables are initialized with personal information about the learner. The goal of creating this personal information is to identify the domain, knowledge/expertise level in that domain and learning style of the user. However, demographic information can be recommended, still not used in the proposed work. Although, behavioral, emotional and cognitive states are considered for creating a learner's profile. To initialize learner's profile, the Big Five Personality Traits Model (Big

Five Personality Traits, 2018) is used to describe the personality aspects. It consists of five factors (refer Figure 2) namely: Openness, Conscientiousness, Extraversion, Agreeableness, and Neuroticism.

1. **Openness:** It is used to measure the learner's degree of creativity, novelty, imagination, and curiosity. However, a learner with a very high value of openness could be very unpredictable. On the other hand lower values signify that learner could be close-minded.
2. **Conscientiousness:** It is used to measure efficiency and self-discipline. Higher the value, a learner could be more organized whereas a lower value signifies flexible behavior with spontaneity with the lack of reliability.
3. **Extraversion:** It is used to measure learner's energy and positivity towards the teaching-learning process.
4. **Agreeableness:** It is used to measure learner's temperament and degree of disengagement while learning.
5. **Neuroticism:** It is used to measure emotional stability and psychological stress of the learner.

Figure 2. The Big Five Personality Traits Model (Big Five Personality Traits, 2018)

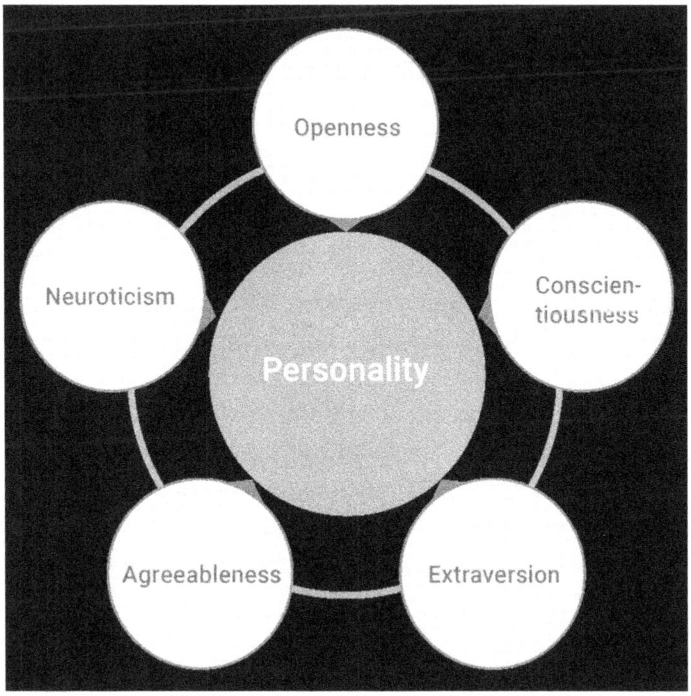

In the self-learning environment, the Big Five Personality Trait test is performed initially on personality survey data (Personality test, 2018) for a better adaptation of the learner model. Cognitive and affective states of the learners are recorded with these five factors.

Since learning is a continuous process, a learner with poor values can get better variable values for these factors, therefore behavioral states are also considered, that will be covered later in the section. The real problem arises because of the large number of variable and how to analyze them (Refer Issue and Problem number 1). When analyzing a large set of variables, a straightforward approach is to parse these variables in a top-down manner. This approach provides flexibility and reusability when the learner wants to shift from one domain to another. A universal set of variables can be shared to infer similar concept variable for such cases. Time and cost of learning will significantly be reduced.

Another solution would go for a fixed structure of knowledge-base that provides better scalability with flexibility and reusability. A tree-based ontology is created to model knowledge-base. This knowledge-based repository is essentially required for storage and retrieval of learning content. Different learning contents like definition, explanation, mathematical formulation, exercise, assignments, quizzes, tutorial, audio, and video, etc. are contained in the repository. The idea is to make a standard structure that can be searchable. A standard meta-data based learning object standard IEEE Learning Object Metadata (IEEE Standard for Learning Object, 2002) is used. It is an XML based conceptual data model used to describe metadata for learning objects. Although extensions and modifications of IEEE Learning Object Metadata (IEEE LOM) are available for annotations of knowledge-base, a standard IEEE LOM is considered as a standard reference (refer Figure 3). Different attributes of IEEE LOM are used for information retrieval.

A hierarchical domain ontology is used for domain model (Roy, 2006). A domain/subject/topic is decomposed into a finite set of concepts. Concepts are further decomposed into sub-concept and each sub-concept has different terms (refer Figure 4). Each node of the tree is populated with meta-data based learning object. The advantage of using such a hybrid structure is that it provides some sort of standardization that is one of the issues (refer Issue 2). Concepts are now pushed to the second level of the hierarchy, therefore, provide flexibility and reusability. The concepts are still domain-dependent but lower hierarchical position doesn't make that much issue (refer Issue 3). An array of information blocks on every node provides a course of pedagogical strategies for the learner.

Initial cognitive and affective states are initialized from Big Five Personality Traits. For Issue 4, the instructional strategy should depend on user attitude, behavior, and knowledge-level. Facial expression and gesture recognition is key to identify the confidence of the learner while learning. Inconsistency between

Figure 3. A schematic representation of the hierarchy of elements in the LOM data model (Learning object metadata, 2018)

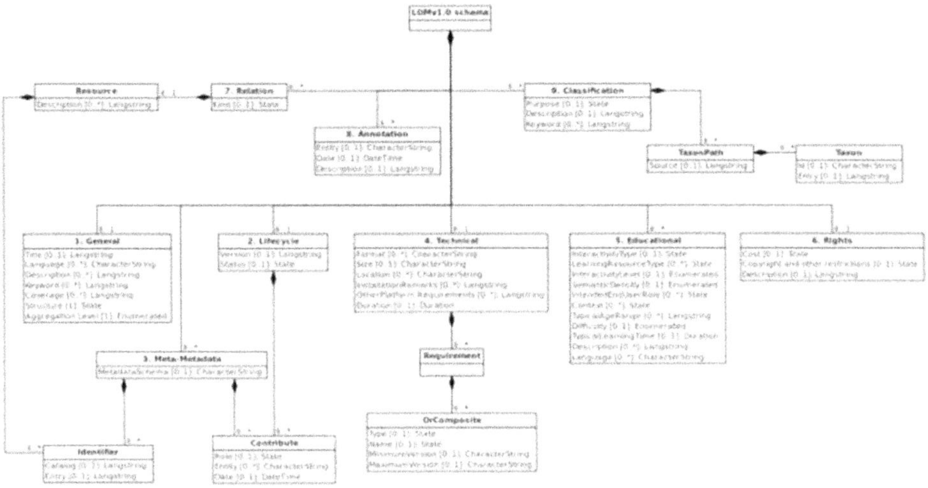

standard baselines with the recorded during learning helps in identifying learner's confidence. Additionally, learner interaction with user-interface will help in identifying learner's confidence for a particular concept. A gesture recognition toolkit (Gillian & Paradiso, 2014) is employed to identify different gestures while emotions from facial expressions are calculated by Affectiva SDK: A Cross-Platform RealTime Multi-Face Expression Recognition Toolkit (Affectiva SDK: A Cross-Platform RealTime Multi-Face Expression Recognition Toolkit, 2018). Behavioral Analysis of user includes the action performed by the user over a period of time. It includes the time spent by the user for particular "*term*", skipped particular "*term/ concept*", page-up/ page-down to revise "*term/ concept*", visiting back to revise particular "*term/ concept*" along with cognitive and affective states of the user during learning and evaluation.

For each "*term*," the evaluation model has a set of questions to test the learner's understanding. Questions in each question set are categorized as per Bloom's Taxonomy (Bloom, 1956) with different learning styles (Felder & Silverman, 1988). Time spent over a "*term/ concept*" with affect, behavior and cognitive states is added in the evaluation model to map learner's confidence. Based on this evaluation, the ITS updates learner's profile. This model estimates the probability for a learner to recommend what to learn next or repeat those concepts again. It attempts to make personalized recommendations by creating complex relations between events, learner states, and time-dependent scenarios. Cognitive theory of affect (emotions) and behavior (interaction with UI), cognitive states (for the mental process) are

Figure 4. Hierarchical Structure of Ontology (Roy, 2006)

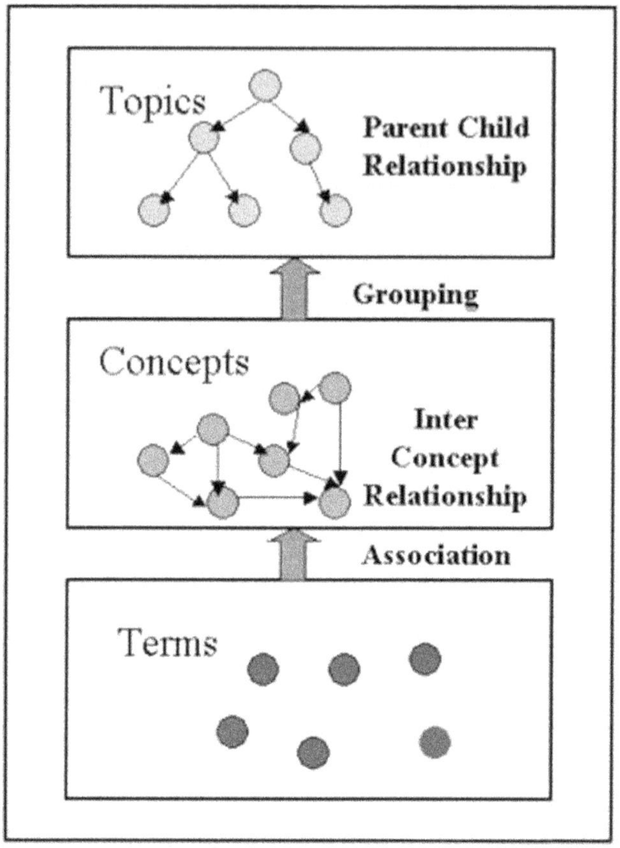

also the parameters to create a learner profile. It categorizes knowledge-level along with cognitive theory & time-dependent scenarios and makes a relationship with the learner model.

When optimizing a learning process with respect to time, a behavioral disengagement is also a problem. Behavioral engagement is defined as a learner's positive attitude towards learning, active participation in the learning process and /or contribution in the discussion (Fredricks, Blumenfeld, & Paris, 2004). The evaluation process may be time-bound, but the learning process could not be limited to time. A simple solution to this problem is not allowing a learner to switch to another process until exiting the ITS. It seems to be very hard and most of the learner will not like such restrictions. Another option would be through displaying a notification to the learner and reminding them to switch back to ITS. Another problem is an act of carelessness. Identifying mouse movement on the user interface might be a simpler solution for such a problem. Carelessness would not be a single reason for behavioral disengagement, learner's attitude and cognitive states may be other reasons too. Therefore, it is better to predict the time taken to complete a learning task. The time is calculated on:

1. Time taken by other learner's of similar profile to complete that particular learning task.
2. Time taken by the learner to complete similar learning tasks.
3. Time taken by the learner to complete recent *n* number of tasks.

Another solution is to provide highly interactive & interesting learning content and act on learner's feedback. Usually, the feedback system works on automatic text processing (refer Issue 9). A conversational based feedback system is applied in the ITS. The Google Assistant (Google Assistant SDK for devices, 2018) is embedded in the ITS for more precise automatic text processing.

To evaluate the ITS, the first import thing is to create datasets. Although the concepts are domain dependent, a uniform hybrid hierarchical ontology with IEEE LOM based domain structure is suggested in this chapter. It helps to improve reusability and transferability of learner models. Classifier accuracy can be used on learners' preferences. ITS recommendations and learning style predictions. Human-computer interaction is usually employed in ITS for emotional intelligence and it is the key to personalization. Accurate prediction of emotional intelligence with improvement in learning is recommended for effective ITS (refer issue 1 to 12).

FUTURE RESEARCH DIRECTIONS

The objective of the learning is to provide easy understanding and encourage innovations and creativity. Creativity and innovations are the most vital factors in today's competitive environment and promote productivity. The Openness factor of Big Five Personality Traits Model covers the creativity and innovative personality of the learner. But creativity is not included in the learner model.

Another recommendation is to enhance the learning gains of the learner. Ease of learning and interactive teaching can improve learning gains. Learning with high confidence and minimum disengagement is still an issue. The key is to provide a domain-independent generalized instruction technique that will include both macro-adaptive and micro-adaptive strategies. The prior strategy includes historical data while later rely on real-time data. For better personalization, an adaptive hybrid strategy should be available to consider both types of data. The context-aware and context-based factor are still missing for globally generalized techniques.

IEEE LOM is employed in ITS to provide a metadata-based description of learning content. Different modifications and updates are available for IEEE LOM. Dublin Core and IEEE LOM based repository are recommended for flexible and reusable structure. Future ITS should optimize the learning process with respect to time.

The major issues with ITS are empirical evaluation. No standard techniques are still available on measure effectiveness of the teaching-learning process. ITS is an integration of four basic models. Some standards are recommended for these models for integration.

CONCLUSION

The motivation of this work is to provide the impact of artificial intelligence in the learning process. The basic architecture of the Intelligent Tutoring System is discussed with the main objective is to provide personalized teaching-learning process. It mimics the learning style of a human tutor and makes an adaptation for future learning recommendations. Different issues related to ITS are discussed in the chapter. A hybrid ontology based on IEEE LOM is employed for standardization of the domain model to achieve flexibility and reusability. It provides some sort of integrations of the domain model in any ITS. Another contribution of the study is to identify the personality traits of the learner to initialize the learner. In the later stages, the cognitive theory is employed in learning and evaluation phase to model emotions and attitude of the learner over a period of time. This could model both momentary and prolonged emotional intelligence of the learner.

REFERENCES

Affectiva SDK: A Cross-Platform RealTime Multi-Face Expression Recognition Toolkit. (2018, May). Retrieved from Affectiva: https://www.affectiva.com/science-resource/affdex-sdk-a-cross-platform-realtime-multi-face-expression-recognition-toolkit/

Al Emran, M., & Shaalan, K. (2014). A survey of intelligent language tutoring systems. *International Conference on Advances in Computing,Communications and Informatics*, 393-399. 10.1109/ICACCI.2014.6968503

Al-Muhaideb, S., & Menai, M. E. (2011). Evolutionary computation approaches to the curriculum sequencing problem. *Natural Computing*, *10*(2), 891–920. doi:10.100711047-010-9246-5

Alharthi, A. D., Spichkova, M., & Hamilton, M. (2018). Sustainability requirements for eLearning systems: A systematic literature review and analysis. *Requirements Engineering*, 1–21.

Amela, V., Diez, J. L., & Valles, M. (2011). A new framework for the control of lms in intelligent tutoring systems. *Proceedings of the 18th World Congress The International Federation of Automatic Control*. 10.3182/20110828-6-IT-1002.01817

Anh, N. V., Ha, N. V., & Dam, H. S. (2008). Constructing a Bayesian belief network to generate learning path in adaptive hypermedia system. *Journal of Computer Science and Cybernetics*, *24*(1), 12–19.

Arevalillo-Herráez, M., Arnau, D., & Marco-Giménez, L. (2013). Domain-specific knowledge representation and inference engine for an intelligent tutoring system. *Knowledge-Based Systems*, *49*, 97–105. doi:10.1016/j.knosys.2013.04.017

Arevalillo-Herraez, M., Marco-Gim'enez, L., Arnau, D., & Gonz'alez Calero, J. A. (2017). Adding sensor-free intention-based affective support to an Intelligent Tutoring System. *Knowledge-Based Systems*, *132*, 85–93. doi:10.1016/j.knosys.2017.06.024

Baker, R., & Rossi, L. M. (2013). Assessing the Disengaged Behaviors of Learners. In R. Sottilare, A. Graesser, X. Hu, & H. Holden (Eds.), Design Recommendations for Intelligent Tutoring Systems - Volume 1: Learner Modeling (pp. 153-163). U.S. Army Research Laboratory.

Baker, R. S., Gowda, S. M., Wixon, M., Kalka, J., Wagner, A. Z., Salvi, A., ... Rossi, L. (2012). Towards Sensor-Free Affect Detection in Congnitive Tutor Algebra. *5th International Conference on Educational Data Mining*, 126-133.

Baldiris, S., Santos, O. C., Barrera, C., Boticario, J. G., Velez, J., & Fabreget, R. (2008). Integration of Educational Specifications and Standards to Support Adaptative Learning Scenarios in ADAPTAPlan. *International Journal of Computers and Applications*, *5*(1), 88–107.

Big Five Personality Traits. (2018). Retrieved from Wikipedia: https://en.wikipedia.org/wiki/Big_Five_personality_traits

Bloom, B. S. (1956). *Taxonomy of educational objectives: Handbook 1: Cognitive domain*. New York: Longmans, Green and Company.

Bradac, V., & Kostolanyova, K. (2017). Intelligent Tutoring Systems. In G. Vincenti, A. Bucciero, M. Helfert, & M. Glowatz (Eds.), *E-Learning, E-Education, and Online Training. Lecture Notes of the Institute for Computer Sciences, Social Informatics and Telecommunications Engineering* (pp. 71–78). Springer. doi:10.1007/978-3-319-49625-2_9

Bradley, M. M., & Lang, P. J. (1994). Measuring emotion: The self-assessment manikin and the semantic differential. *Journal of Behavior Therapy and Experimental Psychiatry, 25*(1), 49–59. doi:10.1016/0005-7916(94)90063-9 PMID:7962581

Brusilovsky. (1996). Methods and techniques of adaptive hypermedia. *User Modeling and User-Adapted Interaction, 6*, 87-129.

Brusilvosky, P. (2001). Adaptive hypermedia. *User Modeling and User-Adapted Interaction, 11*(1-2), 87–110. doi:10.1023/A:1011143116306

Butz, C. J., Hua, S., & Maguire, R. B. (2006). A web-based bayesian intelligent tutoring system for computer programming. *Web Intelligence and Agent Systems, 4*(1), 77–97.

Chen, C. (2008). Intelligent web-based learning system with personalized learning path guidance. *Computers & Education, 51*(2), 787–814. doi:10.1016/j.compedu.2007.08.004

Chrysafiadi, K., & Virvou, M. (2015). Fuzzy logic for adaptive instruction in an e-learning environment for computer programming. *IEEE Transactions on Fuzzy Systems, 23*(1), 164–177. doi:10.1109/TFUZZ.2014.2310242

Chrysafiadi, K., Virvou, M., & Sakkopoulos, E. (2020). Optimizing Programming Language Learning Through Student Modeling in an Adaptive Web-Based Educational Environment. In Machine Learning Paradigms. Intelligent Systems Reference Library (Vol. 158, pp. 205-223). Springer. doi:10.1007/978-3-030-13743-4_11

Clore, G. L., & Huntsinger, J. R. (2007). How emotions inform judgment and regulate thought. *Trends in Cognitive Sciences, 11*(9), 393–399. doi:10.1016/j.tics.2007.08.005 PMID:17698405

Creane, S., Crotty, Y., & Farren, M. (2015). A proposed use of Virtual And Augmented Reality for supporting inquiry based learning. *International conference on interactive mobile communication technologies and learning*, 393–395. 10.1109/IMCTL.2015.7359628

Crockett, K., Latham, A., & Whitton, N. (2017). On Predicting Learning Styles in Conversational Intelligent Tutoring Systems using Fuzzy Decision Trees. *Journal of Human Computer Studies*, *97*, 98–115. doi:10.1016/j.ijhcs.2016.08.005

Curilem, S. G., Barbosa, A. R., & de Azevedo, F. M. (2007). Intelligent tutoring systems: Formalization as automata and interface design using neural networks. *Computers & Education*, *49*(3), 545–561. doi:10.1016/j.compedu.2005.10.005

D'Mello, S., Blanchard, N., Baker, R., Ocumpaugh, J., & Brawner, K. (2014). I Feel Your Pain: A Selective Review of Affect-Sensitive Instructional Strategies. In R. Sottilare, A. Graesser, X. Hu, & B. Goldberg (Eds.), Design Recommendations for Intelligent Tutoring Systems - Volume 2: Instructional Management (pp. 35-48). U.S. Army Research Laboratory.

D'Mello, S., & Graesser, A. (2012). Dynamics of affective states during complex learning. *Learning and Instruction*, *22*(2), 145–157. doi:10.1016/j.learninstruc.2011.10.001

Dwivedi, P., Kant, V., & Bhardwaj, K. K. (2018). Learning path recommendation based on modified variable length genetic algorithm. *Education and Information Technologies*, *23*(2), 819–836. doi:10.100710639-017-9637-7

Dzikovska, M. O., Bental, D., Moore, J. D., Steinhauser, N. B., Campbell, G. E., Farrow, E., & Callaway, C. B. (2010). *Intelligent Tutoring with Natural Language Support in the Beetle II System. In Sustaining TEL: From Innovation to Learning and Practice* (pp. 620–625). Springer. doi:10.1007/978-3-642-16020-2_64

El-Khouly, M. M., Far, B. H., & Koono, Z. (2000). Expert tutoring system for teaching computer programming languages. *Expert Systems with Applications*, *18*(1), 27–32. doi:10.1016/S0957-4174(99)00047-0

Felder, R., & Silverman, L. (1988). Learning and Teaching Styles in Engineering Education. *Engineering Education*, *78*(7), 674–881.

Fiedler, K. (2001). Affective states trigger processes of assimilation and accommodation. *Theories of mood and cognition: A user's guidebook*, 85-98.

Fletcher, J. D., & Sottilare, R. A. (2018). Shared Mental Models in Support of Adaptive Instruction for Teams Using the GIFT Tutoring Architecture. *International Journal of Artificial Intelligence in Education*, *28*(2), 265–285. doi:10.100740593-017-0147-y

Fredricks, J. A., Blumenfeld, P. C., & Paris, A. H. (2004). School engagement: Potential of the concept, state of the evidence. *Review of Educational Research, 74*(1), 59–109. doi:10.3102/00346543074001059

Gao, Z., Ries, C., Simon, H. U., & Zilles, S. (2017). Preference-based Teaching. *Journal of Machine Learning Research, 18*, 1–32.

Gardner, J., & Brooks, C. (2018). Student success prediction in MOOCs. *User Modeling and User-Adapted Interaction, 28*(2), 127–203. doi:10.100711257-018-9203-z

Gillian, N., & Paradiso, A. J. (2014). The Gesture Recognition Toolkit. *Journal of Machine Learning Research, 15*, 3483–3487.

Goldman, S. A., & Mathias, H. D. (1996). Teaching a smarter learner. *Journal of Computer and System Sciences, 52*(2), 255–267. doi:10.1006/jcss.1996.0020

Goleman, D. (1995). *Emotional Intelligence*. New York: Bantam Books.

Gonzãlez, C., Burguillo, J. C., & Llamas, M. (2007). Cooperative CBR System for Sharing Student Models in Cooperative Intelligent Tutoring Systems. In H. D. Burkhard, G. Lindemann, R. Verbrugge, & L. Z. Varga (Eds.), *Multi-Agent Systems and Applications V. CEEMAS 2007, LNCS* (Vol. 4696, pp. 313–315). Berlin: Springer. doi:10.1007/978-3-540-75254-7_35

Google Assistant SDK for devices. (2018, May). Retrieved from Google Developers: https://developers.google.com/assistant/sdk/

Gunel, K., & Asliyan, R. (2010). Extracting learning concepts from educational texts in intelligent tutoring systems automatically. *Expert Systems with Applications, 37*(7), 5017–5022. doi:10.1016/j.eswa.2009.12.011

Gutierrez, F., & Atkinson, J. (2011). Adaptive feedback selection for intelligent tutoring systems. *Expert Systems with Applications, 38*(5), 6146–6152. doi:10.1016/j.eswa.2010.11.058

Hsieh, T. C., & Wang, T. (2010). A mining-based approach on discovering courses pattern for constructing suitable learning path. *Expert Systems with Applications, 37*(6), 4156–4167. doi:10.1016/j.eswa.2009.11.007

Huertas, C., & Juarez-Ramirez, R. (2013). Developing an Intelligent Tutoring System for Vehicle Dynamics. *Procedia: Social and Behavioral Sciences, 106*, 838–847. doi:10.1016/j.sbspro.2013.12.096

IEEE Standard for Learning Object. (2002). New York: IEEE. doi:10.1109/IEEESTD.2002.94128

Jesukiewicz, P. (2009). *SCORM 2004*. Advanced Distributed.

Jung, S. Y., & VenLehn, K. (2010). Developing an Intelligent Tutoring System Using Natural Language for Knowledge Representation. In V. Aleven, J. Kay, & J. Mostow (Eds.), *Intelligent Tutoring Systems* (pp. 355-358). Berlin: Springer.

Keles, A., Ocak, R., Keles, A., & Gulcu, A. (2009). ZOSMAT: Web-based intelligent tutoring system for teaching–learning process. *Expert Systems with Applications*, *36*(2), 1229–1239. doi:10.1016/j.eswa.2007.11.064

Khalfallah, J., & Slama, J. B. (2015). Facial expression recognition for intelligent tutoring systems in remote laboratories platform. *AWICT*, *73*, 274–281.

Kim, K., & Moon, N. (2018). Activity index model for self-regulated learning with learning analysis in a TEL environment. *The Journal of Supercomputing*, 1–19.

Kularbphettong, K., Kedsiribut, P., & Roonrakwit, P. (2015). Developing an Adaptive Web-Based Intelligent Tutoring System using Mastery Learning Technique. *Procedia: Social and Behavioral Sciences*, *191*, 686–691. doi:10.1016/j.sbspro.2015.04.619

Kwasnicka, H., Szul, D., Markowska Kaczmar, U., & Myszkowski, P. B. (2008). Learning assistant: Personalizing learning paths in e-learning environments. In 7th Computer Information Systems and Industrial Management Applications, (pp. 308-314). Academic Press.

Latham, A., Crockett, K., & McLean, D. (2014). An adaptation algorithm for an intelligent natural language tutoring system. *Computers & Education*, *71*, 97–110. doi:10.1016/j.compedu.2013.09.014

Latham, A., Crockett, K., McLean, D., & Edmonds, B. (2012). A conversational intelligent tutoring system to automatically predict learning styles. *Computers & Education*, *59*(1), 95–109. doi:10.1016/j.compedu.2011.11.001

Learning object metadata. (2018, May). Retrieved from Wikipedia: https://en.wikipedia.org/wiki/Learning_object_metadata

Lee, S., Choi, J., & Park, J. (2009). Interactive e-learning systems using pattern recognition and Augmented reality. *IEEE Transactions on Consumer Electronics*, *55*(2), 883–890. doi:10.1109/TCE.2009.5174470

Lia, J., Zhang, L., Meng, F., & Lia, F. (2014). Recommendation algorithm based on link prediction and domain knowledge in retail transactions. In *2nd International Conference on Information Technology and Qantitative Management*, (pp. 875–881). Moscow, Russia: Academic Press. 10.1016/j.procs.2014.05.339

Mahmoud, M. H., & El-Hamayed, S. H. (2016). An intelligent tutoring system for teaching the grammar of the Arabic language. *Journal of Electrical Systems and Information Technology*, *3*(2), 282–294. doi:10.1016/j.jesit.2016.04.001

Marciniak, J. (2014). Building intelligent tutoring systems immersed in repositories of e-learning content. *18th International Conference on Knowledge-Based and Intelligent Information & Engineering Systems*, 35, 541-550. 10.1016/j.procs.2014.08.135

Martinez, A., & Du, S. (2012). A Model of the Perception of Facial Expressions of Emotion by Humans: Research Overview and Perspectives. *Journal of Machine Learning Research*, *12*, 1589–1608. PMID:23950695

Noh, N. M., Ahmed, A., Halim, S. A., & Ali, A. M. (2011). Intelligent Tutoring System Using Rule-Based And Case-Based: A Comparision. *The 3rd International Conference on e-Learning ICEL2011*.

Pavlik, P. I. Jr, Brawner, K., Olney, A., & Mitrovic, A. (2013). A Review of models Used in Intelligent Tutoring Systems. In R. Sottilare, A. Graesser, X. Hu, & H. Holden (Eds.), *Design Recommendations for Intelligent Tutoring Systems* (pp. 39–68). U.S. Army Research Laboratory.

Personality Test. (2018). Retrieved from Wikipedia: https://en.wikipedia.org/wiki/Personality_test

Petrovica, S., Anohina-Naumeca, A., & Ekenel, H. K. (2017). Emotion Recognition in Affective Tutoring Systems: Collection of Ground-Truth Data. *ICTE*, *2016*(104), 437–444.

Phobun, P., & Vicheanpanya, J. (2010). Adaptive intelligent tutoring systems for e-learning systems. *Procedia: Social and Behavioral Sciences*, *2*(2), 4064–4069. doi:10.1016/j.sbspro.2010.03.641

Ramírez-Noriega, A., Juárez-Ramírez, R., & Martínez-Ramírez, Y. (2017). Evaluation module based on Bayesian networks to Intelligent Tutoring Systems. *International Journal of Information Management*, *37*(1), 1488–1498. doi:10.1016/j.ijinfomgt.2016.05.007

Rouse, W. B., & Morris, N. M. (1986). On looking into the black box: Prospects and limits in the search for mental models. *Psychological Bulletin, 100*(3), 349–363. doi:10.1037/0033-2909.100.3.349

Roy, D. (2006). *Automatic Annotation of Learning Materials*. Kharagpur: Indian Institute of Technology.

Samuelis, L. (2007). Notes on the Components for Intelligent Tutoring Systems. *Acta Polytechnica Hungarica, 4*(2).

Sathia Bhama, P. R., Hariharasubramanian, V., Mythili, O. P., & Ramachandran, M. (2017). Users' domain knowledge prediction in e-learning with speech Users' domain knowledge prediction in e-learning with speech interfaced. *Virtual Reality (Waltham Cross)*, 1–11.

Sottilare, R., Ragusa, C., Hoffman, M., & Goldberg, B. (2013). *Characterizing an adaptive tutoring learning effect chain for individual and team tutoring*. Orlando, FL: Interservice/Industry Training Simulation & Education Conference.

Taraus, J. K., Niu, Z., & Mustafa, G. (2018). Knowledge-based recommendation: A review of ontology-based recommender systems for e-learning. *Artificial Intelligence Review, 50*(1), 21–48. doi:10.100710462-017-9539-5

Tomar, A., & Nielson, A. D. (2013). Affective-Behavioral-Cognitive (ABC) Learner Modeling. In R. Sottilare, A. Graesser, X. Hu, & H. Holden (Eds.), Design Recommendations for Intelligent Tutoring Systems - Volume 1: Learner Modeling (Vol. 1, pp. 75-85). U.S. Army Research Laboratory.

Troussas, C., Krouska, A., & Virvou, M. (2020). Using a Multi Module Model for Learning Analytics to Predict Learners' Cognitive States and Provide Tailored Learning Pathways and Assessment. In Machine Learning Paradigms. Intelligent Systems Reference Library (Vol. 158, pp. 9-22). Springer.

Vanlehn, K., Jordan, P. W., Rose, C. P., Bhembe, D., Boettner, M., Gaydos, A., . . . Srivastava, R. (2002). The architecture of Why2-Atlas: A coach for qualitative physics essay writing. The Proceedings of 6th InternationalConference on ITS, 158-167.

Vélez-Langs, O., & Argüello, X. (2007). Adaptation in Intelligent Tutoring Systems: Development of Tutoring and Domain Models. In J. Jacko (Ed.), *Human-Computer Interaction (LNCS)* (Vol. 3, pp. 527–534). Springer-Verlag Berlin Heidelberg. doi:10.1007/978-3-540-73110-8_57

Zhang, M., Zhu, J., Wang, Z., & Chen, Y. (2018). Providing personalized learning guidance in MOOCs by multi-source data analysis. *World Wide Web (Bussum)*, 1–31.

Zilles, S., Lange, S., Holte, R., & Zinkevich, M. (2011). Models of cooperative teaching and learning. *Journal of Machine Learning Research*, *12*, 349–384.

Related Readings

To continue IGI Global's long-standing tradition of advancing innovation through emerging research, please find below a compiled list of recommended IGI Global book chapters and journal articles in the areas of massively open online courses, higher education, and learning analytics. These related readings will provide additional information and guidance to further enrich your knowledge and assist you with your own research.

Ackerman, G. L. (2018). Open Source Online Learning in Rural Communities. In I. Bouchrika, N. Harrati, & P. Vu (Eds.), *Learner Experience and Usability in Online Education* (pp. 61–84). Hershey, PA: IGI Global. doi:10.4018/978-1-5225-4206-3.ch003

Alharbi, H., & Sandhu, K. (2018). Robust Data Findings of E-Learning Analytics Recommender Systems and Their Impact on System Adoption for Student Experiences. *International Journal of Organizational and Collective Intelligence*, *8*(3), 1–12. doi:10.4018/IJOCI.2018070101

Alharbi, H., & Sandhu, K. (2019). New Discoveries for User Acceptance of E-Learning Analytics Recommender Systems in Saudi Arabia. *International Journal of Innovation in the Digital Economy*, *10*(1), 31–42. doi:10.4018/IJIDE.2019010103

Alharbi, H., & Sandhu, K. (2019). New Empirical Data Findings for Student Experiences of E-Learning analytics Recommender Systems and their Impact on System Adoption. *International Journal of Innovation in the Digital Economy*, *10*(2), 54–63. doi:10.4018/IJIDE.2019040104

Almjeld, J. (2017). Getting "Girly" Online: The Case for Gendering Online Spaces. In E. Monske & K. Blair (Eds.), *Handbook of Research on Writing and Composing in the Age of MOOCs* (pp. 87–105). Hershey, PA: IGI Global. doi:10.4018/978-1-5225-1718-4.ch006

Alomyan, H. (2018). Issues in Web-Based Learning. In I. Bouchrika, N. Harrati, & P. Vu (Eds.), *Learner Experience and Usability in Online Education* (pp. 235–255). Hershey, PA: IGI Global. doi:10.4018/978-1-5225-4206-3.ch009

Ammenwerth, E., Hackl, W. O., Hoerbst, A., & Felderer, M. (2019). Indicators for Cooperative, Online-Based Learning and Their Role in Quality Management of Online Learning. In M. Boboc & S. Koç (Eds.), *Student-Centered Virtual Learning Environments in Higher Education* (pp. 1–20). Hershey, PA: IGI Global. doi:10.4018/978-1-5225-5769-2.ch001

Babb, J. (2017). Reshaping Institutional Mission: OWI and Writing Program Administration. In E. Monske & K. Blair (Eds.), *Handbook of Research on Writing and Composing in the Age of MOOCs* (pp. 202–215). Hershey, PA: IGI Global. doi:10.4018/978-1-5225-1718-4.ch013

Bader, J. D., & Lowenthal, P. R. (2018). Using Visual Design to Improve the Online Learning Experience: A Synthesis of Research on Aesthetics. In I. Bouchrika, N. Harrati, & P. Vu (Eds.), *Learner Experience and Usability in Online Education* (pp. 1–35). Hershey, PA: IGI Global. doi:10.4018/978-1-5225-4206-3.ch001

Baker, N. L., & Buck, E. H. (2017). Conducting Programmatic Assessments of Online Writing Instruction: CCCC's OWI Principles in Practice. In E. Monske & K. Blair (Eds.), *Handbook of Research on Writing and Composing in the Age of MOOCs* (pp. 385–405). Hershey, PA: IGI Global. doi:10.4018/978-1-5225-1718-4.ch023

Borgman, J. C. (2017). The Online Writing Program Administrator (OWPA): Maintaining a Brand in the Age of MOOCs. In E. Monske & K. Blair (Eds.), *Handbook of Research on Writing and Composing in the Age of MOOCs* (pp. 188–201). Hershey, PA: IGI Global. doi:10.4018/978-1-5225-1718-4.ch012

Bourelle, T., & Hewett, B. L. (2017). Training Instructors to Teach Multimodal Composition in Online Courses. In E. Monske & K. Blair (Eds.), *Handbook of Research on Writing and Composing in the Age of MOOCs* (pp. 348–369). Hershey, PA: IGI Global. doi:10.4018/978-1-5225-1718-4.ch021

Branson, T. (2017). Problematic Partnerships: An Analysis of Three Composition MOOCs Funded by the Gates Foundation. In E. Monske & K. Blair (Eds.), *Handbook of Research on Writing and Composing in the Age of MOOCs* (pp. 169–187). Hershey, PA: IGI Global. doi:10.4018/978-1-5225-1718-4.ch011

Browning, L. G., & Dorner, L. M. (2018). Missing Opportunity?: Rural School Board Members and Data Use. In E. Mense & M. Crain-Dorough (Eds.), *Data Leadership for K-12 Schools in a Time of Accountability* (pp. 184–205). Hershey, PA: IGI Global. doi:10.4018/978-1-5225-3188-3.ch010

Cocquyt, C., Diep, A. N., Zhu, C., De Greef, M., & Vanwing, T. (2019). Towards Blended Learning Designs Fostering Adults' Social Capital: What Do Empirical Findings Reveal? In E. Ossiannilsson (Ed.), *Ubiquitous Inclusive Learning in a Digital Era* (pp. 55–80). Hershey, PA: IGI Global. doi:10.4018/978-1-5225-6292-4.ch003

Colby, R. (2017). A Typology of MOOCS. In E. Monske & K. Blair (Eds.), *Handbook of Research on Writing and Composing in the Age of MOOCs* (pp. 1–16). Hershey, PA: IGI Global. doi:10.4018/978-1-5225-1718-4.ch001

Colby, R. S. (2017). Using Online Writing Communities to Teach Writing MOOCs. In E. Monske & K. Blair (Eds.), *Handbook of Research on Writing and Composing in the Age of MOOCs* (pp. 317–330). Hershey, PA: IGI Global. doi:10.4018/978-1-5225-1718-4.ch019

Crain-Dorough, M., & Elder, A. C. (2018). Making Research Methods Instruction Relevant for Prospective Principals: The Development of Data Literacy for Effective Data Use. In E. Mense & M. Crain-Dorough (Eds.), *Data Leadership for K-12 Schools in a Time of Accountability* (pp. 260–283). Hershey, PA: IGI Global. doi:10.4018/978-1-5225-3188-3.ch013

Cypret-Mahach, R. (2018). Transformational Shifts of Pedagogy Through Professional Development, Essential Questions, and Self-Directed Learning. In F. Giuseffi (Ed.), *Emerging Self-Directed Learning Strategies in the Digital Age* (pp. 160–178). Hershey, PA: IGI Global. doi:10.4018/978-1-5225-3465-5.ch008

Dash, A. R., & Patra, M. R. (2018). Ensuring Quality of Web Portals Through Accessibility Analysis. In I. Bouchrika, N. Harrati, & P. Vu (Eds.), *Learner Experience and Usability in Online Education* (pp. 194–234). Hershey, PA: IGI Global. doi:10.4018/978-1-5225-4206-3.ch008

Galaige, J., & Torrisi-Steele, G. (2019). Unpacking the 'Learning' in Student-Facing Analytics: Metacognition and the Zone of Proximal Development. *International Journal of Adult Vocational Education and Technology, 10*(1), 1–12. doi:10.4018/IJAVET.2019010101

Giesteira, B., & Pereira, E. (2018). HCI4D Guidelines for Interactive Content. In R. Queirós (Ed.), *Emerging Trends, Techniques, and Tools for Massive Open Online Course (MOOC) Management* (pp. 49–77). Hershey, PA: IGI Global. doi:10.4018/978-1-5225-5011-2.ch003

Gomes, M. A., Sharma, R. C., Matta, A. E., & Robatto, L. (2019). Three Dimensional (3D) Simulation for Ubiquitous and Inclusive Learning in a Digital Era. In E. Ossiannilsson (Ed.), *Ubiquitous Inclusive Learning in a Digital Era* (pp. 228–251). Hershey, PA: IGI Global. doi:10.4018/978-1-5225-6292-4.ch010

Grant-Smith, D., Donnet, T., Macaulay, J., & Chapman, R. (2019). Principles and Practices for Enhanced Visual Design in Virtual Learning Environments: Do Looks Matter in Student Engagement? In M. Boboc & S. Koç (Eds.), *Student-Centered Virtual Learning Environments in Higher Education* (pp. 103–133). Hershey, PA: IGI Global. doi:10.4018/978-1-5225-5769-2.ch005

Hambrock, H. B., & Richter, R. G. (2019). A Pedagogical Approach Towards Curating Mobile Apps in an Educational Context. In E. Ossiannilsson (Ed.), *Ubiquitous Inclusive Learning in a Digital Era* (pp. 81–106). Hershey, PA: IGI Global. doi:10.4018/978-1-5225-6292-4.ch004

Hayag, M. R. Jr. (2018). Learning Analytics: Application on Curriculum Design and Assessment. In M. Kumar Singh, Z. Zerihun, & N. Singh (Eds.), *Impact of Learning Analytics on Curriculum Design and Student Performance* (pp. 113–124). Hershey, PA: IGI Global. doi:10.4018/978-1-5225-5369-4.ch008

Hayes, S. D., & Lee, C. G. (2018). The Principal as a Data-Driven Instructional Leader: Using PLCs to Improve Teaching and Learning. In E. Mense & M. Crain-Dorough (Eds.), *Data Leadership for K-12 Schools in a Time of Accountability* (pp. 76–97). Hershey, PA: IGI Global. doi:10.4018/978-1-5225-3188-3.ch005

Henry, T. P. (2017). What's a "Technician" to Do?: Theorizing and Articulating MOOC Maintenance Concerns. In E. Monske & K. Blair (Eds.), *Handbook of Research on Writing and Composing in the Age of MOOCs* (pp. 216–231). Hershey, PA: IGI Global. doi:10.4018/978-1-5225-1718-4.ch014

Herring, T. (2018). Data Dissemination Practices of Elementary School Principals. In E. Mense & M. Crain-Dorough (Eds.), *Data Leadership for K-12 Schools in a Time of Accountability* (pp. 19–38). Hershey, PA: IGI Global. doi:10.4018/978-1-5225-3188-3.ch002

Hewett, B. L., & Warnock, S. (2017). Writing MOOEEs?: Reconsidering MOOCs in Light of the OWI Principles. In E. Monske & K. Blair (Eds.), *Handbook of Research on Writing and Composing in the Age of MOOCs* (pp. 17–38). Hershey, PA: IGI Global. doi:10.4018/978-1-5225-1718-4.ch002

Hill, V. (2017). Digital Citizens as Writers: New Literacies and New Responsibilities. In E. Monske & K. Blair (Eds.), *Handbook of Research on Writing and Composing in the Age of MOOCs* (pp. 56–74). Hershey, PA: IGI Global. doi:10.4018/978-1-5225-1718-4.ch004

Hood, N., & Littlejohn, A. (2019). Disruptive Democratisers?: The Complexities and Incongruities of Scale, Diversity and Personalisation in MOOCs. In E. Ossiannilsson (Ed.), *Ubiquitous Inclusive Learning in a Digital Era* (pp. 1–28). Hershey, PA: IGI Global. doi:10.4018/978-1-5225-6292-4.ch001

Howard, L. (2017). A (Critical) Distance: Contingent Labor, MOOCs, and Teaching Online. In E. Monske & K. Blair (Eds.), *Handbook of Research on Writing and Composing in the Age of MOOCs* (pp. 232–253). Hershey, PA: IGI Global. doi:10.4018/978-1-5225-1718-4.ch015

Hsu, Y., Meyen, E. L., & Lee, Y. (2019). Understanding Emotional Analytics for Student Engagement: An Instructional Design Perspective. In M. Boboc & S. Koç (Eds.), *Student-Centered Virtual Learning Environments in Higher Education* (pp. 70–102). Hershey, PA: IGI Global. doi:10.4018/978-1-5225-5769-2.ch004

Irwin, L. H., & Reames, E. H. (2018). Towards Partnerships for Student Success: Teacher Collaboration in Data Analysis and Common Formative Assessment Systems. In E. Mense & M. Crain-Dorough (Eds.), *Data Leadership for K-12 Schools in a Time of Accountability* (pp. 140–156). Hershey, PA: IGI Global. doi:10.4018/978-1-5225-3188-3.ch008

Jenkins, P. (2017). Arguing for Proactivity: Talking Points for Owning Accessibility in Online Writing Instruction. In E. Monske & K. Blair (Eds.), *Handbook of Research on Writing and Composing in the Age of MOOCs* (pp. 106–122). Hershey, PA: IGI Global. doi:10.4018/978-1-5225-1718-4.ch007

Johnson, M. L. (2018). Empowering Educators to Make Data-Informed Decisions: A District's Journey of Effective Data Use. In E. Mense & M. Crain-Dorough (Eds.), *Data Leadership for K-12 Schools in a Time of Accountability* (pp. 158–183). Hershey, PA: IGI Global. doi:10.4018/978-1-5225-3188-3.ch009

Johnston, E. A., Olivas, G. W., Steele, P., Smith, C., & Bailey, L. W. (2019). Virtual Reality Pedagogical Considerations in Learning Environments. In M. Boboc & S. Koç (Eds.), *Student-Centered Virtual Learning Environments in Higher Education* (pp. 21–39). Hershey, PA: IGI Global. doi:10.4018/978-1-5225-5769-2.ch002

Jurado, F., & Rodriguez, P. (2018). The Learning Style of Gamers: Exploring a Multidimensional Profile Aimed at Gamifying MOOCs. In R. Queirós (Ed.), *Emerging Trends, Techniques, and Tools for Massive Open Online Course (MOOC) Management* (pp. 106–129). Hershey, PA: IGI Global. doi:10.4018/978-1-5225-5011-2.ch005

Kashtwari, D. M., & Wani, Z. A. (2019). MOOCs: The Indian Journey So Far. In E. Ossiannilsson (Ed.), *Ubiquitous Inclusive Learning in a Digital Era* (pp. 29–54). Hershey, PA: IGI Global. doi:10.4018/978-1-5225-6292-4.ch002

Khan, M. S., Nambobi, M., & Ali, M. S. (2018). MOOCs in TVET Sectors of Developing Countries: Benefits, Possibilities, and Challenges. In F. Giuseffi (Ed.), *Emerging Self-Directed Learning Strategies in the Digital Age* (pp. 22–47). Hershey, PA: IGI Global. doi:10.4018/978-1-5225-3465-5.ch003

Lancaster, S. J., & Topper, A. (2019). Designing and Implementing a Student-Centered Online Graduate Program: A Case Study in a College of Education. In M. Boboc & S. Koç (Eds.), *Student-Centered Virtual Learning Environments in Higher Education* (pp. 157–184). Hershey, PA: IGI Global. doi:10.4018/978-1-5225-5769-2.ch007

Lin, L. (2018). Student Learning and Engagement in a Blended Environment: A Mixed Methods Study. In I. Bouchrika, N. Harrati, & P. Vu (Eds.), *Learner Experience and Usability in Online Education* (pp. 256–269). Hershey, PA: IGI Global. doi:10.4018/978-1-5225-4206-3.ch010

Liu, M., Pardo, A., & Liu, L. (2017). Using Learning Analytics to Support Engagement in Collaborative Writing. *International Journal of Distance Education Technologies*, *15*(4), 79–98. doi:10.4018/IJDET.2017100105

Liu, S., Hu, Z., Peng, X., Liu, Z., Cheng, H. N., & Sun, J. (2017). Mining Learning Behavioral Patterns of Students by Sequence Analysis in Cloud Classroom. *International Journal of Distance Education Technologies*, *15*(1), 15–27. doi:10.4018/IJDET.2017010102

Liu, S., Ni, C., Liu, Z., Peng, X., & Cheng, H. N. (2017). Mining Individual Learning Topics in Course Reviews Based on Author Topic Model. *International Journal of Distance Education Technologies*, *15*(3), 1–14. doi:10.4018/IJDET.2017070101

Long, J. D. (2018). The Intersection of Andragogy and Dissertation Writing: How Andragogy Can Improve the Process. In F. Giuseffi (Ed.), *Emerging Self-Directed Learning Strategies in the Digital Age* (pp. 81-108). Hershey, PA: IGI Global. doi:10.4018/978-1-5225-3465-5.ch005

Luo, T., & Baaki, J. (2019). Scaffolding Problem-Solving and Instructional Design Processes: Engaging Students in Reflection-in-Action and External Representations in Three Online Courses. In M. Boboc & S. Koç (Eds.), *Student-Centered Virtual Learning Environments in Higher Education* (pp. 40–69). Hershey, PA: IGI Global. doi:10.4018/978-1-5225-5769-2.ch003

Lusta, A. F. (2018). Investigating MOOC Arabic Learners' Motivation in Language Online Courses (MOOCs). In R. Queirós (Ed.), *Emerging Trends, Techniques, and Tools for Massive Open Online Course (MOOC) Management* (pp. 156–179). Hershey, PA: IGI Global. doi:10.4018/978-1-5225-5011-2.ch007

Mahmoudi, L., & Gronseth, S. (2019). Video-Based Discussion: Promoting Presence Through Interactions in Online Higher Education Courses. In E. Ossiannilsson (Ed.), *Ubiquitous Inclusive Learning in a Digital Era* (pp. 128–153). Hershey, PA: IGI Global. doi:10.4018/978-1-5225-6292-4.ch006

Malik, N. (2018). Learning Analytics in the Perspective of Enhancing Students' Performance. In M. Kumar Singh, Z. Zerihun, & N. Singh (Eds.), *Impact of Learning Analytics on Curriculum Design and Student Performance* (pp. 125–141). Hershey, PA: IGI Global. doi:10.4018/978-1-5225-5369-4.ch009

Mariano, G. J., & Batchelor, K. (2018). The Role of Metacogntion and Knowledge Transfer in Self-Directed Learning. In F. Giuseffi (Ed.), *Emerging Self-Directed Learning Strategies in the Digital Age* (pp. 141–159). Hershey, PA: IGI Global. doi:10.4018/978-1-5225-3465-5.ch007

Martini, R. H., & Webster, T. (2017). What Online Writing Spaces Afford Us in the Age of Campus Carry, "Wall-Building," and Orlando's Pulse Tragedy. In E. Monske & K. Blair (Eds.), *Handbook of Research on Writing and Composing in the Age of MOOCs* (pp. 278–293). Hershey, PA: IGI Global. doi:10.4018/978-1-5225-1718-4.ch017

McEachern, R. W. (2017). Challenging Evaluation: The Complexity of Grading Writing in Hybrid MOOCs. In E. Monske & K. Blair (Eds.), *Handbook of Research on Writing and Composing in the Age of MOOCs* (pp. 370–384). Hershey, PA: IGI Global. doi:10.4018/978-1-5225-1718-4.ch022

Mense, E. G., Griggs, D. M., & Shanks, J. N. (2018). School Leaders in a Time of Accountability and Data Use: Preparing Our Future School Leaders in Leadership Preparation Programs. In E. Mense & M. Crain-Dorough (Eds.), *Data Leadership for K-12 Schools in a Time of Accountability* (pp. 235–259). Hershey, PA: IGI Global. doi:10.4018/978-1-5225-3188-3.ch012

Mihăeş, L. C., & Epure, M. (2019). Insights Into University-Business Cooperation in the Information Society: A Romanian Project for Higher Education. In E. Ossiannilsson (Ed.), *Ubiquitous Inclusive Learning in a Digital Era* (pp. 199–227). Hershey, PA: IGI Global. doi:10.4018/978-1-5225-6292-4.ch009

Miteva, D., Stefanov, K., & Stefanova, E. (2017). e-Analytics for e-Learning. *International Journal of Human Capital and Information Technology Professionals, 8*(4), 1–13. doi:10.4018/IJHCITP.2017100101

Mouri, K., Ren, Z., Uosaki, N., & Yin, C. (2019). Analyzing Learning Patterns Based on Log Data from Digital Textbooks. *International Journal of Distance Education Technologies, 17*(1), 1–14. doi:10.4018/IJDET.2019010101

Murray, R. W., & Murray, M. A. (2018). Behind the Scenes of Data-Driven Leadership: Intentionality of Leadership. In E. Mense & M. Crain-Dorough (Eds.), *Data Leadership for K-12 Schools in a Time of Accountability* (pp. 1–18). Hershey, PA: IGI Global. doi:10.4018/978-1-5225-3188-3.ch001

Nobre, A., Mallmann, E. M., Nobre, V., & Mazzardo, M. D. (2018). MOOC and OER: Identity Management. In R. Queirós (Ed.), *Emerging Trends, Techniques, and Tools for Massive Open Online Course (MOOC) Management* (pp. 1–23). Hershey, PA: IGI Global. doi:10.4018/978-1-5225-5011-2.ch001

Novak, J. I. (2019). Self-Directed Learning in the Age of Open Source, Open Hardware and 3D Printing. In E. Ossiannilsson (Ed.), *Ubiquitous Inclusive Learning in a Digital Era* (pp. 154–178). Hershey, PA: IGI Global. doi:10.4018/978-1-5225-6292-4.ch007

Nunes, F. B., Zunguze, M. C., Hannel, K., Antunes, F. F., Franco, S. R., & De Lima, J. V. (2018). Analysis of Users in an Immersive Environment for Teaching Science. In I. Bouchrika, N. Harrati, & P. Vu (Eds.), *Learner Experience and Usability in Online Education* (pp. 149–173). Hershey, PA: IGI Global. doi:10.4018/978-1-5225-4206-3.ch006

Odom, S., & Lindsey, L. (2017). Hacking the Lecture: Transgressive Praxis and Presence Using Online Video. In E. Monske & K. Blair (Eds.), *Handbook of Research on Writing and Composing in the Age of MOOCs* (pp. 331–347). Hershey, PA: IGI Global. doi:10.4018/978-1-5225-1718-4.ch020

Önaçan, M. B., Uluağ, M., Önel, T., & Medeni, T. D. (2018). Selection of Plagiarism Detection Software and Its Integration Into Moodle for Universities: An Example of Open Source Software Use in Developing Countries. In R. Queirós (Ed.), *Emerging Trends, Techniques, and Tools for Massive Open Online Course (MOOC) Management* (pp. 239–258). Hershey, PA: IGI Global. doi:10.4018/978-1-5225-5011-2.ch010

Orlando, M., & Howard, L. (2018). Setting the Stage for Success in an Online Learning Environment. In F. Giuseffi (Ed.), *Emerging Self-Directed Learning Strategies in the Digital Age* (pp. 1–9). Hershey, PA: IGI Global. doi:10.4018/978-1-5225-3465-5.ch001

Ossiannilsson, E. (2018). Increasing Access, Social Inclusion, and Quality Through Mobile Learning. *International Journal of Advanced Pervasive and Ubiquitous Computing, 10*(4), 29–44. doi:10.4018/IJAPUC.2018100103

Oswal, S. K. (2017). MOOCs in the Global Context. In E. Monske & K. Blair (Eds.), *Handbook of Research on Writing and Composing in the Age of MOOCs* (pp. 39–55). Hershey, PA: IGI Global. doi:10.4018/978-1-5225-1718-4.ch003

Overstreet, M. (2017). Principled/Digital: Composition's "Ethics of Attunement" and the Writing MOOC. In E. Monske & K. Blair (Eds.), *Handbook of Research on Writing and Composing in the Age of MOOCs* (pp. 75–86). Hershey, PA: IGI Global. doi:10.4018/978-1-5225-1718-4.ch005

Paneva-Marinova, D., & Pavlov, R. (2018). Improving Learner Experience Within Educational Nooks in Digital Libraries. In I. Bouchrika, N. Harrati, & P. Vu (Eds.), *Learner Experience and Usability in Online Education* (pp. 174–193). Hershey, PA: IGI Global. doi:10.4018/978-1-5225-4206-3.ch007

Pérez-Juárez, M. A., Antón-Rodríguez, M., Díaz-Pernas, F. J., Martínez-Zarzuela, M., & González-Ortega, D. (2018). An Analysis of the Possibilities of the Use of Technology for the Learning of Languages: From CSCL to Cloud Computing and MOOCs. In R. Queirós (Ed.), *Emerging Trends, Techniques, and Tools for Massive Open Online Course (MOOC) Management* (pp. 180–212). Hershey, PA: IGI Global. doi:10.4018/978-1-5225-5011-2.ch008

Petrosino, K. L. (2017). Developmental Writing and MOOCs: Reconsidering Access, Remediation, and Development in Large-Scale Online Writing Instruction. In E. Monske & K. Blair (Eds.), *Handbook of Research on Writing and Composing in the Age of MOOCs* (pp. 153–168). Hershey, PA: IGI Global. doi:10.4018/978-1-5225-1718-4.ch010

Quezada, T., Brunk-Chavez, B., & Posey, E. (2017). Connecting Writing Studies with Online Programs: UTEP's Graduate Technical and Professional Writing Certificate Program. In E. Monske & K. Blair (Eds.), *Handbook of Research on Writing and Composing in the Age of MOOCs* (pp. 123–136). Hershey, PA: IGI Global. doi:10.4018/978-1-5225-1718-4.ch008

Rajabi, E., & Greller, W. (2019). Exposing Social Data as Linked Data in Education. *International Journal on Semantic Web and Information Systems, 15*(2), 92–106. doi:10.4018/IJSWIS.2019040105

Rock, H. M. (2019). A Framework for Effective Online Professional Development. In M. Boboc & S. Koç (Eds.), *Student-Centered Virtual Learning Environments in Higher Education* (pp. 210–232). Hershey, PA: IGI Global. doi:10.4018/978-1-5225-5769-2.ch009

Rodrigues, R. L., Ramos, J. L., Silva, J. C., Dourado, R. A., & Gomes, A. S. (2019). Forecasting Students' Performance Through Self-Regulated Learning Behavioral Analysis. *International Journal of Distance Education Technologies, 17*(3), 52–74. doi:10.4018/IJDET.2019070104

Rysavy, M. D., Michalak, R., & Hunt, K. (2018). Information Literacy Education for First-Year Composition Students: A Case Study of Three Deployment Modes. In I. Bouchrika, N. Harrati, & P. Vu (Eds.), *Learner Experience and Usability in Online Education* (pp. 85–121). Hershey, PA: IGI Global. doi:10.4018/978-1-5225-4206-3.ch004

Sanchez-Gordon, S., & Luján-Mora, S. (2018). Lifecycle for MOOC Development and Management. In R. Queirós (Ed.), *Emerging Trends, Techniques, and Tools for Massive Open Online Course (MOOC) Management* (pp. 24–48). Hershey, PA: IGI Global. doi:10.4018/978-1-5225-5011-2.ch002

Sani-Bozkurt, S. (2019). Universal Design Principles and Technology-Supported Learning in the Digital Era: Assistive Technologies in Inclusive Learning. In E. Ossiannilsson (Ed.), *Ubiquitous Inclusive Learning in a Digital Era* (pp. 107–127). Hershey, PA: IGI Global. doi:10.4018/978-1-5225-6292-4.ch005

Schildkamp, K., & Poortman, C. L. (2018). Leadership to Support and Sustain Data Use in Data Teams. In E. Mense & M. Crain-Dorough (Eds.), *Data Leadership for K-12 Schools in a Time of Accountability* (pp. 98–118). Hershey, PA: IGI Global. doi:10.4018/978-1-5225-3188-3.ch006

Shanks, J. N. (2018). Establishing a Data Culture Using a Data-Driven Instructional System for School Improvement. In E. Mense & M. Crain-Dorough (Eds.), *Data Leadership for K-12 Schools in a Time of Accountability* (pp. 39–53). Hershey, PA: IGI Global. doi:10.4018/978-1-5225-3188-3.ch003

Shi, H., & Witte, M. M. (2018). Self-Directed Language Learning, Asian Cultural Influences, and the Teacher's Role. In F. Giuseffi (Ed.), *Emerging Self-Directed Learning Strategies in the Digital Age* (pp. 109–140). Hershey, PA: IGI Global. doi:10.4018/978-1-5225-3465-5.ch006

Shoukry, L., Konert, J., & Göbel, S. (2018). The Evaluation of Learner Experience in Serious Games. In I. Bouchrika, N. Harrati, & P. Vu (Eds.), *Learner Experience and Usability in Online Education* (pp. 122–148). Hershey, PA: IGI Global. doi:10.4018/978-1-5225-4206-3.ch005

Silva, J. C., Zambom, E., Rodrigues, R. L., Ramos, J. L., & de Souza, F. D. (2018). Effects of Learning Analytics on Students' Self-Regulated Learning in Flipped Classroom. *International Journal of Information and Communication Technology Education, 14*(3), 91–107. doi:10.4018/IJICTE.2018070108

Singh, M. K. (2018). Challenges of Learning Analytics Execution in the Educational System. In M. Kumar Singh, Z. Zerihun, & N. Singh (Eds.), *Impact of Learning Analytics on Curriculum Design and Student Performance* (pp. 28–40). Hershey, PA: IGI Global. doi:10.4018/978-1-5225-5369-4.ch003

Singh, M. K. (2018). Implementation and Impact of Learning Analytics on Multifarious Educational Systems: Technique and Process. In M. Kumar Singh, Z. Zerihun, & N. Singh (Eds.), *Impact of Learning Analytics on Curriculum Design and Student Performance* (pp. 142–152). Hershey, PA: IGI Global. doi:10.4018/978-1-5225-5369-4.ch010

Singh, N. (2018). A Study on the Impact of Learning Analytics to Evaluate Students' Performance in Higher Education. In M. Kumar Singh, Z. Zerihun, & N. Singh (Eds.), *Impact of Learning Analytics on Curriculum Design and Student Performance* (pp. 19–27). Hershey, PA: IGI Global. doi:10.4018/978-1-5225-5369-4.ch002

Singh, N. (2018). Impact of Learning Analytics on the Assessment of a Curriculum-Based Test. In M. Kumar Singh, Z. Zerihun, & N. Singh (Eds.), *Impact of Learning Analytics on Curriculum Design and Student Performance* (pp. 56–70). Hershey, PA: IGI Global. doi:10.4018/978-1-5225-5369-4.ch005

Singh, R. P. (2018). Learning Analytics: Potential, Protection, and Privacy in the Educational System. In M. Kumar Singh, Z. Zerihun, & N. Singh (Eds.), *Impact of Learning Analytics on Curriculum Design and Student Performance* (pp. 1–18). Hershey, PA: IGI Global. doi:10.4018/978-1-5225-5369-4.ch001

Soares, F., & Lopes, A. P. (2018). M100S Project: Math MOOCs From Polytechnic of Porto – Development, Continuance, and Use. In R. Queirós (Ed.), *Emerging Trends, Techniques, and Tools for Massive Open Online Course (MOOC) Management* (pp. 213–238). Hershey, PA: IGI Global. doi:10.4018/978-1-5225-5011-2.ch009

Steffen, V. T. (2017). Contact and Interactivity in Televised Learning: 15 Years Later. In E. Monske & K. Blair (Eds.), *Handbook of Research on Writing and Composing in the Age of MOOCs* (pp. 137–152). Hershey, PA: IGI Global. doi:10.4018/978-1-5225-1718-4.ch009

Stewart, J. (2017). Introduction Discussion Board Forums in Online Writing Courses Are Essential: No, Really, They Are. In E. Monske & K. Blair (Eds.), *Handbook of Research on Writing and Composing in the Age of MOOCs* (pp. 294–316). Hershey, PA: IGI Global. doi:10.4018/978-1-5225-1718-4.ch018

Stone, J. (2019). Fostering Social Presence on Virtual Learning Teams. In M. Boboc & S. Koç (Eds.), *Student-Centered Virtual Learning Environments in Higher Education* (pp. 134–156). Hershey, PA: IGI Global. doi:10.4018/978-1-5225-5769-2.ch006

Strang, K. D. (2017). Predicting Student Satisfaction and Outcomes in Online Courses Using Learning Activity Indicators. *International Journal of Web-Based Learning and Teaching Technologies*, *12*(1), 32–50. doi:10.4018/IJWLTT.2017010103

Sutha, J. (2018). Exploring the Role of Adult Learning Theory in Understanding Employees' Participation in Non-Mandatory Training. In F. Giuseffi (Ed.), *Emerging Self-Directed Learning Strategies in the Digital Age* (pp. 48–80). Hershey, PA: IGI Global. doi:10.4018/978-1-5225-3465-5.ch004

Tahiri, J. S., Bennani, S., & Idrissi, M. K. (2018). Differentiated Instruction Supporting MOOC: A Pedagogical Framework to Improve the Dropout Rate. In R. Queirós (Ed.), *Emerging Trends, Techniques, and Tools for Massive Open Online Course (MOOC) Management* (pp. 130–154). Hershey, PA: IGI Global. doi:10.4018/978-1-5225-5011-2.ch006

Teine, M. (2018). A Prototypical Participatory Design-Process: Bringing Digital Learning and User Experience Together. In I. Bouchrika, N. Harrati, & P. Vu (Eds.), *Learner Experience and Usability in Online Education* (pp. 36–60). Hershey, PA: IGI Global. doi:10.4018/978-1-5225-4206-3.ch002

Tham, J. C. (2017). Audience, User, Producer: MOOCs as Activity Systems. In E. Monske & K. Blair (Eds.), *Handbook of Research on Writing and Composing in the Age of MOOCs* (pp. 254–277). Hershey, PA: IGI Global. doi:10.4018/978-1-5225-1718-4.ch016

Tlili, A., Essalmi, F., Jemni, M., Kinshuk, & Chen, N.-S. (2018). A Complete Validated Learning Analytics Framework: Designing Issues from Data Preparation Perspective. *International Journal of Information and Communication Technology Education*, *14*(2), 1–16. doi:10.4018/IJICTE.2018040101

Topal, M., & Karaca, O. (2018). Gamification in E-Learning. In R. Queirós (Ed.), *Emerging Trends, Techniques, and Tools for Massive Open Online Course (MOOC) Management* (pp. 79–105). Hershey, PA: IGI Global. doi:10.4018/978-1-5225-5011-2.ch004

Umar, M. A., Shuru, A., Kufena, A. M., Tanko, M. Y., Sambo, A. A., & Hassan, S. A. (2018). Mobile CGPA Monitoring System: A Tool to Guide Self-Directed Learning. In F. Giuseffi (Ed.), *Emerging Self-Directed Learning Strategies in the Digital Age* (pp. 10–21). Hershey, PA: IGI Global. doi:10.4018/978-1-5225-3465-5.ch002

Ünal, E., & Çakır, H. (2019). Use of Dynamic Web Technologies in Collaborative Problem-Solving Method at Community Colleges. In M. Boboc & S. Koç (Eds.), *Student-Centered Virtual Learning Environments in Higher Education* (pp. 185–209). Hershey, PA: IGI Global. doi:10.4018/978-1-5225-5769-2.ch008

Varanasi, M. R., Fischetti, J. C., & Smith, M. W. (2018). Analytics Framework for K-12 School Systems. In E. Mense & M. Crain-Dorough (Eds.), *Data Leadership for K-12 Schools in a Time of Accountability* (pp. 206–233). Hershey, PA: IGI Global. doi:10.4018/978-1-5225-3188-3.ch011

Velliaris, D. M. (2018). An Intervention Program for Advancing the Academic Performance of International Pathway "STAR". In M. Kumar Singh, Z. Zerihun, & N. Singh (Eds.), *Impact of Learning Analytics on Curriculum Design and Student Performance* (pp. 71–95). Hershey, PA: IGI Global. doi:10.4018/978-1-5225-5369-4.ch006

Wani, S. A., Wani, Z. A., & Bhat, A. R. (2019). Identification and Evaluation of Quality of Open Access Journals Cited by Researchers of MIT, CIT and STANFORD. In E. Ossiannilsson (Ed.), *Ubiquitous Inclusive Learning in a Digital Era* (pp. 179–198). Hershey, PA: IGI Global. doi:10.4018/978-1-5225-6292-4.ch008

Wheat, J. (2018). Assessment Literacy Within Middle School-Level Math Professional Learning Communities. In E. Mense & M. Crain-Dorough (Eds.), *Data Leadership for K-12 Schools in a Time of Accountability* (pp. 119–139). Hershey, PA: IGI Global. doi:10.4018/978-1-5225-3188-3.ch007

White, C. C., & Johnson, J. (2018). Change Management in K-12 Education for Data-Driven Decisions: Moving From Professional Judgment to Evidence. In E. Mense & M. Crain-Dorough (Eds.), *Data Leadership for K-12 Schools in a Time of Accountability* (pp. 54–74). Hershey, PA: IGI Global. doi:10.4018/978-1-5225-3188-3.ch004

Willis, J. E. III, & Strunk, V. A. (2017). The Ethics of Machine-Based Learning: Advancing without Losing Humanity. *International Journal of Sociotechnology and Knowledge Development*, *9*(1), 53–66. doi:10.4018/IJSKD.2017010104

Zeirhun, Z. (2018). Learning Analytics: A Critical Review of the Role and Implementation in Educational Institutions. In M. Kumar Singh, Z. Zerihun, & N. Singh (Eds.), *Impact of Learning Analytics on Curriculum Design and Student Performance* (pp. 41–55). Hershey, PA: IGI Global. doi:10.4018/978-1-5225-5369-4.ch004

Zesu, S. (2018). Assessment and Evaluation of Students' Performance Without Learning Analytics. In M. Kumar Singh, Z. Zerihun, & N. Singh (Eds.), *Impact of Learning Analytics on Curriculum Design and Student Performance* (pp. 96–112). Hershey, PA: IGI Global. doi:10.4018/978-1-5225-5369-4.ch007

About the Contributors

Chintan Bhatt (Ph.D.) is currently working as an Assistant Professor in Computer Engineering department, Chandubhai S. Patel Institute of Technology, CHARUSAT. He is a member of IEEE, EAI, ACM, CSI, AIRCC and IAENG (International Association of Engineers). His areas of interest include Internet of Things, Data Mining, Web Mining, Networking, Security Mobile Computing, Big Data and Software Engineering. He has more than 5 years of teaching experience and research experience, having good teaching and research interests. He has chaired a track in CSNT 2015 and ICTCS 2014. He has been working as Reviewer in Wireless Communications, IEEE (Impact Factor-6.524) and Internet of Things Journal, IEEE, Knowledge-Based Systems, Elsevier (Impact Factor-2.9) Applied Computing and Informatics, Elsevier and Mobile Networks and Applications, Springer. He has delivered an expert talk on Internet of Things at Broadcast Engineering Society Doordarshan, Ahmedabad on 30/09/2015. He has been awarded Faculty with Maximum Publication in CSIC Award and Paper Presenter Award at International Conference in CSI-2015, held at New Delhi.

Priti Srinivas Sajja (b.1970) has been working at the Post Graduate Department of Computer Science, Sardar Patel University, India since 1994 and presently holds the post of Professor. She received her M.S. (1993) and Ph.D (2000) in Computer Science from the Sardar Patel University. Her research interests include knowledge-based systems, soft computing, multiagent systems, and software engineering. She has produced 208 publications in books, book chapters, journals, and in the proceedings of national and international conferences out of which five publications have won best research paper awards. She is author of Essence of Systems Analysis and Design (Springer, 2017) published at Singapore and co-author of Intelligent Techniques for Data Science (Springer, 2016); Intelligent Technologies for Web Applications (CRC, 2012) and Knowledge-Based Systems (J&B, 2009) published at Switzerland and USA, and four books published in India. She is supervising work of a few doctoral research scholars while seven candidates have completed their Ph.D research under her guidance. She has served as Principal Investigator of a major research project funded by University Grants Commission, India.

Sidath R Liyanage graduated from University of Kelaniya with BSc Honours in Statistics and Computer Science in 2005, he completed Master of Philosophy in Computer Engineering from University of Peradeniya in 2009 and received PhD from National University of Singapore in 2013. His research interests are in Brain Computer Interfaces, Data Science and applications of Machine Learning and pattern recognition. He has published over 40 publications.He is the Head of Department and a Senior Lecturer attached to Department of Software Engineering, Faculty of Computing and Technology, University of Kelaniya . He is a member of IEEE and a Council member of Sri Lanka Association for Artificial Intelligence.

* * *

Rangel Arthur has a degree in Electrical Engineering from the Paulista State University Júlio de Mesquita Filho (1999), a Master's degree in Electrical Engineering (2002) and a PhD in Electrical Engineering (2007) from the State University of Campinas. Over the years from 2011 to 2014 he was Coordinator and Associate Coordinator of Technology Courses in Telecommunication Systems and Telecommunication Engineering of FT, which was created in its management. From 2015 to 2016 he was Associate Director of the Technology (FT) of Unicamp. He is currently lecturer and advisor to the Innovation Agency (Inova) of Unicamp. He has experience in the area of Electrical Engineering, with emphasis on Telecommunications Systems, working mainly on the following topics: computer vision, embedded systems and control systems.

Reinaldo França has a B.Sc. in Computer Engineering in 2014. Currently, he is an Ph.D. degree candidate by Department of Communications (DECOM), Instruments and Photonics, Faculty of Electrical and Computer Engineering at the LCV-UNICAMP working with technological and scientific research as well as in programming and development in C / C ++, Java and .NET languages. His main topics of interest are simulation, operating systems, software engineering, wireless networks, internet of things, broadcasting and telecommunications systems.

Deepam Goyal is pursuing doctoral program at National Institute of Technical Teachers Training & Research, Chandigarh, India under the AORC scheme of the INSPIRE Program of the Department of Science & Technology (DST), New Delhi. He holds an excellent academic record throughout his studies and is Gold medalist in

M.E. Mechanical Engineering (Manufacturing Technology) from Panjab University, Chandigarh. He has contributed technical and non-technical papers in the refereed journals and conference proceedings besides writing a book. He also has a patent and a copyright to his credit.

Yuzo Iano, B.Sc. (1972), M.Sc. (1974), and Ph.D. degrees (1986) in Electrical Eng. at UNICAMP, Brazil. Since then he has been working in the technological production field, with 1 patent granted, 8 filed patent applications and 36 projects completed with research and development agencies. He has supervised 29 doctoral theses, 49 master's dissertations, 74 undergraduate and 48 scientific initiation works. He has participated in 100 master's examination boards, 50 doctoral degrees, author of 2 books and more than 250 published articles. He is currently Professor at UNICAMP, Editor-in-Chief of the SET International Journal of Broadcast Engineering and General Chair of the Brazilian Symposium on Technology (BTSym). He has experience in Electrical Engineering, with knowledge in Telecommunications, Electronics and Information Technology, mainly in the field of audio-visual communications and multimedia.

K.T.S Kasthuriarachchi has a B.Sc. in Information Technology and M.Sc. in Information Technology. Currently, she is a Ph.D. degree candidate by Department of Software Engineering, Faculty of Information and Communication Technology at University of Kelaniya, Sri Lanka. Her main topics of interest are data mining, data analysis and education.

Arun Raj L. is an Assistant Professor (Sr.Grade) in the Department of Computer Science and Engineering at B.S.Abdur Rahman Crescent University, Chennai. He has published many research papers in reputed journals and his major research interests include Multimedia Applications, Wireless Networks, and Mobile Communication.

A. Anny Leema is an Associate Professor in School of Computer Science and Engineering SCOPE VIT, Vellore. She has published more than 30 International papers reputed journals. Her major research interests include RFID, E-learning, Data Mining, and Web-Mining.

Pamela A. Lemoine has Ed. D. in Educational Leadership from the University of Louisiana at Lafayette, a master's degree in Educational Technology, and a bachelor's degree in English. Dr. Lemoine's P12 experiences include serving as a librarian, teacher, principal, district supervisor of 33 elementary and middle schools, and a director of federal programs. Dr. Lemoine also lived and worked in Okinawa, Japan, Germany, and Canada. She has been working in higher education since 2011, most recently serving as the Program Coordinator for Educational Leadership at Columbus State University, Columbus, Georgia and now as an assistant professor in the Department of Professional Studies at Troy University. As an educational leadership professor, her current research interests include educational leader preparation programs, educational technology, and student achievement. Most recently, Dr. Lemoine has written about the VUCA (volatility, uncertainty, chaos, and ambiguity) world of higher education, cyberlearning, and the effects of globalization in higher education.

Evan G. Mense is currently an Associate Professor in the Department of Educational Leadership and Technology and has served as the Director of the Masters and Doctoral Program at Southeastern Louisiana University. Dr. Mense has extensive background in Educational Administration and Leadership as a public school administrator. Dr. Mense holds a Doctorate in Educational Leadership from Saint Louis University-Saint Louis, Missouri, a Master of Science degree in Administration from Pittsburg State University – Pittsburg, Kansas, and a Bachelor of Science degree in Education from Missouri Southern State University – Joplin Missouri. Dr. Evan G. Mense Assistant Professor and Director of Masters in Educational Leadership Southeastern Louisiana University Department of Educational Leadership and Technology.

Ana Carolina Borges Monteiro has a B.Sc. in Biomedicine in 2015. Currently, she is a Ph.D. degree candidate by Department of Communications (DECOM), Faculty of Electrical and Computer Engineering (FEEC) at State University of Campinas (UNICAMP), and a researcher at the Laboratory of Visual Communications (LCV). She has expertise in the areas of Clinical Analysis and digital image processing through MATLAB software, knowledge acquired through the realization of research projects and internship in municipal hospital, as also experience in the revision of scientific works by acting as a reviewer in congresses.

Michael D. Richardson is Professor of Educational Leadership at Columbus State University. He previously held faculty and administrative appointments at Western Kentucky University, Clemson University, Georgia Southern University, Mercer University and Southeastern Louisiana University. He completed a B.S. and M.A. in Education at Tennessee Technological University and was awarded the Ed.D. in Educational Administration from the University of Tennessee. Dr. Richardson served as Founding Editor of the Journal of School Leadership an internationally refereed journal of educational leadership and as Editor of The Journal of At-Risk Issues. He has authored or edited 17 books, published more than 135 articles in professional journals, authored more than 45 book chapters and made more than 250 presentations to state, regional, national and international professional organizations. He has chaired more than ninety dissertations and actively collaborates in conducting research and writing for publication. His current research areas are organizational theory, resiliency of leaders, and phenomenology.

Index

A

Active learning 5
Adaptive learning 57, 125
Agreeableness 131
Artificial Immune Network (AIN) 42
artificial intelligence 122, 124, 136
asynchronous media 7
attainment gap 99-100
Attribute Selection 60, 85
AWGN (Additive White Gaussian Noise) 20

B

big data 17-18, 101-102
Big Five Personality Traits Model 130-131, 135
bit error rate (BER) 24
blended learning 4

C

Case Deletion 68, 85
CBEDE 13, 22-23, 25-27, 29-31
classification 41-42, 48-49, 61-64, 85, 126
cluster 17, 42, 85
Coding of Bits for Entities by Means of Discrete Events (CBDE) 22
Collaborative Deep Learning (CDL) 42
Collaborative Filtering (CF) 42
collaborative learning 5, 57, 127
Collaborative Topic Regression (CTR) 42
communication 1-8, 13-20, 29-31, 36-37, 61, 81, 122
communication systems 13, 29-30
communication technologies 1-8, 14, 30
Conscientiousness 131
Content-Based Filtering (CBF) 42
Content-Based Recommender System (CBRS) 43
Creative Learning 5
cross validation 71, 74, 85

D

data 3, 13-22, 24, 29-31, 35-36, 38-40, 43, 45, 47-48, 56-65, 67-68, 70-71, 74, 79, 82, 85-103, 121-122, 126-127, 132-133, 135
Data Interpretation 61, 85
data mining 35-36, 39-40, 47-48, 56-64, 68, 70-71, 74, 79, 85-102, 126
Data Science 17-18
Decision Tree 58, 61-62, 74, 76, 79, 126
Differential Phase Shift Keying (DPSK) 20, 22-23
Differential Quadrature Phase Shift Keying (DQPSK) 13, 21-22, 24-28
discrete events 18-19, 22-24, 27, 29-31
Discrete Events (DES) 18

E

Education 1-10, 15-16, 31, 36-37, 39-40, 47, 56-59, 61-64, 68, 79-82, 86-99, 101-103, 122, 124
Educational Data Mining (EDM) 36, 57
e-learning 4, 35-41, 43-44, 47, 49-51, 57, 61, 121-122, 124, 127

e-learning system 35, 37, 39-40, 44, 49-51
enrollment 87, 91, 94, 96-97, 101
Enrollment management 87, 96-97
Evaluative Learning 5
expert model 123-126
expert system 122
Extraversion 131

F

Fuzzy cognitive maps (FCM) 127

G

Global higher education 86-88, 90-92, 94, 99, 103
globalization 9, 88
Google Assistant 135

H

Hybrid Recommender System 45, 47, 51
Hybrid Systems (HS) 42

I

ICT Integration 4
Imperative Learning 5
information retrieval 36, 45, 49-51, 132
Intelligent Tutoring Systems (ITS) 122
interestingness 64-65, 76-77, 80

K

Kappa Statistic 85
K Means Algorithm 85
K-Nearest Neighbor (KNN) 61
Knowledge-Based Systems (KBS) 42
Knowledge Discovery in Databases (KDD) 59

L

learner model 47, 123, 125, 130, 132, 134-135
learning analytics 92, 95-96
Learning Management 36-37, 40, 57, 61, 96, 100
Learning Management System (LMS) 36, 57
learning style 124-125, 130, 135-136

M

mining algorithms 58-59, 61, 64, 68, 70-71, 74
modeling systems 19
Modular Object Oriented Developmental Learning Environment (MOODLE) 61
Multi-Input Multi-Output Student Academic Performance Prediction (MIMOSAPP) 2

N

Neural Network (NN) 43
Neuroticism 131

O

ontology 44-45, 50, 63, 125, 132, 134-136
Ontology-Based Recommender System (OBRS) 44
Openness 131, 135
Outliers 60, 85

P

Pedagogy 1, 4-5, 40, 96
personalization 35, 38-40, 42, 45, 50-51, 121-122, 125-127, 130, 135
Precision 45, 85
Programme for International Student Assessment (PISA) 8

Q

Quadrature Phase Shift Keying (QPSK) 21-22

R

Recommendation Systems (RSs) 35, 38-51
Recurrent Neural Network (RNN) 43
relationship management 96

S

semantics 44-45, 65
student learning 86, 92-94, 100, 102-103
student performance 91, 93-94, 99-101
Student retention 95, 97
students at risk 95, 98-99
Support Vector Machines 62

T

teaching-learning 1-5, 9, 121-122, 126, 129, 136
test model 123, 125

U

U-learning 6
user interface 123-124, 134

CPSIA information can be obtained
at www.ICGtesting.com
Printed in the USA
BVHW012154080919
557293BV00019B/46/P

9 781799 800101